THE HUMANISTIC TRADITION

SECOND EDITION

2

Medieval Europe and the World Beyond

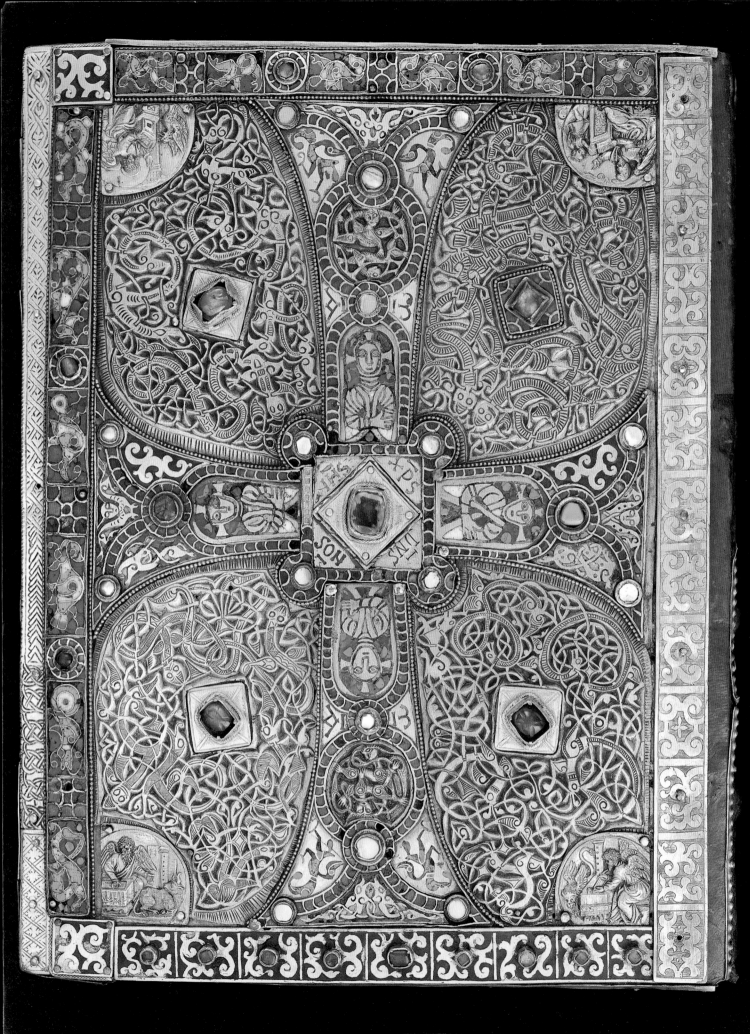

THE HUMANISTIC TRADITION

SECOND EDITION

2

Medieval Europe and the World Beyond

Gloria K. Fiero

University of Southwestern Louisiana

WCB Brown &
Benchmark

PUBLISHERS

Madison, Wisconsin • Dubuque, Iowa

Book Team
Associate Publisher *Rosemary Bradley*
Senior Developmental Editor *Deborah Daniel Reinbold*

Publishing Services Manager *Sherry Padden*

**Brown &
Benchmark**
A Division of Wm. C. Brown Communications, Inc.

Executive Vice President/General Manager *Thomas E. Doran*
Vice President/Editor in Chief *Edgar J. Laube*
Director of Marketing *Eric Ziegler*
Vice President of Production *Vickie Putman Caughron*
Director of Custom and Electronic Publishing *Chris Rogers*

Wm. C. Brown Communications, Inc.

President and Chief Executive Officer *G. Franklin Lewis*
Corporate Senior Vice President and Chief Financial Officer *Robert Chesterman*
Corporate Senior Vice President and President of Manufacturing *Roger Meyer*

The credits section for this book begins on page 154 and is considered an extension of the copyright page.

A Times Mirror Company

Library of Congress Catalog Card Number: 94–072137

ISBN 0–697–24218–8

This book was designed and produced by
CALMANN & KING LTD
71 Great Russell Street, London WC1B 3BN

Designer *Karen Osborne*
Cover designer *Karen Stafford*
Picture researcher *Carrie Haines*
Maps by Oxford Illustrators Ltd.
Timeline artwork by *Richard Foenander*

Typeset by Bookworm Typesetting, Manchester, UK
Printed in Singapore

10 9 8 7 6 5 4 3 2

Front cover
Main image: Detail of South rose window, Chartres Cathedral, France, thirteenth century.
Photo: Sonia Halliday, Weston Turville.
Insets: (top) Epicetus, Cup (detail), ca. 510 B.C.E. Diameter 13 in. Reproduced by courtesy of
the Trustees of the British Museum, London.
(center) Raphael, *The School of Athens* (detail), 1509–1511. Fresco, 26 ft. × 18 ft. Stanza della Segnatura, Vatican, Rome.
Scala/Art Resource, New York.
(bottom) *Shiva Nataraja* from Chidambaram, ca. eleventh century. Bronze, height 21¼ in. Museum van Asiatische
Kunst Amsterdam. Photo: Bildarchiv preussischer kulturbesitz, Berlin.

Frontispiece
Back cover of Lindau Gospels, ca. 800 C.E. Silver gilt with enamel and precious stones, 13⅜ × 10⅜ in.
The J. Pierpont Morgan Library, New York.

Series Contents

Book 2
Contents

PART II

The Medieval West 57

11 Patterns of Medieval Life 58

12 The Christian Church and the Medieval Mind 80

13 The Medieval Synthesis in the Arts 102

PART III

The World Beyond the West   *131*

MUSIC LISTENING SELECTIONS

Preface

"It's the most curious thing I ever saw in all my life!" exclaimed Lewis Carroll's Alice in Wonderland, as she watched the Cheshire Cat slowly disappear, leaving only the outline of a broad smile. "I've often seen a cat without a grin, but a grin without a cat!" A student who encounters an ancient Greek epic, a Yoruba mask, or a Mozart opera – lacking any context for these works – might be equally baffled. It may be helpful, therefore, to begin by explaining how the artifacts (the "grin") of the humanistic tradition relate to the larger and more elusive phenomenon (the "cat") of human culture.

The Humanistic Tradition and the Humanities

In its broadest sense, the term *humanistic tradition* refers to humankind's cultural legacy – the sum total of the significant ideas and achievements handed down from generation to generation. This tradition is the product of responses to conditions that have confronted all people throughout history. Since the beginnings of life on earth, human beings have tried to ensure their own survival by controlling nature. They have attempted to come to terms with the inevitable realities of disease and death. They have endeavored to establish ways of living collectively and communally. And they have persisted in the desire to understand themselves and their place in the universe. In response to these ever-present and universal challenges – *survival*, *communality*, and *self-knowledge* – human beings have created and transmitted the tools of science and technology, social and cultural institutions, religious and philosophic systems, and various forms of personal expression, the sum total of which we call culture.

Even the most ambitious survey cannot assess all manifestations of the humanistic tradition. This book therefore focuses on the creative legacy referred to collectively as *the humanities*: literature, philosophy, history (in its literary dimension), architecture, the visual arts (including photography and film), music, and dance. Selected examples from each of these disciplines constitute our *primary sources*. Primary sources (that is, works original to the age that produced them) provide first-hand evidence of human inventiveness and ingenuity. The primary sources in this text have been chosen on the basis of their authority, their beauty, and their enduring value. They are, simply stated, the masterpieces of their time and, in some cases, of all time. Because of their universal appeal, they have been imitated and transmitted from generation to generation. Such works are, as well, the landmark examples of a specific time and place: they offer insight into the ideas and values of the society in which they were produced. *The Humanistic Tradition* surveys these landmark works, but joins "the grin" to "the cat" by examining them within their political, economic, and social contexts.

The Humanistic Tradition explores a living legacy. History confirms that the humanities are not frivolous social ornaments, but rather, integral forms of a given culture's values, ambitions, and beliefs. Poetry, painting, philosophy, and music are not, generally speaking, products of unstructured leisure or indulgent individuality; rather, they are tangible expressions of the human quest for the good (one might even say the "complete") life. Throughout history, the arts have served the domains of the sacred, the ceremonial, and the communal. And even in modern times, as these domains have come under assault and as artists have openly challenged time-honored traditions, the reciprocal relationship between artist and community prevails. Unquestionably, the creative minds of every age both reflect and shape their culture. In these pages, then, we find works made by individuals with special sensitivities and unique talents for interpreting the conditions and values of their day. The drawings of Leonardo da Vinci, for example, reveal a passionate determination to understand the operations and functions of nature. And while Leonardo's talent far exceeded that of the average individual of his time, his achievements may be viewed as a mirror of the robust curiosity that characterized his time and place – the Age of the Renaissance in Italy.

The Scope of the Humanistic Tradition

The humanistic tradition is not the exclusive achievement of any one geographic region, race, or class of human beings. For that reason, this text assumes a global and multicultural rather than exclusively Western perspective. At the same time, Western contributions are emphasized, first, because the audience for these books is predominantly Western, but also because in recent centuries the West has exercised a dominant influence on the course and substance of global history. Clearly, the humanistic tradition belongs to all of humankind, and the best way to understand the Western contribution to that tradition is to examine it in the arena of world culture.

As a survey, *The Humanistic Tradition* cannot provide an exhaustive analysis of our creative legacy. The critical reader will discover many gaps. Some aspects of culture that receive extended examination in traditional Western humanities surveys have been pared down to make room for the too often neglected contributions of Islam, Africa, and Asia. This book is necessarily selective – it omits many major figures and treats others only briefly. Primary sources are arranged, for the most part, chronologically, but they are presented as manifestations of *the informing ideas of the age* in which they were produced. The intent is to examine the evidence of the humanistic tradition thematically and topically, rather than to compile a series of mini-histories of the individual arts.

Studying the Humanistic Tradition

To study the creative record is to engage in a dialogue with the past, one that brings us face to face with the values of our ancestors, and, ultimately, with our own. This dialogue is (or should be) a source of personal revelation and delight; like Alice in Wonderland, our strange, new encounters will be enriched according to the degree of curiosity and patience we bring to them. Just as lasting friendships with special people are cultivated by extended familiarity, so our appreciation of a painting, a play, or a symphony depends on close attention and repeated contact. There are no shortcuts to the study of the humanistic tradition, but there are some techniques that may be helpful. It should be useful, for instance, to approach each primary source from the triple perspective of its *text*, its *context*, and its *subtext*.

The Text: The *text* of any primary source refers to its *medium* (that is, what it is made of), its *form* (that is, its outward shape), and its *content* (that is, the subject it describes). All literature, for example, whether intended to be spoken or read, depends on the medium of words – the American poet Robert Frost once defined literature as "performance in words." Literary form varies according to the manner in which words are arranged. So poetry, which shares with music and dance rhythmic organization, may be distinguished from prose, which normally lacks regular rhythmic pattern. The main purpose of prose is to convey information, to narrate, and to describe; poetry, a form that assumes freedom from conventional patterns of grammar, is usually concerned with expressing intense emotions. Philosophy (the search for truth through reasoned analysis) and history (the record of the past) make use of prose to analyze and communicate ideas and information. In literature, as in most kinds of expression, content and form are usually interrelated. The subject matter or the form of a literary work will determine its *genre*. For instance, a long narrative poem recounting the adventures of a hero is an *epic*, while a formal, dignified speech in praise of a person or thing constitutes a *eulogy*.

The visual arts – painting, sculpture, architecture, and photography – employ a wide variety of media, such as wood, clay, colored pigments, marble, granite, steel, and (more recently) plastic, neon, film, and computers. The form or outward shape of a work of art depends on the manner in which the artist manipulates the formal elements of color, line, texture, and space. Unlike words, these formal elements lack denotative meaning. The artist may manipulate form to describe and interpret the visible world (as in such genres as portraiture and landscape painting); to generate fantastic and imaginative kinds of imagery; or, to create nonrepresentational imagery – that is, without identifiable subject matter. In general, however, the visual arts are all spatial in that they operate and are apprehended in space.

The medium of music is sound. Like literature, music is durational: that is, it unfolds over the period of time in which it occurs, rather than all at once. The formal elements of music are melody, rhythm, harmony, and tone color – elements that also characterize the oral life of literature. As with the visual arts, the formal elements of music are without symbolic content, but while literature, painting, and sculpture may imitate or describe nature, music is almost always nonrepresentational – it rarely has meaning beyond the sound itself. For that reason, music is the most difficult of the arts to describe in words, as well as (in the view of some) the most affective of the arts. Dance, the artform that makes the human body itself a medium of expression, is, like music, temporal and performance-oriented. Like music, dance exploits rhythm as a formal tool, but like painting and sculpture, it unfolds in space as well as time.

In analyzing the text of a work of literature, art, or music, we might ask how its formal elements contribute to its meaning and affective power. We might examine the ways in which the artist manipulates medium and form to achieve a characteristic manner of execution and expression that we call *style*. We may try to determine the extent to which a style reflects the personal vision of the artist and the larger vision of his or her time and place. Comparing the styles of various artworks from a single era, we may discover that they share certain defining features and characteristics. Similarities (both formal and stylistic) between, for instance, Golden Age Greek temples and Greek tragedies, between Chinese lyric poems and landscape paintings, and between postmodern fiction and pop sculpture, prompt us to seek the unifying moral and aesthetic values of the cultures in which they were produced.

The Context: We use the word *context* to describe the historical and cultural milieu. To determine the context, we ask: In what time and place did the artifact originate? How did it function within the society in which it was created? Was the purpose of the piece decorative, didactic, magical, propagandistic? Did it serve the religious or political needs of the community? Sometimes our answers to these questions are mere guesses. Nevertheless, understanding the function of an artifact often serves to clarify the nature of its form (and vice-versa). For instance, much of the literature produced prior to the fifteenth century was spoken or sung rather than read; for that reason, such literature tends to feature repetition and rhyme, devices that facilitated memorization. We can assume that literary works embellished with frequent repetitions, such as the *Epic of Gilgamesh* and the Hebrew Bible, were products of an oral tradition. Determining the original function of an artwork also permits us to assess its significance in its own time and place: The paintings on the walls of Paleolithic caves, which are among the most compelling animal illustrations in the history of world art, are not "artworks" in the modern sense of the term; cave art was most probably an extension of sacred hunting rituals, the performance of which was essential to the survival of the community. Understanding the relationship between text and context is one of the principal concerns of any inquiry into the humanistic tradition.

The Subtext: The *subtext* of the literary or artistic object refers to its secondary and implied meanings. The subtext embraces the emotional or intellectual messages embedded in, or implied by, a work of art. The epic poems of the ancient Greeks, for instance, which glorify prowess and physical courage, carry a subtext that suggests such virtues are exclusively male. The state portraits of the seventeenth-century French ruler, Louis XIV, carry the subtext of unassailable and absolute power. In our own century, Andy Warhol's serial adaptations of soup cans and Coca-Cola bottles offer wry commentary on the supermarket mentality of postmodern American culture. Analyzing the implicit message of an artwork helps us to determine the values and customs of the age in which it was produced and to test these values against others.

Beyond *The Humanistic Tradition*

This book offers only small, enticing samples from an enormous cultural buffet. To dine more fully, students are encouraged to go beyond the sampling presented at this table; and for the most sumptuous feasting, nothing can substitute for first-hand experience. Students, therefore, should make every effort to supplement this book with visits to art museums and galleries, concert halls, theaters, and libraries. *The Humanistic Tradition* is designed for typical students, who may or may not be able to read music, but who surely are able to cultivate an appreciation of music in performance. The clefs that appear in the text refer to the forty-five Music Listening Selections found on two accompanying cassettes, available from Brown and Benchmark Publishers. Lists of suggestions for further reading are included at the end of each chapter, while a selected general bibliography of humanities resources appears at the end of each book.

The Second Edition

The second edition of *The Humanistic Tradition* broadens the coverage of non-European cultures, while emphasizing the fertile, reciprocal nature of global interchange. This edition also gives increased attention to the contributions of women artists and writers. Selections from the writings of the Han historian, Ssu-ma Ch'ien; from Li Ju-chen's eighteenth-century satire, *Flowers in the Mirror*; and from modern Chinese and Japanese poetry enhance our appreciation of the Asian literary tradition. A new, more graceful and precise translation of the Koran appears in Book 2. Three Native American tales have been added to Book 3. Short stories by Isabel Allende (Chile) and Chinua Achebe (Africa) now enrich Book 6, which has been updated to include a section on sexual orientation, AIDS art, and the most recent developments in global culture. In response to the requests and suggestions of numerous readers, we have added literary selections from the works of Cervantes, Pushkin, Frederick Douglass, Dostoevsky, Nietzsche, Kate Chopin, and Gwendolyn Brooks; and we have lengthened the excerpts from the *Iliad*, Virgil's *Aeneid*, the Gospel of Matthew, the writings of Augustine, Dante's *Inferno*, *Sundiata*, Chaucer's *Canterbury Tales*, Milton's *Paradise Lost*, and Whitman's *Leaves of Grass*.

The second edition offers a larger selection of high quality color illustrations and a number of new illustrations, some representative of the rich legacy of Japanese art. Expanded timelines and glossaries, updated bibliographies, and color maps provide convenient study resources for readers. In Book 3, materials on the Euro-American encounter have been augmented with text and illustrations. To facilitate the transition from Book 3 to Book 4, we have added to the latter an introductory summary of the Renaissance and the Reformation. Other changes of organization and emphasis have been made in response to the bountiful suggestions of readers.

Acknowledgments

Writing *The Humanistic Tradition* has been an exercise in humility. Without the assistance of learned friends and colleagues, assembling a book of this breadth would have been an impossible task. James H. Dormon read all parts of the manuscript and made extensive and substantive editorial suggestions; as his colleague, best friend, and wife, I am most deeply indebted to him. I owe thanks to the following faculty members of the University of Southwestern Louisiana: for literature, Allen David Barry, Darrell Bourque, C. Harry Bruder, John W. Fiero, Emilio F. Garcia, Doris Meriwether, and Patricia K. Rickels; for history, Ora-Wes S. Cady, John Moore, Bradley Pollack, and Thomas D. Schoonover; for philosophy, Steve Giambrone and Robert T. Kirkpatrick; for geography, Tim Reilly; for the sciences, Mark Konikoff and John R. Meriwether; and for music, James Burke and Robert F. Schmalz.

The following readers and viewers generously shared their insights in matters of content and style: Michael K. Aakhus (University of Southern Indiana), Vaughan B. Baker (University of Southwestern Louisiana), Katherine Charlton (Mt. San Antonio Community College), Bessie Chronaki (Central Piedmont Community College), Debora A. Drehen (Florida Community College – Jacksonville), Paula Drewek (Macomb Community College), William C. Gentry (Henderson State University), Kenneth Ganza (Colby College), Ellen Hofman (Highline Community College), Burton Raffel (University of Southwestern Louisiana), Frank La Rosa (San Diego City College), George Rogers (Stonehill College), Douglas P. Sjoquist (Lansing Community College), Howard V. Starks (Southeastern Oklahoma State University), Ann Wakefield (Academy of the Sacred Heart – Grand Coteau), Sylvia White (Florida Community College – Jacksonville), and Audrey Wilson (Florida State University).

The University of Southwestern Louisiana facilitated my lengthy commitment to this project with two Summer Faculty Research Grants. I am indebted also to the University Honors Program and to the secretarial staff of the Department of History and Philosophy. The burden of preparing the second edition has been considerably lightened by the able and spirited assistance of Rosemary Bradley, Associate Publisher at Brown and Benchmark; and by the editorial efficiency of Melanie White at Calmann and King Limited. Finally, I am deeply grateful to my students; their sense of wonder and enthusiasm for learning are continuing reminders of why this book was written.

In the preparation of the second edition, I have benefited from the suggestions and comments generously offered by numerous readers, only some of whom are listed below. I am indebted to the various members of four fine Humanities "teams" – those at Hampton College (Hampton, Virginia), Kean College (Union, New Jersey), Thiel College (Greenville, Pennsylvania), and Tallahassee Community College (Florida). Special thanks go to Enid Housty at Hampton, James R. Bloomfield at Thiel, and Jim Davis and Roy Barineau at Tallahassee. Useful guidance for the revision was provided by other members of these departments including Muntaz Ahmad and Mabel Khawaja (Hampton); Elizabeth Kirby, Ursula Morgan, and Elizabeth Stein (Tallahassee); and also Elizabeth Folger Pennington (Santa Fe Community College).

Special thanks also to Charles Muenchow (Tallahassee Community College) for critical commentary on Early Christianity and Buddhism; B. Ross Brown (Northern Arizona University) and Anne H. Lisca (Santa Fe Community College) for reviewing the final manuscript of Book 2.

SUPPLEMENTS FOR THE INSTRUCTOR

A number of useful supplements are available to instructors using *The Humanistic Tradition*. Please contact your Brown & Benchmark representative or call 1-800-338 5371 to obtain these resources, or to ask for further details.

Audiocassettes

Two ninety-minute audiocassettes containing a total of forty-five musical selections have been designed exclusively for use with *The Humanistic Tradition*. Cassette One corresponds to the music listening selections discussed in Books 1–3 and Cassette Two contains the music in Books 4–6. Each selection on the cassettes is discussed in the text and includes a voice introduction for easier location. Instructors may obtain copies of the cassettes for classroom use by calling 1-800-338 5371. Individual cassettes may be purchased separately; however, upon the request of instructors who place book orders, Cassette One or Two can be packaged with any of the six texts, so that students may use the musical examples *along with* the text.

Slide Sets

A set of 50 book-specific slides is available to adopters of *The Humanistic Tradition*. These slides have been especially selected to include many of the less well-known images in the books, and will be a useful complement to your present slide resources. Please contact your Brown & Benchmark representative for further details.

A larger set of 200 book-specific slides is available for purchase from Sandak, Inc. For further information, please contact Sandak, 180 Harvard Avenue, Stamford, CT 06902 (phone 1-800-343-2806, fax 203-967-2445).

Instructor's Resource Manual

The Instructor's Resource Manual, written by Paul Antal of Front Range Community College, Boulder, and Regis University, Denver, is designed to assist instructors as they plan and prepare for classes. Course outlines and sample syllabi for both semester and quarter systems are included. The chapter summaries emphasize key themes and topics that give focus to the primary source readings. The study questions for each chapter may be removed and copied as handouts for student discussion or written assignments. The *Factual Questions* allow students to recapture the important points of each chapter, while the *Challenge Questions* force students to think more deeply and critically about the subject matter.

The Test Item File, previously at the end of the manual, has been revised and expanded, and is now divided by chapter. Each chapter also has a correlation list that directs instructors to the appropriate music examples, slides, transparencies, and software sections of the other supplements. A list of suggested videotapes, recordings, videodiscs and their suppliers is included.

MicroTest III

The questions in the test item file are available on MicroTest III, a powerful but easy-to-use test generating program by Chariot Software Group. MicroTest is available for DOS, Windows, and Macintosh personal computers. With MicroTest, an instructor can easily select the questions from the test item file and print a test and answer key. You can customize questions, headings, and instructions, you can add or import questions of your own, and with the Windows and Macintosh versions, you can print your test in a choice of fonts if your printer supports them. You can obtain a copy of MicroTest III by contacting your local Brown & Benchmark sales representative or by phoning Educational Resources at 1-800-338-5371.

Call-In/Mail-In/Fᴀx Service

You may use Brown & Benchmark's convenient call-in/mail-in/FAX service to generate tests. Using this test item file, select the questions to include in the customized test. Then simply call (1-800-338-5371), mail (Brown & Benchmark Publishers/25 Kessel Court/Madison, WI 53711), or FAX (608-277-7351) your request to Educational Resources. Within two working days of receiving your order, Brown & Benchmark will send by first-class mail (or FAX), a test master, a student answer sheet, and an answer key for fast and easy grading.

Brown & Benchmark *Humanities Transparencies*

A set of 71 acetate transparencies is available with *The Humanistic Tradition*. These show examples of art concepts, architectural styles, art media, maps, musical notation, musical styles, and musical elements.

Culture 2.0 ©

Developed by Cultural Resources, Inc., for courses in interdisciplinary humanities, Culture 2.0 © is a fascinating journey into humanity's cultural achievements on Hypercard © software. Available in either IBM PC or Macintosh formats, this seven-disk program allows students to explore the achievements of humanity through essays, almanacs, visual, or musical examples. Each time period contains historical, political, religious, philosophical, artistic, and musical categories, creating an interactive, Socratic method of learning for the students. Culture 2.0 © also features note-taking capabilities, report capabilities, and a student workbook for more guided learning. Contact your Brown & Benchmark representative for preview disks or ordering information.

	0 C.E.	250	500	600	700	800

WORLD EVENTS

Jesus crucified ca. 33
Paul's missionary journeys
Council of Nicaea 325
Benedict establishes monasticism
Battle of Tours 732

MEDIEVAL EUROPE
EAR[LY]
Charlemag[ne]
ROMAN EMPIRE
West Visigoths Fall of
sack Rome
Rome 410
East
Gregory the Great sends out Christian missionaries

Rome destroys Jerusalem 70
BYZANTINE EMPIRE
Diocletian divides Roman Empire 286
Battle of Adrianople 378
Justinian codifies Roman law 533
Constantine issues Edict of Milan 313
ISLAMIC CIVILIZATION
Mystery cults
Barbarian migrations: Goths, Huns
Birth of Muhammad 570
North Africa and Spain under Muslim rule

India: — GUPTA EMPIRE — Hun invasion — Regional Indian kingdoms — Muslim rul[e] in India

China: — HAN ERA — T'ANG ERA —
Mahayana Buddhism in China

Japan:
Buddhism enters Japan

LITERATURE AND PHILOSOPHY

Apuleius: *"Cult of Isis"*
Plotinus and Neoplatonism
Tacitus: *History of the Germans*
Carolingian Renaissance: religious and secular manuscripts

Gospels
Paul's letters
Nicene Creed
St. Jerome: *Vulgate*
St. Augustine: *Confessions, City of God*
Germanic epics: *Beowulf*
Plato's Academy closed 529
The Koran
Romance of Antar

Zen Buddhism

Asvaghosha: *Sermons of the Buddha*

The Golden Age [of]
Li Po
Tu Fu

Sanskrit poetry

VISUAL ARTS AND ARCHITECTURE

Christian catacombs
EARLY CHRISTIAN basilicas: Old St. Peter's, St. Paul's
BYZANTINE STYLE
Hagia Sophia, Constantinople
San Vitale, Ravenna
Sant' Apollinaire Nuovo, Ravenna
Lindisfarne gospels
Sutton Hoo treasure
Ardagh chalice

Christ as Good Shepherd

Great Mosq[ue] at Cordoba

Sarcophagus of Theodorus

Great Stupa at Sanchi
Indian Gandhara sculpture: *Buddha Teaching the Law*
Buddhist pagoda at Nara

Chaitya caves
Ajanta frescoes
Chinese/Buddhist altarpieces
Buddhist pagoda at Mt. Sung
T'ang tomb figurin[es]

MUSIC AND DANCE

St. Ambrose: "Ancient Morning Hymn"
Gregorian chant monophony

Tarafa: odes

Indian classical dance: *raga, tala, sitar*
Buddhist chant
Muezzin call to prayer
Arabic *ud* (lute)
Muslim Spain: orchestral compositions

900	1000	1100	1200	1300	1400

Viking invasions   Norman Conquest   First universities founded in Europe
of England 1066

Rise of towns and guilds   Philip IV ruler
of France

DLE AGES ——————————————— HIGH MIDDLE AGES ———————

bands his empire   Split between the   Medieval papacy
Roman Catholic and   Christian   Establishment of   at its height   Boniface VIII:
the Greek Orthodox   crusades   Franciscan order   Unam Sanctum
Church   1094-1204   1302

Baghdad becomes   Mongols conquer
important center   Baghdad 1258

Delhi
sultanate

lock printing   SUNG ERA   Movable type   Introduction of   Marco Polo reaches
nvented   invented   paper currency   China ca. 1275

HEIAN ERA   KAMAKURA
SHOGUNATE
Rise of the
Samurai

Lindau Gospels   MEDIEVAL SCHOLASTICISM

Song of Roland   Abelard: Sic   Aquinas: Summa
transcribed   et Non   Troubadour and   Theologica
trouvère lyrics

Dante: Divine
Avicenna: Canon of   Comedy
Medicine   Medieval romance
Chrétien de Troyes: Lancelot

Mystery and miracle plays
Morality play: Everyman

hinese poetry
Po Chu-i

World's earliest   Vidyakara: Japanese novels,   Sung Dynasty: Chinese novels, short
printed book: Treasury of   short stories: painted album   stories, popular theater:
Diamond Sutra   Well-Tuned   Murasakii: Tale of   leaves and   Luo Guanzhong: Three
Verse   Genii   scrolls   Kingdoms

Carolingian Abbey Church   ROMANESQUE STYLE   GOTHIC STYLE
St. Gall   Pilgrimage Church: St. Sernin   St. Denis Abbey Church
Chapel at Aachen   Gislebertus at Autun Cathedral   Chartres Cathedral   Cimabue:
Norman architecture: Notre Dame of Paris   Madonna Enthroned
Bayeux tapestry   Notre Dame of Amiens   Martini: Annunciation
Dover Castle   Ste. Chapelle, Paris

Chinese landscape
painting: Hindu temple:
Li Ch'eng: A   Kandriya Mahadeo
Solitary Temple   Chola bronzes:
Chinese porcelains   Shiva Lord of the Dance

Antiphons, tropes,   Organum/early polyphony   Bernart de   Leonin: Magnus Liber
sequences   The Play of Herod   Ventadour: Organi
Jongleurs: troubadour songs   Perotin: 3- and 4- part   Estampie
chansons   Guido of Arezzo: polphony
de geste   musical notation

Al-Isfahani: Great   Motets   Dies irae
Book of Songs

Chinese opera and
court music

PART
I
TRANSITION TO THE MIDDLE AGES

Scholars once described the thousand-year period between the fall of Rome and the age of the Renaissance as a "dark" age whose cultural achievements fell far short of those of ancient Greece and Rome. Our present understanding of the Middle Ages suggests otherwise. As the following chapters indicate, the Middle Ages was one of the most brilliant chapters in the history of Western culture. During the Early Middle Ages, that is, the first seven centuries of the first millennium, a transition from classical to Christian culture took place in the West. Elsewhere in the world, the same period witnessed the vitalizing effects of two world religions: Buddhism and Islam. So powerful were these religious faiths – Christianity, Buddhism, and Islam – that by the year 1000, the Eastern hemisphere could be described as being divided among them (Map **8.1**).

From the perspective of world history, the transition to the Middle Ages encompassed several significant developments: the decline of classical civilization in the West and the rise of Christianity; the expansion of Germanic tribal peoples into the Roman Empire; the Golden Age of Byzantine civilization; the spread of Buddhism from India to China; and finally, the birth and expansion of Islam in the Near East and beyond.

Chapter 8, "A Flowering of Faith," examines the climate of religious renewal that produced Christianity in the West and Buddhism in the East, and reviews the spiritual message of each of these world faiths. Chapter 9, "The Language of Faith," surveys the establishment of the Early Christian Church, the shift from classical to Christian art in Byzantium and the West, and the evidence of Buddhism in the art, architecture, and music of India and China. Chapter 10, "Expansive Cultures," describes the ways in which the Germanic tribes entering the West affected the cultural identity of the Christian Middle Ages. The chapter also explores the rich cultural heritage of Islam – a religion practiced today by almost a billion people – and analyzes the influence of Islam on the medieval West.

(opposite) Detail of Figure 9.17 *Jesus calling the first apostles, Peter and Andrew*. From the north-wall upper-register mosaic in Sant' Apollinare Nuovo, Ravenna, Italy, early sixth century C.E. Scala, Florence.

8

A Flowering of Faith:
Religious Renewal West and East

Shortly after the reign of the Roman Emperor Octavian, in the province of Judaea (the Roman name for Palestine), an obscure Jewish preacher named Joshua (in Greek, *Jesus*) brought forth a message that became the basis for a new world religion: Christianity. Christianity came to provide an alternative to the secular, rational values associated with classical culture in the West. The pursuit of reason and earthly wisdom gave way to the promise of messianic deliverance and eternal life.

As Christianity began to win converts within the Roman Empire, an equally significant world faith — Buddhism — was spreading throughout the Far East. The message of Siddhartha Gautama, the fifth-century B.C.E.* founder of Buddhism, swept through Asia, and by the first century C.E., Buddhism had become the principal religious faith of Han China. The similarities and differences between Buddhism and Christianity offer valuable insight into humankind's cultural history. And while no in-depth analysis of either religion can be offered here, a brief look at the formative stages of Christianity and Buddhism sheds light on their importance to the humanistic tradition.

The Background to Christianity
Roman Religion and Religious Philosophies

Roman religion, like Roman culture itself, was a blend of native and borrowed traditions. Ancient pagan religious rituals celebrated seedtime and harvest. Augury, the interpretation of omens – a practice borrowed from the Etruscans – was important to Roman religious life. Such Roman deities as Vesta, who guarded the hearthfire, and Mars, God of War, protected household and state. At the same time, the Romans worshiped

Greek gods such as Zeus, Hera, and Aphrodite, among others, to whom they had given Latin names: Jupiter, Juno, and Venus. The fact that the Romans welcomed the gods of other cultures and honored them along with the greater and lesser Roman gods meant that there was little religious uniformity in the empire. Furthermore, while many Romans anticipated an otherworldly realm (similar to the Greek Hades or the Hebrew Sheol) in which the souls of the dead survived, Roman religion offered no clear promise of life after death.

Rome hosted a wide variety of religious beliefs and practices, along with a number of quasireligious Hellenistic philosophies, including Epicureanism, Stoicism, and Neoplatonism. Based on the writings of Plato and the Platonic Theory of Forms, Neoplatonism aimed at the attainment of a mystical union between the individual soul and "the One," or Ultimate Being, a concept comparable to Plato's Form of Goodness. According to Plotinus, a third-century C.E. Egyptian-born Neoplatonist, the soul's purification was accomplished by its ascent through a series of levels or degrees of spiritual purification. Neoplatonism was to have a far-reaching influence on the development of Christian thought.

Following the decline of the Roman Republic and in the wake of increased contacts with Egypt and the Near East, Rome absorbed a number of uniquely Eastern traditions. Roman emperors came to be regarded as theocratic monarchs and were given titles such as *dominus* (lord) and *deus* (god). By the second century, Rome enjoyed a full-blown imperial cult honoring the living emperor as semidivine and deifying him after his death. At the same time, an increasing distrust of reason and a growing impulse toward mysticism accompanied widespread social, political, and economic unrest. These circumstances led many to seek salvation in a heavenly rather than an earthly kingdom. The mystery cults of the Near and Middle East and, ultimately, Christianity, would answer these needs.

---

*Dates are designated as B.C.E., "Before the Christian (or Common) Era," or C.E., "Christian (or Common) Era."

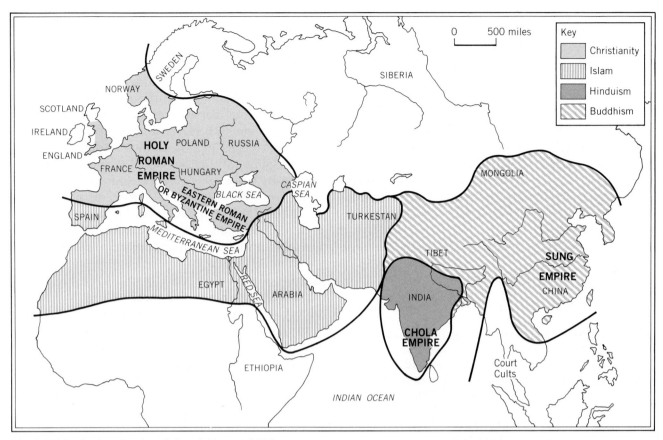

Map 8.1 Distribution of major religious faiths, ca. 1000 c.e.

The Mystery Cults

In the Near East, there had long flourished numerous religious cults whose appeal was less intellectual than Neoplatonism and far more personal than that of the prevailing Greco-Roman religious philosophies. The promise of personal immortality was the central feature of these cults, known as "mystery cults" – from the fact that their initiation rituals were secret (in Greek *mysterios*). The cults of Isis in Egypt, Cybele in Phrygia, Dionysus in Greece, and Mithra in Persia, to name but four, had a heritage dating back to Neolithic times. As we have seen in earlier chapters, ancient agricultural societies celebrated seasonal change by means of symbolic performances of the birth, death, and rebirth of gods and goddesses associated with the regeneration of the crops. The mystery cults perpetuated these practices. Their initiates participated in symbolic acts of spiritual death and rebirth, including ritual baptism and a communal meal at which they might partake of the flesh or blood of the deity.

The cult of Isis originated in the Egyptian myth of the descent of the goddess Isis into the underworld to find and resurrect her mate Osiris (see chapter 2). Followers of this cult identified Isis as earth mother and Queen of Heaven and looked to her to ensure their own salvation (Figure 8.1). Initiation into the cult included

Figure 8.1 *Isis and Horus enthroned*, Middle Egyptian, fourth century c.e. Limestone, height 35 in. Staatliche Museum, Berlin.

formal processions, a ritual meal, purification of the body, and a ten-day period of fasting that culminated in the ecstatic vision of the goddess herself. During the second century C.E., in a Latin novel entitled *The Golden Ass*, or *Metamorphoses*, the Roman writer Lucius Apuleius described the initiation rites of the cult of Isis. At the close of the ceremony, according to Apuleius, the initiate fell prostrate before the image of the Queen of Heaven and recited the prayer that is reproduced in part in the passage that follows. The ecstatic tone of this prayer – a startling departure from the measured, rational tone of most Greco-Roman literature – reflects the mood of religious longing that characterized the late classical era.

READING 29

From Apuleius' *Initiation into the Cult of Isis*

"O holy and eternal savior of mankind, you who ever   1
bountifully nurture mortals, you apply the sweet affection of a mother to the misfortunes of the wretched. Neither a day nor a night nor even a tiny moment passes empty of your blessings: you protect men on sea and land, and you drive away the storm-winds of life and stretch forth your rescuing hand, with which you unwind the threads of the Fates even when they are inextricably twisted, you calm the storms of Fortune, and you repress harmful motions of the stars. The spirits above revere you, the spirits below   10
pay you homage. You rotate the earth, light the sun, rule the universe, and tread Tartarus[1] beneath your heel. The stars obey you, the seasons return at your will, deities rejoice in you, and the elements are your slaves. At your nod breezes breathe, clouds give nourishment, seeds sprout, and seedlings grow. Your majesty awes the birds travelling the sky, the beasts wandering upon the mountains, the snakes lurking in the ground, and the monsters that swim in the deep. But my talent is too feeble to speak your praises and my inheritance too meagre to   20
bring you sacrifices. The fullness of my voice is inadequate to express what I feel about your majesty; a thousand mouths and as many tongues would not be enough, nor even an endless flow of inexhaustible speech. I shall therefore take care to do the only thing that a devout but poor man can: I shall store your divine countenance and sacred godhead in the secret places of my heart, forever guarding it and picturing it to myself . . . ."

— ◆ —

While the worship of Isis, Dionysus, and Cybele were peculiar to the Mediterranean, the most popular of the many Near Eastern mystery cults – the cult of Mithra – centered in Persia. Associated with the sun and with the forces of Light and Goodness in ancient Persian religion, the man-god Mithra was believed to have achieved immortality by slaughtering the Bull of Fertility. Mithra's followers, who sought in this hero-god the blessing of immortality, celebrated his birth on the twenty-fifth of December, that is, just after the winter solstice. Mithraism, which excluded the participation of women, involved strict initiation rites, periods of fasting, ritual baptism, and a communal meal of bread and wine. The favorite religion of Roman soldiers, who readily identified with Mithra's heroism and self-discipline, Mithraism spread throughout Europe and North Africa, where archeologists have discovered numerous Mithraic chapels. Indeed, for the first two centuries of this millennium, Mithraism was the chief rival of Christianity. The similarities between Mithraism and Christianity – a man-god hero, ritual baptism, a communal meal, and the promise of personal immortality – suggest that some of the basic features of Christianity already existed as a pattern in the religious history of the Near East prior to the time of Jesus. It is no surprise that many educated Romans considered Christianity to be an imitation of Mithraism.

Although the mystery cults often involved costly and demanding rituals, they were successful in attracting devotees. The Romans readily accommodated the exotic gods and goddesses of these cults as long as their worship did not violate the demands of the Roman imperial cult or threaten the security of the Roman state.

The Jewish Background

Judaism differed from the other religions of the classical world in its ethical bias and its commitment to monotheism. Judaism, the main religion of Judaea (which had become a Roman province in 63 B.C.E.), forbade the worship of the Roman emperor and the gods of the Roman state. Hence the Roman presence in Jerusalem caused nothing but animosity and discord, and, ultimately, conflict between Rome and Judaea came to a head in the Roman destruction of Jerusalem in 70 C.E.* (see Figure 7.18). During the first century B.C.E., however, political unrest in Judaea was complicated by disunity within the Jewish community. The leading groups of **rabbis** (Jewish teachers) disagreed over such important matters of biblical interpretation as the question of life after death and the nature of the **Messiah** ("Anointed One") anticipated by some of the Hebrew prophets. The Sadducees, a learned sect of Jewish aristocrats who advocated cultural and religious unity among the Jews, envisioned the Messiah as a temporal leader who would consolidate Jewish ideals and lead the Jews to political freedom. They denied that

---

[1]In Greek mythology, a part of the underworld where the wicked are punished.

*Hereafter, unless otherwise designated, all dates refer to the Christian (or Common) era.

the soul survived the death of the body. The Pharisees, the more influential group of Jewish teachers and the principal interpreters of Hebrew law, believed in the advent of a spiritual redeemer who would lead the righteous to salvation. In their view, the soul was imperishable and the souls of the wicked would suffer eternal punishment.

In addition to the Sadducees and the Pharisees, there existed in Judaea a minor religious sect called the Essenes, whose members lived in monastic communities near the Dead Sea. The Essenes renounced worldly goods and practiced **asceticism**, strict self-denial and self-discipline. The Essenes believed in the immortality of the soul and its ultimate release and liberation from the body. They anticipated the coming of a teacher of truth who would ultimately suffer martyrdom. The Dead Sea Scrolls — some of the oldest extant fragments of the Hebrew Bible — have been found in caves near Essene ruins in the desert cliffs near the western shore of the Dead Sea. In Judaea, where all of these groups along with scores of self-proclaimed miracle workers and preachers competed for an audience, the climate of intense religious expectation was altogether receptive to the appearance of a charismatic leader.

The Message of Jesus

That charismatic leader proved to be a young Jewish rabbi from the city of Nazareth (Figure 8.2). Since Jesus of Nazareth (0–33 C.E) is not mentioned in non-Christian literature until almost the end of the first century C.E., the historical Jesus is an elusive figure. Our most important source of information concerning Jesus is the Christian Gospels (literally, "good news"). The Gospels, the earliest of which dates from at least forty years after Jesus' death, provide the earliest biographical evidence of the life of Jesus. Yet, since the authors of the Gospels — the evangelists Mark, Matthew, Luke, and John — gave most of their attention to the last months of Jesus' life, the Gospels are not biographies in the true sense of the word. Perhaps because Jesus' followers anticipated his imminent return, they made no effort to keep a careful historical record of their master's life.

Recorded in Greek, the Gospels describe the life and miracles of an elusive but inspiring teacher. Like all great teachers, Jesus was concerned with ethical matters. His message, cast in simple and direct language and in parables that carried moral lessons, was essentially pacifistic and antimaterialistic. He warned of the perils of riches and the temptations of the temporal world. Jesus' insistence upon the evils of material wealth represented a radically new direction in ancient culture. Despite such exceptions as the Essenes, the Neoplatonists, and the Stoics, the classical world

Figure 8.2 *Christ Enthroned*, ca. 350–360 C.E. Marble, smaller than life size. National Museum, Rome. © Hirmer Fotoarchiv.

was fundamentally materialistic and secular. Jesus preached the renunciation of material goods ("do not lay up for yourselves treasures on earth") not merely as a means of freeing the soul from temporal enslavement, but as a preparation for eternal life.

With a reformer's zeal, Jesus criticized the Judaism of his day, and especially its emphasis on the observance of ritual. He embraced the spirit (rather than the letter) of Hebrew law and proclaimed the primacy of faith over ritual. Asked which of the laws were primary, Jesus cited love of God and love of one's neighbor (Matthew 22:34–40). He pictured God as stern but merciful, loving and protective, rather than chastising (recall Job's Yahweh) or remote and inaccessible (as with the deities of the mystery cults). Finally, and most importantly, Jesus preached the cultivation of compassion, righteousness, and trust in God, the rewards for which would be reaped in the "kingdom of heaven." For all its simplicity and directness, the message of Jesus prescribed an almost impossibly altruistic ideal, an ideal of unconditional love linked to an equally lofty imperative: "You must be perfect just as your heavenly Father is perfect."

The Sermon on the Mount, as recorded by the apostle Matthew, is probably the most representative of Jesus' sermons. Here Jesus sets forth the basic injunctions of an uncompromising ethic to which moral intention is more important than outward behavior: Love your neighbor; accept persecution with humility; pass no judgement on others; and treat others as you would have them treat you.

READING 30

From the Sermon on the Mount
(Matthew 5; 6:1–21; 7:1–14)

Chapter 5: The Beatitudes
[1]Seeing the crowds, he went onto the mountain. And when he was seated his disciples came to him. [2]Then he began to speak. This is what he taught them:

[3]How blessed are the poor in spirit:
the kingdom of Heaven is theirs.
[4]Blessed are *the gentle*:
they shall have the earth as inheritance.
[5]Blessed are those who mourn:
they shall be comforted.
[6]Blessed are those
who hunger and thirst for uprightness:
they shall have their fill.
[7]Blessed are the merciful:
they shall have mercy shown them.
[8]Blessed are the pure in heart:
they shall see God.
[9]Blessed are the peacemakers:
they shall be recognised
as children of God.
[10]Blessed are those who are persecuted
in the cause of uprightness:
the kingdom of Heaven is theirs.

[11]"Blessed are you when people abuse you and persecute you and speak all kinds of calumny against you falsely on my account. [12]Rejoice and be glad, for your reward will be great in heaven; this is how they persecuted the prophets before you.

Salt for the earth and light for the world
[13]"You are salt for the earth. But if salt loses its taste, what can make it salty again? It is good for nothing, and can only be thrown out to be trampled under people's feet.

[14]"You are light for the world. A city built on a hill-top cannot be hidden. [15]No one lights a lamp to put it under a tub; they put it on the lamp-stand where it shines for everyone in the house. [16]In the same way your light must shine in people's sight, so that, seeing your good works, they may give praise to your Father in heaven.

The fulfilment of the Law
[17]"Do not imagine that I have come to abolish the Law or the Prophets. I have come not to abolish but to complete them. [18]In truth I tell you, till heaven and earth disappear, not one dot, not one little stroke, is to disappear from the Law until all its purpose is achieved. [19]Therefore, anyone who infringes even one of the least of these commandments and teaches others to do the same will be considered the least in the kingdom of Heaven; but the person who keeps them and teaches them will be considered great in the kingdom of Heaven.

The new standard higher than the old
[20]"For I tell you, if your uprightness does not surpass that of the scribes and Pharisees, you will never get into the kingdom of Heaven.

[21]"You have heard how it was said to our ancestors, *You shall not kill*; and if anyone does kill he must answer for it before the court. [22]But I say this to you, anyone who is angry with a brother will answer for it before the court; anyone who calls a brother 'Fool' will answer for it before the Sanhedrin; and anyone who calls him 'Traitor' will answer for it in hell fire. [23]So then, if you are bringing your offering to the altar and there remember that your brother has something against you, [24]leave your offering there before the altar, go and be reconciled with your brother first, and then come back and present your offering. [25]Come to terms with your opponent in good time while you are still on the way to the court with him, or he may hand you over to the judge and the judge to the officer, and you will be thrown into prison. [26]In truth I tell you, you will not get out till you have paid the last penny.

[27]"You have heard how it was said, *You shall not commit adultery*. [28]But I say this to you, if a man looks at a woman lustfully, he has already committed adultery with her in his heart. [29]If your right eye should be your downfall, tear it out and throw it away; for it will do you less harm to lose one part of yourself than to have your whole body thrown into hell. [30]And if your right hand should be your downfall, cut it off and throw it away; for it will do you less harm to lose one part of yourself than to have your whole body go to hell.

[31]"It has also been said, *Anyone who divorces his wife must give her a writ of dismissal*. [32]But I say this to you, everyone who divorces his wife, except for the case of an illicit marriage, makes her an adulteress; and anyone who marries a divorced woman commits adultery.

[33]"Again, you have heard how it was said to our ancestors, *You must not break your oath, but must fulfil your oaths to the Lord*. [34]But I say this to you, do not swear at all, either by *heaven*, since that is *God's throne*; [35]or by *earth*, since that is *his footstool*; or by Jerusalem, since that is *the city of the great King*. [36]Do not swear by your own head either, since you cannot turn a single hair white or black. [37]All you need say is 'Yes' if you mean yes, 'No' if you mean no; anything more than this comes from the Evil One.

[38]"You have heard how it was said: *Eye for eye and tooth for tooth.* [39]But I say this to you: offer no resistance to the wicked. On the contrary, if anyone hits you on the right cheek, offer him the other as well; [40]if someone wishes to go to law with you to get your tunic, let him have your cloak as well. [41]And if anyone requires you to go one mile, go two miles with him. [42]Give to anyone who asks you, and if anyone wants to borrow, do not turn away.

[43]"You have heard how it was said, *You will love your neighbour* and hate your enemy. [44]But I say this to you, love your enemies and pray for those who persecute you; [45]so that you may be children of your Father in heaven, for he causes his sun to rise on the bad as well as the good, and sends down rain to fall on the upright and the wicked alike. [46]For if you love those who love you, what reward will you get? Do not even the tax collectors do as much? [47]And if you save your greetings for your brothers, are you doing anything exceptional? [48]Do not even the gentiles do as much? You must therefore be perfect, just as your heavenly Father is perfect."

Chapter 6: Almsgiving in secret

[1]"Be careful not to parade your uprightness in public to attract attention; otherwise you will lose all reward from your Father in heaven. [2]So when you give alms, do not have it trumpeted before you; this is what the hypocrites do in the synagogues and in the streets to win human admiration. In truth I tell you, they have had their reward. [3]But when you give alms, your left hand must not know what your right is doing; [4]your almsgiving must be secret, and your Father who sees all that is done in secret will reward you.

Prayer in secret

[5]"And when you pray, do not imitate the hypocrites; they love to say their prayers standing up in the synagogues and at the street corners for people to see them. In truth I tell you, they have had their reward. [6]But when you pray, *go to your private room*, shut yourself in, and so pray to your Father who is in that secret place, and your Father who sees all that is done in secret will reward you.

How to pray. The Lord's Prayer

[7]"In your prayers do not babble as the gentiles do, for they think that by using many words they will make themselves heard. [8]Do not be like them; your Father knows what you need before you ask him. [9]So you should pray like this:

Our Father in heaven,
may your name be held holy,
[10]your kingdom come,
your will be done,
on earth as in heaven.
[11]Give us today our daily bread.
[12]And forgive us our debts,
as we have forgiven those
who are in debt to us.
[13]And do not put us to the test,
but save us from the Evil One.

[14]"Yes, if you forgive others their failings, your heavenly Father will forgive you yours; [15]but if you do not forgive others, your Father will not forgive your failings either.

Fasting in secret

[16]"When you are fasting, do not put on a gloomy look as the hypocrites do: they go about looking unsightly to let people know they are fasting. In truth I tell you, they have had their reward. [17]But when you fast, put scent on your head and wash your face, [18]so that no one will know you are fasting except your Father who sees all that is done in secret; and your Father who sees all that is done in secret will reward you.

True treasures

[19]"Do not store up treasures for yourselves on earth, where moth and woodworm destroy them and thieves can break in and steal. [20]But store up treasures for yourselves in heaven, where neither moth nor woodworm destroys them and thieves cannot break in and steal. [21]For wherever your treasure is, there will your heart be too."

Chapter 7: Do not judge

[1]"Do not judge, and you will not be judged; [2]because the judgements you give are the judgements you will get, and the standard you use will be the standard used for you. [3]Why do you observe the splinter in your brother's eye and never notice the great log in your own? [4]And how dare you say to your brother, 'Let me take that splinter out of your eye,' when, look, there is a great log in your own? [5]Hypocrite! Take the log out of your own eye first, and then you will see clearly enough to take the splinter out of your brother's eye.

Do not profane sacred things

[6]"Do not give dogs what is holy; and do not throw your pearls in front of pigs, or they may trample them and then turn on you and tear you to pieces.

Effective prayer

[7]"Ask, and it will be given to you; search, and you will find; knock, and the door will be opened to you. [8]Everyone who asks receives; everyone who searches finds; everyone who knocks will have the door opened. [9]Is there anyone among you who would hand his son a stone when he asked for bread? [10]Or would hand him a snake when he asked for a fish? [11]If you, then, evil as you are, know how to give your children what is good, how much more will your Father in heaven give good things to those who ask him!

The golden rule

[12]"So always treat others as you would like them to treat you; that is the Law and the Prophets.

The two ways

[13]"Enter by the narrow gate, since the road that leads to destruction is wide and spacious, and many take it; [14]but it is a narrow gate and a hard road that leads to life, and only a few find it."

———————————◆———————————

The Teachings of Paul

Jesus' urgent and prophetic words, along with the stories of his miraculous acts, spread like wildfire throughout Judaea; but his message won few converts from among the Jewish population. Both the Pharisees and the Sadducees opposed Jesus and accused him of violating Jewish law. While the learned community of Judaea rejected Jesus as the biblical Messiah, the Romans condemned him as a subversive and a threat to imperial stability. By the authority of the Roman governor, Pontius Pilate, Jesus was put to death by crucifixion, the punishment that the Romans dispensed to thieves and traitors.

Despite the missionary activities of the apostles, a dedicated group of Jesus' followers, only a small percentage of the population of the Roman Empire — scholarly estimates range from ten to fifteen percent — became Christians in the first hundred years after Jesus' death. And those who did convert came mainly from communities where Jewish tradition was not strong. However, through the efforts of the best-known of the apostles, Paul (d. 65), the message of Jesus gained widespread appeal. A Jewish tent-maker from Tarsus in Asia Minor, Paul had been schooled in both Greek and Hebrew. Though he probably never met Jesus, he became a passionate convert to the teachings of the preacher from Nazareth. Paul is generally believed to have written ten to fourteen of the twenty-seven books of the Christian Scriptures or "New Testament." Paul's most important contributions lie in his having universalized and systematically explained Jesus' message. While Jesus preached only to the Jews, Paul spread the message of Jesus in the non-Jewish communities of Greece, Asia Minor, and Rome, thus earning the title "Apostle to the Gentiles." Preaching among non-Jews, Paul stressed the universal elements in Jesus' teachings, especially salvation by faith. Paul also clarified the meaning of Jesus' life on earth and explained the reason for his death. Calling Jesus the Christ (*Christos*, Greek for Messiah), he described Jesus as a sacrifice for human sin, which had entered the world through Adam and Eve's defiance of God in the Garden of Eden. Finally, Paul interpreted the death of Jesus as an act of atonement that "acquitted" humankind from the condemnation merited by Original Sin.

These concepts, which indelibly separated Christianity from both its parent faith, Judaism, and from the classical belief in the innate goodness and freedom of human nature, were set forth in Paul's Epistle to the Church in Rome, parts of which follow. Written ten years before his death, the epistle imparts a message of faith laden with a view of humankind as condemned by "the law of sin and death." Paul anticipated, however, that those who are "baptized in Christ" would "live a new life." Emphasizing the promise of eternal life, Paul thus interpreted the mission of Jesus in terms that were basic to the mystery cults: the death and resurrection of a savior god as redemption for humankind. So important was Paul's contribution to the foundations of the new faith that he has been called "the co-founder of Christianity."

READING 31

From Paul's Epistle to the Church in Rome
(Romans 1:8–17; 2:1–11; 5:1–21; 6:1–11; 8:1–8)

Chapter 1: Thanksgiving and prayer

[8]First I give thanks to my God through Jesus Christ for all of you because your faith is talked of all over the world. [9]God, whom I serve with my spirit in preaching the gospel of his Son, is my witness that I continually mention you in my prayers, [10]asking always that by some means I may at long last be enabled to visit you, if it is God's will. [11]For I am longing to see you so that I can convey to you some spiritual gift that will be a lasting strength, [12]or rather that we may be strengthened together through our mutual faith, yours and mine. [13]I want you to be quite certain too, brothers, that I have often planned to visit you — though up to the present I have always been prevented — in the hope that I might work as fruitfully among you as I have among the gentiles elsewhere. [14]I have an obligation to Greeks as well as barbarians, to the educated as well as the ignorant, [15]and hence the eagerness on my part to preach the gospel to you in Rome too.

Chapter 2: The Jews are not exempt from the retribution of God

[1]So no matter who you are, if you pass judgement you have no excuse. It is yourself that you condemn when you judge others, since you behave in the same way as those you are condemning. [2]We are well aware that people who behave like that are justly condemned by God. [3]But you — when you judge those who behave like this while you are doing the same yourself — do you think you will escape God's condemnation? [4]Or are you not disregarding his abundant goodness, tolerance and patience, failing to realise that this generosity of God is meant to bring you to repentance? [5]Your stubborn refusal to repent is only storing up retribution for yourself on that Day of retribution when God's just verdicts will be made known. [6]*He will repay everyone as their deeds deserve.* [7]For those who aimed for glory and honour and immortality by persevering in doing good, there will be eternal life; [8]but for those who out of jealousy have taken for their guide not truth but injustice, there will be the fury of retribution. [9]Trouble and distress will come to every human being who does evil — Jews first, but Greeks as well; [10]glory and honour and peace will come to everyone who does good — Jews first, but Greeks as well. [11]*There is no favouritism with God.*

Chapter 5: Faith guarantees salvation

[1]So then, now that we have been justified by faith, we are at peace with God through our Lord Jesus Christ; [2]it is through him, by faith, that we have been admitted into God's favour in which we are living, and look forward exultantly to God's glory. [3]Not only that; let us exult, too, in our hardships, understanding that hardship develops perseverance, [4]and perseverance develops a tested character, something that gives us hope, [5]and a hope which will not let us down, because the love of God has been poured into our hearts by the Holy Spirit which has been given to us. [6]When we were still helpless, at the appointed time, Christ died for the godless. [7]You could hardly find anyone ready to die even for someone upright; though it is just possible that, for a really good person, someone might undertake to die. [8]So it is proof of God's own love for us, that Christ died for us while we were still sinners. [9]How much more can we be sure, therefore, that, now that we have been justified

by his death, we shall be saved through him from the retribution of God. [10]For if, while we were enemies, we were reconciled to God through the death of his Son, how much more can we be sure that, being now reconciled, we shall be saved by his life. [11]What is more, we are filled with exultant trust in God, through our Lord Jesus Christ, through whom we have already gained our reconciliation.

Adam and Jesus Christ

[12]Well then; it was through one man that sin *came into the world*, and through sin death, and thus death has spread through the whole human race because everyone has sinned. [13]Sin already existed in the world before there was any law, even though sin is not reckoned when there is no law. [14]Nonetheless death reigned over all from Adam to Moses, even over those whose sin was not the breaking of a commandment, as Adam's was. He prefigured the One who was to come . . . .

[15]There is no comparison between the free gift and the offence. If death came to many through the offence of one man, how much greater an effect the grace of God has had, coming to so many and so plentifully as the free gift through the one man Jesus Christ! [16]Again, there is no comparison between the gift and the offence of one man. One single offence brought condemnation, but now, after many offences, have come the free gift and so acquittal! [17]It was by one man's offence that death came to reign over all, but how much greater the reign in life of those who receive the fullness of grace and the gift of saving justice, through the one man, Jesus Christ. [18]One man's offence brought condemnation on all humanity; and one man's good act has brought justification and life to all humanity. [19]Just as by one man's disobedience many were made sinners, so by one man's obedience are many to be made upright. [20]When law came on the scene, it was to multiply the offences. But however much sin increased, grace was always greater; [21]so that as sin's reign brought death, so grace was to rule through saving justice that leads to eternal life through Jesus Christ our Lord.

Chapter 6: Baptism

[1]What should we say then? Should we remain in sin so that grace may be given the more fully? [2]Out of the question! We have died to sin; how could we go on living in it? [3]You cannot have forgotten that all of us, when we were baptised into Christ Jesus, were baptised into his death. [4]So by our baptism into his death we were buried with him, so that as Christ was raised from the dead by the Father's glorious power, we too should begin living a new life. [5]If we have been joined to him by dying a death like his, so we shall be by a resurrection like his; [6]realising that our former self was crucified with him, so that the self which belonged to sin should be destroyed and we should be freed from the slavery of sin. [7]Someone who has died, of course, no longer has to answer for sin.

[8]But we believe that, if we died with Christ, then we shall live with him too. [9]We know that Christ has been raised from the dead and will never die again. Death has no power over him any more. [10]For by dying, he is dead to sin once and for all, and now the life that he lives is life with God. [11]In the same way, you must see yourselves as being dead to sin but alive for God in Christ Jesus.

Chapter 8: The life of the spirit

[1]Thus, condemnation will never come to those who are in Christ Jesus, [2]because the law of the Spirit which gives life in Christ Jesus has set you free from the law of sin and death. [3]What the Law could not do because of the weakness of human nature, God did, sending his own Son in the same human nature as any sinner to be a sacrifice for sin, and condemning sin in that human nature. [4]This was so that the Law's requirements might be fully satisfied in us as we direct our lives not by our natural inclinations but by the Spirit. [5]Those who are living by their natural inclinations have their minds on the things human nature desires; those who live in the Spirit have their minds on spiritual things. [6]And human nature has nothing to look forward to but death, while the Spirit looks forward to life and peace, [7]because the outlook of disordered human nature is opposed to God, since it does not submit to God's Law, and indeed it cannot, [8]and those who live by their natural inclinations can never be pleasing to God.

◆

The Spread of Christianity

A variety of historical factors contributed to the slow but growing reception to Christianity within the Roman Empire. The decline of the Roman Republic had left in its wake large gaps between the rich and the poor. Octavian's efforts to restore the old Roman values of duty and civic pride failed to offset increasing impersonalism and bureaucratic corruption. Furthermore, as early as the second century B.C.E., Germanic tribes had been migrating into the West and assaulting Rome's borders (see chapter 9). Repeatedly, these nomadic people put Rome on the defensive and added to the prevailing sense of insecurity. Amidst widespread oppression and grinding poverty, Christianity promised personal immortality and a life to come from which material adversities were absent. Jesus' message was easy to understand, free of cumbersome regulations and costly rituals, and (in contrast to many of the mystery cults) accessible to all – male and female, rich and poor, freeman and slave. The unique feature of the new faith, however, was its historical credibility, that is, the fact that Jesus – unlike the elusive gods of the mystery cults or the remote Yahweh – had actually lived among men and women and had practiced the morality he preached.

Nevertheless, at the outset, the new religion failed to win official approval. While both Roman religion and the mystery cults were receptive to many gods, Christianity – like Judaism – professed monotheism. Christians not only refused to worship the emperor as divine but also denied the existence of the Roman gods. Even more threatening to the state was the fact that Christians refused to serve in the Roman army. While the Romans dealt with the Jews by destroying Jerusalem, how might they annihilate a people whose kingdom was in heaven? Between the second and fourth centuries, Roman emperors imposed sporadic, inhumane persecution upon the Christian minority. In the amphitheaters of Rome, Christian martyrs astonished Roman audiences by going to their deaths joyously proclaiming their anticipation of a better life in the hereafter. Despite such public persecution, converts to the faith increased. By the end of the fourth century, the minor religious sect called Christianity had become the official religion of the Roman Empire.

Buddhism and the Message of the Buddha

The reasons why similar world-historical developments occur at approximately the same time within two remotely related cultures is a mystery that historians have never solved. One of the most interesting such parallels is that between the spread of Buddhism in the East and the emergence of Christianity in the West, both of which took place during the first century of the Christian era. Siddhartha Gautama (ca. 563– ca. 483 B.C.E.), known as the Buddha (or the "Enlightened One"), lived in India some five centuries before Jesus. Although born into a princely Hindu family and protected from all knowledge of pain and suffering, Siddhartha discovered the three "truths" of existence: sickness, old age, and death. At the age of twenty-nine, he renounced his wealth, abandoned his wife and child, and began a quest for inner illumination. With shaven head, yellow robe, and begging bowl, he followed the way of the Hindu ascetic for six years, until he realized that his life of self-denial was futile. Turning inward, Siddhartha rose in consciousness to the full perception of the cause of human sufferings: Meditating beneath a Bo (fig) tree (Figure 8.3), he achieved enlightenment – the omniscient consciousness of reality. Thereafter, he spent the rest of his life preaching a message of humility and compassion, the pursuit of which might lead his followers to *nirvana*, the ultimate release from the Wheel of Rebirth.

The Buddha's message was simple: It promised escape from reincarnation by avoiding all extremes and by practicing the Eightfold Path: right views, right intention, right speech, right action, right livelihood, right effort, right mindfulness, and right concentration. The Buddhist's reward was not – as with Christianity – the achievement of personal immortality, but rather, an enlightened release from the endless cycle of death and rebirth. To extinguish the Self and its desire was the goal of the Buddhist. The Buddha preached the Hindu rejection of material wealth and annihilation of worldly desires. But in contrast to the caste-oriented Hinduism of his time, he promised spiritual bliss to all people, not just to those at the highest level of the caste system (see chapter 3). He renounced reliance on the popular gods of the Vedas (see chapter 2) and urged his

Figure 8.3 Seated Buddha, Gandharan region, N.W. Pakistan, ca. 200 C.E. Gray schist, 51 × 31 in. The Cleveland Museum of Art. Leonard Hanna, Jr. Bequest (CMA 61.418).

followers to work out their own salvation by embracing the Middle Path which consists of the Four Noble Truths: Pain is universal, desire causes pain, ceasing to desire relieves pain, and the practice of the Eightfold Path leads to release from pain. (The second and third Truths may be compared with Stoic thought, while the Truth of the Middle Path resembles Aristotle's Golden Mean.)

Like Jesus, Siddhartha was an eloquent teacher whose concerns were profoundly ethical. As with Jesus, Siddhartha's life came to be surrounded by miraculous tales, which, along with his sermons, were preserved by his followers and recorded long after his death. Just as Jesus criticized Judaism's heavy emphasis on ritual, so Siddhartha attacked the existing forms of Hindu worship, including animal sacrifice and the authority of the Vedas. And both religions – Christianity and Buddhism – began as reformations of older world faiths: Judaism and Hinduism.

The Buddha himself wrote nothing, but his disciples memorized his sermons and set them down during the first century B.C.E. in three main books, the *Pitakas* or "Baskets of the Law." These works, written in Pali and Sanskrit, were divided into instructional chapters known as *sutras* (Sanskrit for "thread"). The most famous of the Buddha's sermons is one that he preached to five of his disciples at a deer park in Benares in northeast India. The *Sermon at Benares*, part of which is reproduced here, urges the abandonment of behavioral extremes and the pursuit of the Eightfold Path of right conduct. In its emphasis on faith over good works and on the renunciation of worldly pleasures, the *Sermon at Benares* has much in common with Jesus' Sermon on the Mount. Comparable also to Jesus' teachings (see Matthew 5:11, for instance) is the Buddha's regard for loving kindness that "commends the return of good for evil" – a concept central to the *Sermon on Abuse,* as we see in the following excerpts.

READING 32

From the Buddha's *Sermon at Benares*

"There are two extremes, O bhikkhus,[1] which the man who has given up the world ought not to follow — the habitual practice, on the one hand, of self-indulgence which is unworthy, vain and fit only for the worldly-minded — and the habitual practice, on the other hand, of self-mortification, which is painful, useless and unprofitable. 1

"Neither abstinence from fish or flesh, nor going naked, nor shaving the head, nor wearing matted hair, nor dressing in a rough garment, nor covering oneself with dirt, nor sacrificing to Agni,[2] will cleanse a man who is not free from delusions. 10

"Reading the Vedas, making offerings to priests, or sacrifices to the gods, self-mortification by heat or cold, and many such penances performed for the sake of immortality, these do not cleanse the man who is not free from delusions.

"Anger, drunkenness, obstinacy, bigotry, deception, envy, self-praise, disparaging others, superciliousness and evil intentions constitute uncleanness; not verily the eating of flesh. 20

"A middle path, O bhikkhus, avoiding the two extremes, had been discovered by the Tathāgata[3] — a path which opens the eyes, and bestows understanding, which leads to peace of mind, to the higher wisdom, to full enlightenment, to Nirvāna!

"What is that middle path, O bhikkhus, avoiding these two extremes, discovered by the Tathāgata — that path which opens the eyes, and bestows understanding, which leads to peace of mind, to the higher wisdom, to full enlightenment, to Nirvāna? 30

"Let me teach you, O bhikkhus, the middle path, which keeps aloof from both extremes. By suffering, the emaciated devotee produces confusion and sickly thoughts in his mind. Mortification is not conducive even to worldly knowledge; how much less to a triumph over the senses!

"He who fills his lamp with water will not dispel the darkness, and he who tries to light a fire with rotten wood will fail. And how can any one be free from self by leading a wretched life, if he does not succeed in quenching the fires of lust, if he still hankers after either worldly or heavenly pleasures. But he in whom self has become extinct is free from lust; he will desire neither worldly nor heavenly pleasures, and the satisfaction of his natural wants will not defile him. However, let him be moderate, let him eat and drink according to the needs of the body. 40

"Sensuality is enervating; the self-indulgent man is a slave to his passions, and pleasure-seeking is degrading and vulgar.

"But to satisfy the necessities of life is not evil. To keep the body in good health is a duty, for otherwise we shall not be able to trim the lamp of wisdom, and keep our mind strong and clear. Water surrounds the lotus-flower, but does not wet its petals. 50

"This is the middle path, O bhikkhus, that keeps aloof from both extremes."

And the Blessed One spoke kindly to his disciples, pitying them for their errors, and pointing out the uselessness of their endeavors, and the ice of ill-will that chilled their hearts melted away under the gentle warmth of the Master's persuasion. 60

Now the Blessed One set the wheel of the most excellent law[4] rolling, and he began to preach to the five bhikkhus, opening to them the gate of immortality, and showing them the bliss of Nirvāna.

The Buddha said:

"The spokes of the wheel are the rules of pure conduct: justice is the uniformity of their length; wisdom is the tire; modesty and thoughtfulness are the hub in which the immovable axle of truth is fixed. 70

"He who recognizes the existence of suffering, its cause, its remedy, and its cessation has fathomed the four noble truths. He will walk in the right path.

"Right views will be the torch to light his way. Right aspirations will be his guide. Right speech will be his dwelling-place on the road. His gait will be straight, for it is right behavior. His refreshments will be the right way of earning his livelihood. Right efforts will be his steps: right thoughts his breath; and right contemplation will give him the peace that follows in his footprints. 80

"Now, this, O bhikkhus, is the noble truth concerning suffering:

"Birth is attended with pain, decay is painful, disease is painful, death is painful. Union with the unpleasant is painful, painful is separation from the pleasant; and any craving that is unsatisfied, that too is painful. In brief, bodily conditions which spring from attachment are painful.

"This, then, O bhikkhus is the noble truth concerning suffering. 90

---

[1] Disciples.
[2] The Vedic god of fire, associated with sun and lightning.
[3] "The successor to his predecessors in office," another name for the Buddha.

---

[4] The Wheel of Law, or *Dharma*.

"Now this, O bhikkhus, is the noble truth concerning the origin of suffering:

"Verily, it is that craving which causes the renewal of existence, accompanied by sensual delight, seeking satisfaction now here, now there, the craving for the gratification of the passions, the craving for a future life, and the craving for happiness in this life.

"This, then, O bhikkhus, is the noble truth concerning the origin of suffering.

"Now this, O bhikkhus, is the noble truth concerning the destruction of suffering: 100

"Verily, it is the destruction, in which no passion remains, of this very thirst; it is the laying aside of, the being free from, the dwelling no longer upon this thirst.

"This, then, O bhikkhus, is the noble truth concerning the destruction of suffering.

"Now this, O bhikkhus, is the noble truth concerning the way which leads to the destruction of sorrow. Verily! it is this noble eightfold path; that is to say:

"Right views; right aspirations; right speech; right 110 behavior; right livelihood; right effort, right thoughts; and right contemplation.

"This, then, O bhikkhus, is the noble truth concerning the destruction of sorrow.

"By the practice of loving kindness I have attained liberation of heart, and thus I am assured that I shall never return in renewed births. I have even now attained Nirvāna."

And when the Blessed One had thus set the royal chariot wheel of truth rolling onward, a rapture thrilled through the 120 universes . . . .

From the Buddha's *Sermon on Abuse*

And the Blessed One observed the ways of society and 1 noticed how much misery came from malignity and foolish offenses done only to gratify vanity and self- seeking pride.

And the Buddha said: "If a man foolishly does me wrong, I will return to him the protection of my ungrudging love; the more evil comes from him, the more good shall go from me; the fragrance of goodness always comes to me, and the harmful air of evil goes to him."

A foolish man learning that the Buddha observed the principle of great love which commends the return of good 10 for evil, came and abused him. The Buddha was silent, pitying his folly.

When the man had finished his abuse, the Buddha asked him, saying: "Son, if a man declined to accept a present made to him, to whom would it belong?" And he answered: "In that case it would belong to the man who offered it."

"My son," said the Buddha, "thou has railed at me, but I decline to accept thy abuse, and request thee to keep it thyself. Will it not be a source of misery to thee? As the 20 echo belongs to the sound, and the shadow to the substance, so misery will overtake the evil-doer without fail."

The abuser made no reply, and the Buddha continued:

"A wicked man who reproaches a virtuous one is like one who looks up and spits at heaven; the spittle soils not the heaven, but comes back and defiles his own person.

"The slanderer is like one who flings dust at another when the wind is contrary; the dust does but return on him who threw it. The virtuous man cannot be hurt and the 30 misery that the other would inflict comes back on himself."

The abuser went away ashamed, but he came again and took refuge in the Buddha, the Dharma,[1] and the Sangha . . . .[2]

———————◆———————

The Spread of Buddhism

During the third century B.C.E. the Emperor Asoka (273–232 B.C.E.) made Buddhism the state religion of India and sent Buddhist missionaries as far west as Greece and southeast into Ceylon (present-day Sri Lanka). By the first century C.E., there were as many as five hundred major and minor Buddhist sects in India alone. Eventually, two principal divisions of Buddhism emerged: Hinayana Buddhism and Mahayana Buddhism. The former, with an emphasis on the individual's own private pursuit of *nirvana*, remained closer to the original teachings of the Buddha. Mahayana Buddhism, on the other hand, elevated the Buddha to the level of a divine being and established rituals by which he might be worshiped.

While the Buddha had urged his followers to work out their own salvation, Mahayana Buddhists taught that the Buddha was the source of salvation. They also held that there were other divine beings who had postponed reaching *nirvana* in order to help suffering humankind. These enlightened beings, known as *bodhisattvas*, became – much like the Christian saints – the objects of many popular Buddhist cults. The favorite Chinese female *bodhisattva*, Kuan-Yin – originally pictured in Indian art as a mustached male (Figure 8.4) – was widely regarded as a goddess of mercy and worshiped much in the way that Roman Catholics and Orthodox Christians honor the Virgin Mary.

Despite Asoka's efforts, the Buddha's teachings never gained widespread popularity in India. The strength of the established Hindu tradition (like that of Judaism in Judaea) and the resistance of the Brahmins to the Buddha's egalitarianism hindered the success of Buddhism in India, and by the seventh century, Buddhism was absorbed into Hinduism. In China, however, where Mahayana Buddhism became popular, the faith gained a considerable following. Here, as in many other parts of Asia, the Buddha was regarded not simply as a teacher or reformer, but as a savior whose intercession on one's behalf would free the faithful from physical suffering. Indeed, Chinese

---

[1] The law of Righteousness; the Wheel of Law.
[2] An assemblage of those who vow to pursue the Buddhist life.

Buddhism developed the concept of Heaven in place of the more abstract concept of *nirvana*. Buddhism's tolerance for other religions enhanced its popularity and its universal appeal. Mahayana, the "Great Vehicle" of Buddhism, brought a message of hope and salvation to millions of people in China, Korea, Japan, and Vietnam, while the more austere Hinayana or "Little Vehicle" of Buddhism became the major faith in Ceylon (Sri Lanka), Burma (Myanmar), Thailand, and Cambodia (Kampuchea).

Buddhism entered China during the first century C.E., and rose to prominence during the last turbulent decades of the Han Era. Though comparisons reduce subtle differences to facile analogy, the similarities between the Roman and Han Empires are irrefutable (see chapter 7). As in Rome, the late Han Era confronted increasing conflicts between wealthy landowners (who deemed themselves exempt from taxation) and impoverished and dissatisfied peasants. The repeated attacks of Mongolian tribes along the northern borders of the Han Empire, like those of the Germanic tribes along the Roman borders (see chapter 10), aggravated the prevailing internal disorders and fostered a sense of insecurity. And just as classical humanism gave way to mysticism in the West, the strongly humanistic bias of Confucianism in China began to erode beneath competing forms of religious speculation. During the first century C.E., the Buddha's sermons were translated into Chinese, and over the following centuries, Buddhism was popularized in China by the writings of the Indian poet Asvaghosha (d. 150?). Asvaghosha's Sanskrit descriptions of the life of the Buddha, which became available in Chinese in the year 420, provided the literary vehicle for Mahayana Buddhism.

In China, Confucianism and Taoism were easily reconciled with Buddhism, which assumed many different forms. Buddhist "paradise sects" closely resembling the mystery cults of the Near East promised their adherents rebirth in an idyllic, heavenly realm called "the Pure Land of the West." Still another Buddhist sect, strongly influenced by Taoism, emphasized the role of meditation and intuitive knowledge in the achievement of *nirvana*. Known in China as Ch'an ("meditation") and in Japan as Zen, this sect held that enlightenment could not be attained by rational means, but rather, through concentration that led to spontaneous and profound understanding. Among the tools of Zen masters were such mind-sharpening riddles as: "You know the sound of two hands clapping; what, then, is the sound of one hand clapping?" The Zen monk's attention to such queries forced him to move beyond reason. Legend has it that heavily caffeinated tea was introduced from India to China and Japan as an aid to prolonging meditation.

Figure 8.4 Standing Bodhisattva, Gandharan region, N.W. Pakistan, late second century C.E. Gray schist. Height approx. 3 ft. Courtesy, Museum of Fine Arts, Boston. Helen and Alice Colburn Fund.

SUMMARY

The world into which Jesus was born was ripe for religious revitalization. Roman religion focused on nature deities and civic gods who provided little in the way of personal spiritual comfort. Near Eastern and Persian mystery cults featured savior gods and goddesses associated with rebirth and resurrection. The province of Judaea, beset by religious and political factionalism, sought apocalyptic deliverance from the Roman yoke. The message preached by Jesus demanded an abiding faith in God, compassion for one's fellow human beings, and the renunciation of material wealth. In an age when people were required to serve the state, Jesus asked that they serve God. The apostle Paul universalized Jesus' message by preaching among non-Jews. He explained Jesus' death as atonement for sin and anticipated eternal life for the followers of the *Christos*.

The religion that had begun with the teachings of Siddhartha Gautama in India in the fifth century B.C.E. swept through the Far East in the very centuries that Christianity arose in the West. Although emerging out of very different traditions, the two world faiths had much in common, especially in the message of compassion and right conduct preached by their founders. While the Buddha taught that the soul's deliverance could only be achieved by the individual Buddhist, Buddhism as it came to be practiced in China and the Far East, ultimately regarded its founder as a savior. Christianity and Buddhism had only limited impact in the lands in which their founders were born, but both religions gained popularity in empires that flourished at the same time: Christianity in the Roman world-state, and Buddhism under the late Han dynasty in China. With Christianity, as with Mahayana Buddhism, the belief in a savior god, the promise of salvation for all human beings, and an uncompromising ethic of right conduct provided spiritual alternatives to the prevailing materialism of imperial Rome and Han China. On the soil of these great but declining empires were cast the seeds of two world-historical religions that are still followed by millions of people today.

GLOSSARY

asceticism strict self-denial and self-discipline

bodhisattva (Sanskrit, "one whose essence is enlightenment") a being who has postponed his or her own entry into *nirvana* in order to assist others in reaching that goal; worshiped as a deity in Mahayana Buddhism

Messiah Anointed one, or Savior; in Greek, *Christos*

rabbi a Jewish teacher and master, trained in the Jewish law

sutra (Sanskrit, "thread") an instructional chapter or discourse in any of the sacred books of Buddhism

---

SUGGESTIONS FOR READING

Baldwin, Summerfield. *The Organization of Medieval Christianity*. Gloucester, Mass.: Peter Smith, 1962.

Brown, Peter. *The World of Late Antiquity*, A.D. *150–750*. New York: Norton, 1989.

Ferguson, Everett. *Backgrounds of Early Christianity*. Grand Rapids, MI: Eerdmans, 1987.

Goodenough, E. R. *The Church in the Roman Empire*. New York: Holt, 1931.

Humphreys, Christmas. *Buddhism*. London: Cassell, 1962.

Kautsky, Karl. *Foundations of Christianity*. New York: Monthly Review Press, 1972.

Meeks, W.A. *The First Urban Christians: The Social World of the Apostle Paul*. New Haven, Conn.: Yale University Press, 1982.

Ross, Nancy W. *Three Ways of Asian Wisdom*. New York: Simon and Schuster, 1966.

Wilson, A.N. *Jesus*. New York: Norton 1992.

9

The Language of Faith: Religious Symbolism and the Arts

Between the fourth and sixth centuries C.E., Christianity grew from a small, dynamic sect into a full-fledged religion. The rise of Christianity occurred amidst a waning Roman Empire, beset by economic decline and the attacks of barbarian nomads (see chapter 10). The last great Roman emperors, Diocletian (245–316) and Constantine (ca. 274–337), made valiant efforts at reform. Attempting to govern Rome's sprawling territories more efficiently, Diocletian divided the Empire into western and eastern halves and appointed a coemperor to share the burden of administration and defense. After Diocletian retired, Constantine tried to

strengthen the Empire by levying new taxes and reviving a money economy. Failing to revitalize the West, he moved the seat of power from the city of Rome to the Eastern capital of Byzantium, which he renamed Constantinople. Some years earlier, in 313, Constantine had issued the Edict of Milan, an act proclaiming religious toleration in the West. The crucial act liberated Christians from repeated persecution and encouraged the development of Christianity as a legitimate, broadly based religion. Christian leaders formulated a uniform doctrine of faith, an administrative hierarchy, a set of rituals for worship, and a unique style of artistic

Map 9.1 The Byzantine World under Justinian, 565 C.E.

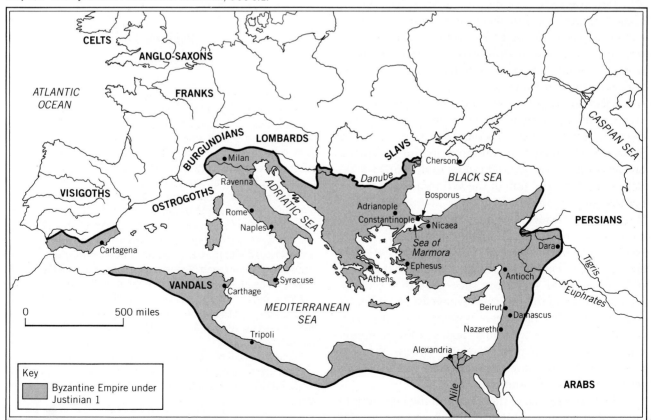

expression. By these means, the Church would ultimately come to replace the Roman Empire as the dominant spiritual and political authority in the West.

While the Roman Empire languished in the West, the East Roman or Byzantine Empire – the economic heart of the Roman world – prospered. Located at the crossroads of Europe and Asia (Map 9.1), Constantinople was the hub of a vital trade network and the heir to the cultural traditions of Greece, Rome, and Asia. Byzantine emperors formed a firm alliance with church leaders and worked to create an empire that flourished until the mid-fifteenth century. The Slavic regions of Eastern Europe (including Russia) converted to Orthodox Christianity during the ninth and tenth centuries, thus sharing the spiritual life of the city that Constantine had designated the "New Rome."

As Christians in Rome and Byzantium worked to formulate a unique language of faith, Buddhists in India, China, and Southeast Asia were developing their own vocabulary of religious expression. Buddhism inspired a glorious outpouring of art, architecture, and music that – like Early Christian art in the West – nourished the spiritual needs of millions of people throughout the East.

The Christian Identity

In the first centuries after the death of Jesus, there was little unity of belief and practice among those who called themselves Christians. But after the legalization of the faith in 313, the followers of Jesus moved toward establishing a ruling hierarchy, Christian **dogma** (prescribed doctrine), and **liturgy** (the rituals for public worship). From Rome, church leaders in the West borrowed the Latin language, the Roman legal system (the basis for **canon law**), and Roman methods of architectural construction. The Church retained Diocletian's administrative divisions and appointed a hierarchy of officials: archbishops in the provinces, bishops in the dioceses, and priests in the parishes. As Rome had been the hub of the Western Empire, so it became the administrative center of the new faith. When church leaders in Constantinople and Antioch stubbornly contested the political primacy of the bishops of Rome, Pope Leo the Great (ca. 390–461) advanced the "Petrine Doctrine," claiming that Roman pontiffs were the legitimate successors to Peter, the First Apostle and the principal evangelist of Rome. As Roman emperors had held supreme authority over the state, so Roman Catholic popes – the temporal representatives of Christ – would govern Western Christendom. The new spiritual order was thus patterned after imperial Rome.

If it was essential to the success of the new faith to create a functional administrative hierarchy, it was equally important to formulate a uniform doctrine of belief. As Christianity spread, the story of Jesus and the meaning of his message had provoked conflicting interpretations. Was Jesus human or divine? What was the status of Jesus in relation to God? Such fundamental questions drew conflicting answers. To resolve them, church officials convened to hammer out a systematic explanation of the life, death, and resurrection of Jesus. The first **ecumenical** (worldwide) council of churchmen was called by the Emperor Constantine. It met at Nicaea in 325 C.E. At the Council of Nicaea, a consensus of opinion among church representatives laid the basis for Christian dogma. It was resolved – to the objection of some dissenting Eastern churchmen – that Jesus was of one substance (or essence) with God the Father. The council issued a statement of Christian belief known as the Nicene Creed. A version of the Nicene Creed issued in 381 and still used by Eastern Orthodox Christians is reproduced below. It pledges commitment to a variety of miraculous phenomena, including virgin birth, the resurrection of the dead, and a mystical Trinity comprised of Jesus, God the Father, and the Holy Spirit. The principal formula of Christian belief, it stands as the turning point between the classical rationalism and Christian mysticism. In place of reason and the evidence of the senses, it advances faith and the intuition of truths that transcend ordinary understanding. As such, it anticipates the shift from a homocentric, classical worldview to the God-centered, medieval worldview.

READING 33
The Nicene Creed

We believe in one God the Father All-Sovereign, maker   1
of heaven and earth, and of all things visible and invisible;
And in one Lord Jesus Christ, the only-begotten Son of
God, Begotten of the Father before all the ages, Light of
Light, true God of true God, begotten not made, of one
substance with the Father, through whom all things were
made; who for us men and for our salvation came down
from the heavens, and was made flesh of the Holy Spirit
and the Virgin Mary, and became man, and was crucified
for us under Pontius Pilate, and suffered and was buried,   10
and rose again on the third day according to the Scriptures,
and ascended into the heavens, and sitteth on the right
hand of the Father, and cometh again with glory to judge
living and dead, of whose kingdom there shall be no end:
And in the Holy Spirit, the Lord and the Life-giver, that
proceedeth from the Father, who with Father and Son is
worshipped together and glorified together, who spake
through the prophets:
In one holy Catholic and Apostolic Church:
We acknowledge one baptism unto remission of sins. We   20
look for a resurrection of the dead, and the life of the age to
come.

————————◆————————

Christian Monasticism

Early Christians looked upon life on earth as a period of probation and preparation for the hereafter. What better way to avoid worldly temptation and preserve Christian ideals than to separate oneself from the secular world? Even before the coming of Christ, asceticism was common among the Essenes in the West and Buddhist monks in Asia. The earliest Christian monastics (the word comes from the Greek *monas*, meaning "alone") lived in the deserts of Egypt. Fasting, poverty, and celibacy were the essential features of the ascetic life-style instituted by the Greek bishop Saint Basil (329–379) and still followed by monastics of the Eastern Church.

In the West, the impulse to withdraw from the affairs of the world became more intense as the last remnants of classical civilization began to disappear. In 529, the same year that Plato's Academy closed its doors in Athens, the first Western monastic community was founded at Monte Cassino in southern Italy. Named after its founder, Benedict of Nursia (ca. 480–543), the Benedictine rule required that its members take vows of poverty (the renunciation of all material possessions), chastity (abstention from sexual activity), and obedience to the governing **abbot**, or father of the monastic community. Benedictine monks followed a routine of work that freed them from dependence on the secular world, balanced by the recitation of a cycle of prayers that marked eight devotional intervals of the day: the Divine Office. The Benedictine motto, *mens sana in corpore sano* ("a sound mind in a sound body"), expresses the standard of moderation that characterized Benedictine monasticism. Among monastics, as among the church fathers, women were regarded as the daughters of Eve, inherently sinful and dangerous as objects of sexual temptation. And although women formed monastic communities on equal terms with men, a negative attitude toward womankind prevailed among churchmen throughout the Middle Ages.

From the fifth century on, members of the **regular clergy**, that is, those following a monastic rule, played an increasingly important role in Western intellectual history. As Greek and Roman sources of education began to dry up and fewer men and women learned to read and write, the task of preserving the history and literature of the past fell to the last bastions of literacy: the monasteries. Benedictine monks and nuns hand-copied and illustrated Christian as well as classical manuscripts, and stored them in their libraries. Over the centuries, Benedictine monasteries sponsored programs of education (usually available only to the upper classes), contributed to the development of sacred music and art, and produced a continuous stream of missionaries, scholars, and church reformers.

The Latin Church Fathers

In the formation of Christian dogma and liturgy in the West, the most important figures were four Latin scholars who lived between the fourth and sixth centuries: Jerome, Ambrose, Gregory, and Augustine. Saint Jerome (ca. 342–420), a Christian educated in Rome, translated into Latin both the Hebrew Bible, which Christians referred to as the "Old Testament," and the Greek books of the "New Testament." This mammoth task resulted in the *Vulgate*, a Latin edition of Scripture that became the official bible of the Roman Catholic church. Although Jerome considered pagan culture a distraction from the spiritual life, he admired the writers of Classical Antiquity and did not hesitate to plunder the spoils of classicism – and Hebraism – to build the edifice of a new faith.

Like Jerome, Ambrose (339–397) fused Hebrew, Greek and Near Eastern traditions in formulating Christian doctrine and liturgy. A Roman aristocrat who became bishop of Milan, Ambrose wrote some of the earliest Christian hymns for congregational use. Influenced by Near Eastern chants and Hebrew psalms, Ambrose's hymns are characterized by a lyrical simplicity that made them models of religious expression. In the hymn that follows, divine light is the unifying theme. The reference to God as the "Light of light" distinctly recalls the cult of Mithras, as well as Plato's analogy between the Good and the Sun. Culminating in a burst of praise for the triune God, the hymn conveys a mood of buoyant optimism similar to that evoked in the Egyptian "Hymn to the Aten" (see chapter 2).

READING 34
Saint Ambrose's "Ancient Morning Hymn"

O Splendor of God's glory bright,   1
O Thou who bringest light from light,
O Light of light, light's living spring,
O Day, all days illumining!

O Thou true Sun, on us Thy glance   5
Let fall in royal radiance;
The Spirit's sanctifying beam
Upon our earthly senses stream.

The Father, too, our prayers implore,
Father of glory evermore,   10
The Father of all grace and might,
To banish sin from our delight.

To guide whate'er we nobly do,
With love all envy to subdue,
To make ill-fortune turn to fair,   15
And give us grace our wrongs to bear.

Rejoicing may this day go hence;
Like virgin dawn our innocence,
Like fiery noon our faith appear,
Nor know the gloom of twilight drear.   20

Morn in her rosy car is borne:
Let him come forth, our perfect morn,
The Word in God the Father one,
The Father perfect in the Son.

All laud to God the Father be;   25
All praise, eternal Son, to Thee;
All glory, as is ever meet,
To God the holy Paraclete.[1]

———————————◆———————————

The contribution of the Roman aristocrat Gregory the Great (540–604) was vital to the development of early church government. Elected to the papacy in 590, Gregory established the administrative machinery by which all subsequent popes would govern the Church of Rome. A born organizer, Gregory sent missionaries to convert England to Christianity; he extended the temporal authority of the Roman church throughout Western Europe; and with equal efficiency, he organized the liturgical music of the early Church (see page 31).

The most profound and influential of all the Latin church fathers was Augustine of Hippo (354–430). A native of Roman Africa and an intellectual who came under the spell of both Plotinus and Paul, Augustine converted to Christianity at the age of thirty-three. His treatises on the nature of the soul, free will, and the meaning of evil made him the greatest philosopher of Christian antiquity. Before his conversion to Christianity, Augustine had enjoyed a sensual and turbulent youth. The ensuing conflict between his love of worldly pleasures, dominated by what he called his "lower self," and his love of God, exercised by the "higher part of our nature," is the focus of his fascinating and self-scrutinizing autobiography known as the *Confessions*. Here, Augustine makes a fundamental distinction between physical and spiritual satisfaction, arguing that "no bodily pleasure, however great it might be . . . [is] worthy of comparison, or even of mention, beside the happiness of the life of the saints." The dualistic model of the human being as the locus of warring elements – the "unclean body" and the "purified soul" – drew heavily on the Neoplatonist duality of Matter and Spirit and the Pauline promise that the sin of Adam might be cleansed by the sacrifice of Jesus.

In the extract below from *Confessions*, Augustine identifies the three everyday temptations that endanger his soul: the lust of the flesh, the lust of the eyes, and the ambition of the world.

—————————————

[1]Holy Spirit

READING 35
From Saint Augustine's *Confessions*

Certainly you command me to restrain myself from the *lust of the flesh, the lust of the eyes, and the ambition of the world*. You commanded me to abstain from sleeping with a mistress, and with regard to marriage you advised me to take a better course than the one that was permitted me. And since you gave me the power, it was done, even before I became a dispenser of your Sacrament. But there still live in that memory of mine, of which I have spoken so much, images of the things which my habit has fixed there. These images come into my thoughts, and, though when I am awake they are strengthless, in sleep they not only cause pleasure but go so far as to obtain assent and something very like reality. These images, though real, have such an effect on my soul, in my flesh, that false visions in my sleep obtain from me what true visions cannot when I am awake. Surely, Lord my God, I am myself when I am asleep? And yet there is a very great difference between myself and myself in that moment of time when I pass from being awake to being asleep or come back again from sleep to wakefulness. Where then is my reason which, when I am awake, resists such suggestions and remains unshaken if the realities themselves were presented to it? Do reason's eyes close with the eyes of the body? Does reason go to sleep when the bodily senses sleep? If so, how does it happen that even in our sleep we do often resist and, remembering our purpose and most chastely abiding by it, give no assent to enticements of this kind? Nevertheless, there is a great difference, because, when it happens otherwise, we return on waking to a peace of conscience and, by the very remoteness of our state now and then, discover that it was not we who did something which was, to our regret, somehow or other done in us.   30

Almighty God, surely your hand is powerful enough to cure all the sickness in my soul and, with a more abundant measure of your grace, to quench even the lustful impulses of my sleep. Lord, you will increase your gifts in me more and more, so that my soul, disentangled from the birdlime of concupiscence, may follow me to you; so that it may not be in revolt against itself and may not, even in dreams, succumb to or even give the slightest assent to those   40
degrading corruptions which by means of sensual images actually disturb and pollute the flesh . . . .

I must now mention another form of temptation which is in many ways more dangerous. Apart from the concupiscence of the flesh which is present in the delight we take in all the pleasures of the senses (and the slaves of it perish as they put themselves far from you), there is also present in the soul, by means of these same bodily senses, a kind of empty longing and curiosity which aims not at taking pleasure in the flesh but at acquiring experience   50
through the flesh, and this empty curiosity is dignified by the names of learning and science. Since this is in the appetite for knowing, and since the eyes are the chief of our senses for acquiring knowledge, it is called in the divine language *the lust of the eyes*. For "to see" is used properly of the eyes; but we also use this word of the other senses when we are employing them for the purpose of

Line markers: 1, 10, 20

gaining knowledge. We do not say: "Hear how it flashes" or "Smell how bright it is" or "Taste how it shines" or "Feel how it gleams"; in all these cases we use the verb "to see." But we not only say: "See how it shines," a thing which can only be perceived by the eyes; we also say "See how it sounds," "See how it smells," "See how it tastes," "See how hard it is." Therefore, the general experience of the senses is, as was said before, called "the lust of the eyes," because seeing, which belongs properly to the eyes, is used by analogy of the other senses too when they are attempting to discover any kind of knowledge.

In this it is easy to see how pleasure and curiosity have different objects in their use of the senses. Pleasure goes after what is beautiful to us, sweet to hear, to smell, to taste, to touch; but curiosity, for the sake of experiment, may go after the exact opposites of these, not in order to suffer discomfort, but simply because of the lust to find out and to know. What pleasure can there be in looking at a mangled corpse, which must excite our horror? Yet if there is one near, people flock to see it, so as to grow sad and pale at the sight. They are actually frightened of seeing it in their sleep, as though anyone had forced them to see it when they were awake or as if they had been induced to look at it because it had the reputation of being a beautiful thing to see. The same is true of the other senses. There is no need to go to the length of producing examples. Because of this disease of curiosity monsters and anything out of the ordinary are put on show in our theaters. From the same motive men proceed to investigate the workings of nature which is beyond our ken — things which it does no good to know and which men only want to know for the sake of knowing. So too, and with this same end of perverted science, people make enquiries by means of magic. Even in religion we find the same thing: God is tempted when signs and portents are demanded and are not desired for any salutary purpose, but simply for the experience of seeing them . . . .

We are tempted, Lord, by these temptations every day; without intermission we are tempted. The tongue of man is the furnace in which we are tried every day. Here too you command us to be continent. Give what you command, and command what you will. You know how on this matter my heart groans to you and my eyes stream tears. For I cannot easily discover how far I have become cleaner from this disease, and I much fear my hidden sins which are visible to your eyes, though not to mine. For in other kinds of temptation I have at least some means of finding out about myself; but in this kind it is almost impossible. With regard to the pleasures of the flesh and the unnecessary curiosity for knowledge I can see how far I have advanced in the ability to control my mind simply by observing myself when I am without these things, either from choice or when they are not available. For I can then ask myself how much or how little I mind not having them. So too with regard to riches, which are desired for the satisfaction of one or two or all of those three concupiscences; if one is not able to be quite sure in one's own mind whether or not one despises them when one has them, it is possible to get rid of them so as to put oneself to the test. But how can we arrange things so as to be without praise and make the same experiment with regard to it? Are we to live a bad life, to live in such a wicked and abandoned way that everyone who knows us

will detest us? Nothing could be madder than such a suggestion as that. On the contrary, if praise both goes with and ought to go with a good life and good works, we should no more part with it than with the good life itself. Yet unless a thing is not there I cannot tell whether it is difficult or easy for me to be without it . . . .

———————◆———————

A living witness to the decline of the Roman Empire, Augustine defended his faith against pagan charges that Christianity was responsible for Rome's downfall. In his multivolume work *The City of God*, he distinguishes between the earthly city of humankind and the heavenly city that is the eternal dwelling place of the Christian soul. Augustine's earthly abode, a place where "wise men live according to man," represents the classical world prior to the coming of Jesus. By contrast, the heavenly city, the spiritual realm where human beings live according to divine precepts, is the destiny of those who embrace the "New Dispensation" of Christ.

Augustine's perception of history as divinely ordered and moving toward a predestined end became fundamental to the Christian philosophy of history. Moreover, his dualistic (and essentially Neoplatonic) view of reality — matter and spirit, body and soul, earth and heaven, Satan and God, state and church — influenced Western thought for centuries to come. The conception of the material world as an imperfect reflection of the divine order determined the allegorical character of medieval literature. According to this tradition, matter was the matrix in which God's message was hidden. In Scripture, as well as in every natural and created thing, God's invisible order might be discovered. For Augustine, the Hebrew Bible was a symbolic guide to Christian belief, and history itself was a cloaked message of divine revelation.

The extract from Augustine's *City of God* illustrates his dual perception of reality and its importance to the tradition of Christian allegory. Augustine's description of Noah's ark as symbolic of the City of God, the Church, and the body of Christ exemplifies the way in which a single image might assume various meanings within the language of Christian faith.

READING 36

From Saint Augustine's
City of God Against the Pagans

On the character of the two cities, the earthly and the heavenly.

The two cities then were created by two kinds of love: the earthly city by a love of self carried even to the point of contempt for God, the heavenly city by a love of God carried even to the point of contempt for self. Consequently, the earthly city glories in itself while the other glories in the Lord.[1] For the former seeks glory from men, but the latter finds its greatest glory in God, the witness of our conscience. The earthly city lifts up its head in its own glory; the heavenly city says to its God: "My glory and the lifter of my head."[2] In the one, the lust for dominion has dominion over its princes as well as over the nations that it subdues; in the other, both those put in charge and those placed under them serve one another in love, the former by their counsel, the latter by their obedience. The earthly city loves its own strength as revealed in its men of power; the heavenly city says to its God: "I will love thee, O Lord, my strength."[3]

Thus in the earthly city its wise men who live according to man have pursued the goods either of the body or of their own mind or of both together; or if any of them were able to know God, "they did not honor him as God or give thanks to him, but they became futile in their thinking and their senseless minds were darkened; claiming to be wise," that is, exalting themselves in their own wisdom under the dominion of pride, "they became fools, and exchanged the glory of the immortal God for images resembling mortal man or birds or beasts or reptiles," for in the adoration of idols of this sort they were either leaders or followers of the populace, "and worshipped and served the creature rather than the creator, who is blessed forever." In the heavenly city, on the other hand, man's only wisdom is the religion that guides him rightly to worship the true God and awaits as its reward in the fellowship of saints, not only human but also angelic, this goal, "that God may be all in all"[4] . . . .

That the ark which Noah was ordered to make symbolizes Christ and the church in every detail.

Now God, as we know, enjoined the building of an ark upon Noah, a man who was righteous and according to the true testimony of Scripture, perfect in his generation,[5] that is, perfect, not as the citizens of the City of God are to become in that immortal state where they will be made equal with the angels of God, but as they can be during their sojourn here on earth. In this ark he was to be rescued from the devastation of the flood with his family, that is, his wife, sons and daughters-in-law, as well as with the animals that came to him in the ark at God's direction. We doubtless have here a symbolic representation of the City of God sojourning as an alien in this world, that is, of the church which wins salvation by virtue of the wood on which the mediator between God and men, the man Christ Jesus,[6] was suspended.

The very measurements of the ark's length, height and breadth symbolize the human body, in the reality of which it was prophesied that Christ would come to mankind, as, in fact, he did come. For the length of the human body from top to toe is six times its breadth from one side to the other and ten times its thickness measured on a side from back to belly. Thus if you measure a man lying on his back or face down, his length from head to foot is six times his breadth from right to left or from left to right and ten times his elevation from the ground. This is why the ark was made three hundred cubits in length, fifty in breadth and thirty in height. And as for the door that it received on its side, that surely is the wound that was made when the side of the crucified one was pierced by the spear.[7] This is the way by which those who come to him enter, because from this opening flowed the sacraments with which believers are initiated. Moreover, the order that it should be made of squared beams contains an allusion to the foursquare stability of saints' lives, for in whatever direction you turn a squared object, it will stand firm. In similar fashion, everything else mentioned in the construction of this ark symbolizes some aspect of the church . . . .

———————◆———————

Symbolism and Early Christian Art

The allegorical tradition in Christian literature had its counterpart in the visual arts, where a symbolic language permeated the **iconography** of the new faith. Before Christianity was legalized in 313, visual symbols served the practical function of identifying the converts to the faith among themselves. Followers of Jesus adopted the sign of the fish because the Greek word for fish (*ichthys*) is an acrostic combination of the first letters of the Greek words, "Jesus Christ, Son of God, Savior." They also used the first and last letters of the Greek alphabet, *alpha* (**A**) and *omega* (**Ω**), to designate Christ's presence at the beginning and the end of time. Roman converts to Christianity saw in the Latin word for peace, *Pax*, a symbolic reference to Christ, since the last and first letters could also be read as *X* (*chi*) and *P* (*rho*), the first two letters in the Greek word *Christos*. Indeed, *Pax* was emblazoned on the banner under which the Emperor Constantine was said to have defeated his enemies. Such symbols soon found their way into Early Christian art.

On a sixth-century **sarcophagus** (stone coffin) of the Archbishop Theodorus of Ravenna (Figure 9.1), the *chi* and *rho* and the *alpha* and *omega* have been made into an insignia that resembles both a crucifix (symbolizing Christ as Savior) and a pastoral cross (symbolizing Christ as shepherd). Three laurel wreaths, Roman imperial symbols of triumph, encircle the medallions on the coffin lid. On either side of the central medallion are grapevines designating the wine that represents the blood of Christ. The tiny birds that stand beneath the vines — derived from Greek funerary art — refer to the human soul. Also included in the iconographic program are two popular Near Eastern symbols of immortality: the peacock or phoenix, a legendary bird that was thought to be reborn from its own ashes, and the rosette, a reference to the "wheel of life." Taken as a whole, the Archbishop's coffin is the vehicle of a sacred

---

[1]Cf. 2 Corinthians 10.17.
[2]Psalms 3.3.
[3]Psalms 18.1.
[4]1 Corinthians 15.28.
[5]Cf. Genesis 6.9
[6]1 Timothy 2.5.

[7]Cf. John 19.34.

Figure 9.1 Sarcophagus of Archbishop Theodorus, sixth century C.E. Marble. Sant' Apollinare in Classe, Ravenna, Italy. Alinari.

language signifying Christ's triumph and the Christian promise of resurrection and salvation.

In Early Christian art, music, and literature, almost every number and combination of numbers was thought to carry allegorical meaning. The number 3, for example, signified the Trinity, 4 signified the evangelists, 5 symbolized the wounds of Jesus, 12 stood for the apostles, and so on. The evangelists were usually represented by four winged creatures: the lion for Mark, the ox for Luke, the man for Matthew, and the eagle for John (upper portion Figure 9.9). Prefigured in the Book of Revelation (4:1–8), each of the four creatures came to be associated with a particular Gospel. The lion, for example, was appropriate to Mark because in his Gospel he emphasized the royal dignity of Christ; the heaven-soaring eagle suited John, who produced the most lofty and mystical of the Gospels.

Some of the earliest evidence of Christian art comes from the **catacombs**, subterranean burial chambers outside the city of Rome. The walls of this vast network of underground galleries and rooms bear frescoes with scenes from the Old and New Testaments. Worshipers are shown in the *orans* position – that is, with arms raised in an attitude of prayer, a gesture priests still use in the performance of the Mass (Figure **9.2**). Like the story of Noah's ark, "decoded" by Augustine to reveal its hidden significance, Early

Figure 9.2 *Orans (Praying Figure)*, ca. 300 C.E. Fresco in the Catacombs of Saint Priscilla, Rome. Scala.

Figure 9.3 *Christ as Good Shepherd*, mid-fourth century c.e. Wall painting from the Catacombs of SS Pietro and Marcellino, Rome. Pontificia Commissione per L'Archeologia Cristiana.

Christian imagery was multilayered and pregnant with symbolic meaning. For example, the popular figure of Jesus as Good Shepherd, an adaptation of the calf or lamb-bearing youth of Greco-Roman art (see Figure 6.6), symbolized Jesus' role as savior-protector (shepherd) and sacrificial victim (lamb). Featured in catacomb frescoes (Figure **9.3**) and in freestanding sculpture (Figure **9.4**), the Good Shepherd evoked the Early Christian theme of deliverance. While the message of the catacomb frescoes is one of salvation and deliverance, the style of these paintings resembles that of secular Roman art (see Figure 7.24): Figures are small but substantial and deftly shaded to suggest three-dimensionality. Setting and specific indications of spatial depth are omitted, however, so that human forms appear to float in ethereal space.

In the centuries following the legalization of Christianity, the story of Jesus' life became increasingly popular. Two specific narrative cycles emerged: *The Youth of Christ*, which included the Annunciation to the Virgin, the Nativity of Jesus, and the Adoration of the Magi; and *The Passion of Christ*, which recounted the events in Jesus' life from the Last Supper through the Resurrection. Not until the fifth century, however, when the manner of Jesus' death began to lose its ignoble associations, was Jesus depicted on the cross.

Figure 9.4 *The Good Shepherd*, ca. 350 c.e. Marble (restored), height 3 ft. 3 in. Vatican Museums, Rome.

Figure 9.5 *Crucifixion*, from the west doors of the Church of Santa Sabina, Rome, ca. 430 C.E. Wood, 11 × 15¾ in. © Hirmer Fotoarchiv.

One of the earliest of such scenes is that carved in low relief on the wooden west doors of the Church of Santa Sabina in Rome (Figure 9.5). Christ assumes the *orans* in a rigid and static frontal position that also signifies a crucified body. The tripartite composition of the relief includes the smaller (because less important) figures of the thieves that flanked Jesus at the crucifixion. Despite its narrative content, the image is far from being a representation of the crucifixion of Jesus. Rather, it is a symbolic statement of Christian redemption.

Early Christians had little use for the Roman approach to art as a window on the world. Roman realism, with its scrupulous attention to time, place, and personalities, was ill-suited to convey the timeless message of a universal faith and the miraculous events surrounding the life of a savior god. Moreover, Christ-

ian artists inherited the Jewish prohibition against "graven images." As a result, little three-dimensional sculpture was produced between the second and eleventh centuries. On the other hand, devotional objects such as hand-illuminated manuscripts and **diptychs** (two-leaved hinged tablets) designed for private use were produced in great numbers. The sixth-century ivory book cover from Murano, Italy, is typical of the Early Christian artist's preoccupation with didactic content and surface adornment (Figure 9.6). Scenes of Jesus' miracles are wedged together in airless compartments surrounding the central image of the enthroned Jesus with Peter and Paul. A royal canopy flanked by **Latin crosses** crowns the holy space. In the top register, two angels modeled on classical **putti** (winged angelic beings) carry a **Greek cross** en-

Figure 9.6 Book cover from Murano, Italy, sixth century c.e. Ivory. Scala/Art Resource, New York.

circled by a triumphal wreath, while below, scenes from the life of Jonah ("reborn" from the belly of the whale) allude to the Resurrection. Despite its classical borrowings, the piece abandons Greco-Roman modes of realistic representation in favor of abstraction and symbolism.

Early Christian Art and Architecture

The legalization of Christianity made possible the construction of monumental houses for public religious worship. In the West, the Early Christian church was modeled on the Roman basilica. Rome's earliest Christian basilicas, Saint Peter's and Saint Paul's, were entered through an atrium, surrounded on three sides by a covered walkway or **ambulatory**, and on the fourth side, directly in front of the church entrance, by a vestibule, or **narthex**. The church interior was divided into a long central hall called the **nave**, flanked by two aisles on each side (Figure **9.7**). The upper wall of the nave bore the **clerestory**, an area consisting of windows

through which light poured into the basilica. Between the clerestory and the nave arcade was the **gallery**, a space often decorated with mosaics or frescoes (Figure **9.8**).

Toward the east end of the church, lying across the axis of the nave, was a rectangular area called the **transept**. The north and south arms of the transept, which might be extended to form a Latin cross, might provide entrances additional to the main entrance at the west end of the church. Entering through the west portal, one proceeded down the colonnaded nave toward the triumphal arch that framed the **apse**, the semicircular space beyond the transept. In the apse, at an altar that stood on a raised platform, the sacrament of Holy Communion was celebrated. As in ancient Egyptian ritual, one sought eternal life in the east, where the sun was "reborn" each day. The journey across the atrium, down the nave, and toward the altar symbolized the soul's progression from the secular world to the spiritual font of salvation.

The Early Christian church served as a place of worship, but it also entombed – usually beneath the

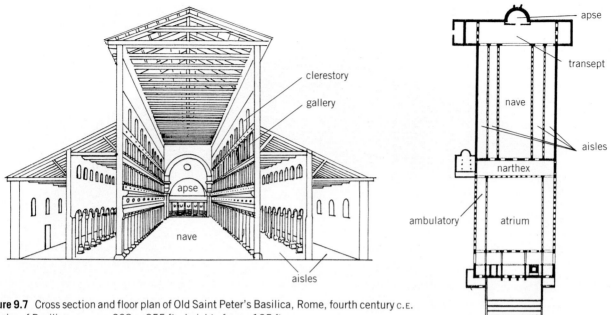

Figure 9.7 Cross section and floor plan of Old Saint Peter's Basilica, Rome, fourth century c.e. Interior of Basilica, approx. 208 × 355 ft., height of nave 105 ft.

Figure 9.8 Interior of Saint Paul's Outside the Walls, Rome, begun 386 c.e. Etching by Giambattista Piranesi, 1749. Photo courtesy of Rudy Turk.

altar – the bones of Christian martyrs. Hence the church was a massive shrine, as well as the setting for the performance of the liturgy. Its spacious interior – Old St. Peter's basilica was 355 feet long and 208 feet wide – accommodated thousands of Christian pilgrims. However, the wood-trussed roofs of these churches made them especially vulnerable to fire. None of the great Early Christian basilicas has survived, except in pictorial records as in Figure 9.8.

The Latin cross plan became the model for the medieval church in the West. The church exterior, which clearly reflected the functional divisions of the

Figure 9.9 *Christ Teaching the Apostles in the Heavenly Jerusalem.* Mosaic in the apse of Santa Pudenziana, Rome, ca. 401–407 C.E. © Hirmer Fotoarchiv.

interior, was usually left plain and unadorned, while the interior was radiantly decorated with mosaics consisting of tiny pieces of colored glass or marble set in wet cement. The mosaic technique had been invented by the Romans, who used the medium largely to decorate the floors of public or private buildings. In the hands of Byzantine craftsmen, however, mosaics became the ideal means of conveying the transcendental character of the Christian message. The mosaic medium encouraged the invention of flat, simplified shapes arranged in radiant color patterns. Small pieces of glass backed with gold leaf added splendor to the total effect. As daylight or candlelight moved across walls embellished with mosaic, it transformed surface designs into sparkling and ethereal apparitions.

In the fifth-century mosaic of Christ teaching the apostles from the apse of Santa Pudenziana in Rome, the Heavenly City unfolds below the hovering image of a magnificent jewelled cross flanked by winged symbols of the four evangelists (Figure **9.9**). The bearded Jesus, conceived as a Roman emperor, rules the world from atop "the throne set in heaven," as described in Revelation 4. Two female figures, personifications of the Old and New Testaments, offer wreaths of victory to Peter and Paul. Looking every bit like an assembly of Roman senators, the apostles receive the Law, symbolized by the open book and the sign of **benediction** by which Jesus blesses the faithful.

Byzantine Art and Architecture

In the churches of Byzantium, the mosaic technique reached its artistic peak. Byzantine church architects favored the Greek cross plan by which all four arms of the structure were of equal length. At the crossing point rose a large and imposing dome. Occasionally, as with the most notable example of Byzantine architecture, the church of Hagia Sophia ("Holy Wisdom"), the longitudinal axis of the Latin cross plan was combined with the Greek cross plan. The crowning architectural glory and principal church of Constantinople, Hagia Sophia (Figures **9.10**, **9.11**) was commissioned in 532 by the East Roman Emperor Justinian (482–565). Its massive dome – 112 feet in diameter – rises 184 feet above the pavement (40 feet higher than the Pantheon, see Figure 7.8). Triangular **pendentives** make the transition between the square base of the building and the dome above (Figure **9.12**). Light filtering through the forty closely set windows at the base of the dome

Figure 9.10 Anthemius of Tralles and Isodorus of Miletus, Hagia Sophia, Constantinople (Istanbul), 532–537 c.e.

Figure 9.11 Interior of Hagia Sophia, Constantinople (Istanbul). Werner Forman Archive.

Figure 9.12 Schematic drawing of the dome of Hagia Sophia, showing pendentives.

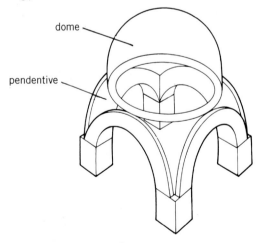

creates the impression that the dome is floating miraculously above the substance of the building. That light, whose symbolic value was as important to Byzantine liturgy as it was to Saint Ambrose's "Ancient Morning Hymn," illumined the resplendent mosaics and colored marble surfaces that once filled the interior of the church. After the fall of Constantinople to the Turks in 1453, the Muslims transformed Hagia Sophia into a mosque and white-washed its mosaics (in accordance

Figure 9.13 *Emperor Justinian and His Courtiers*, ca. 547 c.e. Mosaic in San Vitale, Ravenna, Italy. Giancarlo Costa, Milan.

with the Muslim prohibition against images). Modern Turkish officials, however, have made the building a museum and restored some of the original mosaics.

Hagia Sophia is evidence of the Golden Age of Byzantine art and architecture that took place under the Emperor Justinian. Justinian envisioned Constantinople as the "New Rome." Assuming the throne in 527, he tried unsuccessfully to reunite the two halves of the old Roman Empire. He revised and codified the extensive body of Roman law (see chapter 7). The Justinian Code had an enormous influence on legal and governmental history in the West, especially after the eleventh century, when it became the basis for the law in most of the European states. Justinian's leadership was equally important to the Byzantine economy. By directing his ambassadors to smuggle silkworm eggs out of China, Justinian initiated the silk industry in the West. A devout Christian, he commissioned an ambitious program of church building both in Constantinople and in Ravenna, the north Italian city that served as his Western imperial outpost before it fell into the hands of the Ostrogoths (see chapter 10).

The sixth-century octagonal domed church of San Vitale in Ravenna is one of the small gems of Byzantine architecture (Figure 9.14). Its drab exterior hardly

prepares one for the radiant and ornate interior, the walls of which are embellished with polychromed marble, carved alabaster columns, and magnificent mosaics (Figure 9.16). The mosaics on either side of the altar show Justinian and his capable consort Theodora, each carrying offerings to Christ (Figures 9.13, 9.15).

Figure 9.14 San Vitale, Ravenna, Italy, ca. 526–547 c.e. © Hirmer Fotoarchiv.

Figure 9.15 *Empress Theodora and Retinue*, ca. 547 C.E. Mosaic in San Vitale, Ravenna, Italy. Giancarlo Costa, Milan.

Figure 9.16 Interior of San Vitale, Ravenna, Italy. Scala/Art Resource, New York.

The iconography of the Justinian representation illustrates the vital bond between church and state in Byzantine culture: Justinian is flanked by twelve companions, an allusion to Christ and the apostles. On his right are his soldiers, the defenders of Christ (note the *chi* and *rho* emblazoned on the shield), while on his left are representatives of the clergy, who bear the instruments of the liturgy: the crucifix, the book, and the incense vessel. Crowned by a solar disc or halo, a device often used in Persian and late Roman art to indicate divine status, Justinian personifies the sacred authority of Christ on earth and the unity of temporal and spiritual power.

The style of the mosaic is equally compelling: Justinian and his courtiers stand grave and motionless, as if frozen in ceremonial attention. They are slender, elongated, and rigidly positioned – like the notes of a musical score – against a gold background that works to eliminate spatial depth. Minimally shaded, these "paper cutout" figures with small, flapperlike feet seem to float on the surface of the picture plane, rather than stand anchored in real space. A comparison of this composition with, for instance, the Roman relief of the Spoils of Jerusalem (see Figure 7.18) underlines the vast differences between the aesthetic aims and purposes of classical and Christian art. Whereas the former engaged a realistic narrative style to glorify temporal power, the latter cultivated an abstract language of line and color to celebrate otherworldly glory.

The sixth-century mosaic of the calling of Peter found in Sant' Apollinare Nuovo in Ravenna – a Christian basilica ornamented by Byzantine artisans – provides an extraordinary example of the surrender of narrative detail to symbolic abstraction (Figure 9.17). In the composition, setting is minimal – a gold background shuts out space and provides a supernatural screen against which ritualized action takes place. The figures, stiff and immovable, seem to lack substance. There is almost no sense of muscle and bone beneath the togas of Christ and the apostles. The enlarged eyes and exaggerated gestures – which recall Mesopotamian statuary (see Figure 2.12) – impart a powerful sense of otherworldly vision and omniscience.

Early Christian Music

Early Christians distrusted the sensuous and emotional powers of music, especially instrumental music. Saint Augustine noted the "dangerous pleasure" of music and confessed that on those occasions when he was more "moved by the singing than by what was sung," he felt that he had "sinned criminally." For such reasons, the Early Church was careful to exclude all forms of individual expression from liturgical music. Ancient Jewish religious ritual, especially the practice of chanting daily prayers and singing psalms, directly influenced church music. Hymns of praise such as those produced by Saint Ambrose were sung by the Christian congregation led by a **cantor** (chief solo singer). But the most important music of Christian antiquity, and that

Figure 9.17 *Jesus calling the first apostles, Peter and Andrew.* Detail of north-wall upper-register mosaic in Sant' Apollinare Nuovo, Ravenna, Italy, early sixth century C.E. Scala, Florence.

which became central to the liturgy of the church, was the music of the Mass.

The most sacred rite of the Christian liturgy, the Mass celebrated the sacrifice of Christ's blood and body as enacted at the Last Supper. The service culminated in the sacrament of Holy Communion (or Eucharist), by which Christians symbolically shared the blood and body of their Redeemer. In the West, the service called High Mass featured a series of Latin chants known as either plainsong, plainchant, or Gregorian Chant♭ – the last because Gregory the Great codified and made uniform the many various types of religious chant that existed in Early Christian times. The invariable or "ordinary" parts of the Mass, that is, those used throughout the year, included *Kyrie eleison* (a series of prayers ending with "Lord have mercy"), *Gloria* ("Glory to God"), *Credo* (the affirmation of the Nicene Creed), *Sanctus* ("Holy, Holy, Holy"), *Benedictus* ("Blessed is He that cometh") and *Agnus Dei* ("Lamb of God"). Eventually, the Sanctus and the Benedictus appeared as one chant, making a total of five parts to the ordinary Mass.

One of the oldest bodies of liturgical song still in everyday use, Gregorian chant stands among the great treasures of Western music. It is – like Early Christian hymnody – monophonic, that is, it consists of a single line of melody. Sung *a cappella* (without instrumental accompaniment), the plainsong of the Early Christian era was performed by the clergy and by choirs of monks rather than by members of the congregation – as was the case with the Ambrosian hymns. Both hymns and plainsong might be performed in a **responsorial** style, that is, with the chorus answering the voice of the cantor, or **antiphonally**, that is, with parts of the choir or congregation singing alternating verses. In general, the rhythm of the words dictated the rhythm of the music. Plainsong might be **syllabic** (one note to one syllable), or it might involve **melismatic** (many notes to one syllable) embellishments. Since no method for notating music existed before the ninth century, choristers depended on memory and on **neumes**, that is, marks entered above the words of the text to indicate the rise and fall of the voice. The duration and exact pitch of each note, however, had to be committed to memory.

Drifting without climax, the free rhythms of Gregorian chant echoed throughout the cavernous interiors of Early Christian churches to produce effects that were otherworldly and hypnotic. These qualities, conveyed only to a limited degree by modern recordings, are best appreciated when Gregorian chant is performed in large, acoustically resonant cathedrals such as the remodeled Saint Peter's in Rome.

_____
♭See Music Listening Selections at end of chapter.

The Buddhist Identity

Buddhism, as it spread through India and China, followed a very different path from that of Christianity. While the followers of Jesus created clerical officials and uniform doctrines that laid the basis for the early church, Buddhists established neither an administrative hierarchy nor formulated a systematic program of belief. Under the third-century B.C.E. Emperor Asoka in India, councils of Buddhist monks met to organize the Master's teachings into an official canon. And while a large body of folklore and legend came to ornament the history of the Buddha, Buddhist Scripture remained essentially a body of discourses informed by the Master's injunction that his followers should strive to work out their own salvation. There is no Buddhist equivalent of the Nicene Creed, the Mass, or the secular priesthood, in short, no "authority" other than the words of the Buddha. If indeed there is a Buddhist "creed," it calls for adherence to the Law of Righteousness (*Dharma*) and the Eightfold Path. Monasteries arose as centers for Buddhist meditation and instruction. The Buddhist monk was the model of religious life for a faith that remained aloof from dogma. To this day, religious "services" consist only of the chanting of Buddhist texts (mainly Buddha's sermons), the recitation of hymns and *mantras* (word and sound formulas), meditation, and confession. Unencumbered by an elaborate liturgy, Buddhism remained grounded in reverence for the Buddha and his teachings. And despite the deification of the Buddha among Mahayana Buddhists and the worship of *bodhisattvas* who might aid humans to achieve *nirvana*, Buddhism never abandoned its profoundly contemplative character.

Buddhist Art and Architecture in India

When the Emperor Asoka made Buddhism the state religion of India in the third century B.C.E. he commissioned the construction of thousands of shrines – over 80,000 within three years – to house the relics of the Buddha and mark the places at which he had taught. The most typical Buddhist structure was the *stupa*, a beehivelike mound of earth encased by brick or stone, at the top of which were enshrined the relics of the Buddha or his disciples. More than a reliquary shrine, however, the *stupa* is the symbolic representation of the cosmos – the mountain dwelling of the ancient gods and the sacred womb of the universe. Stone balustrades carved with symbols of the Buddha's teachings and gates marking the four cardinal points of the compass separate the sanctuary from the secular world. Circling the shrine clockwise, Buddhist pilgrims make the sacred journey that, like the act of meditating, brings them into harmony with the cosmos.

Figure 9.18 The Great Stupa, Sanchi, India, completed first century c.e. Shown are the west and south gateways. Government of India, Archaeological Survey of India.

Figure 9.19 (a) Interior of carved chaitya cave, Karli, India, ca. 50 c.e. Government of India, Archaeological Survey of India. (b and c) Elevation and ground plan of chaitya cave, Karli, India, ca. 50 c.e.

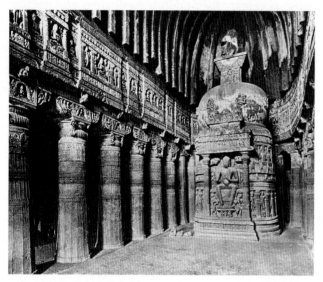

(a)

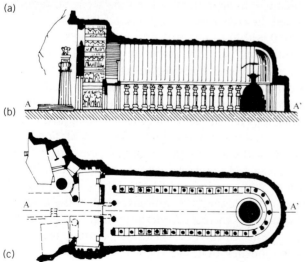

(b)

(c)

Begun in the third century B.C.E., the Great Stupa at Sanchi in central India was one of Asoka's greatest achievements (Figure 9.18). Elevated on a twenty-foot drum and surrounded by a circular stone railing, the shrine is 105 feet in diameter and rises to a height of fifty feet above the ground. It is surmounted by a series of *chatras*, umbrellalike shapes that signify the sacred Bo tree under which the Buddha reached *nirvana*. The *chatras* also symbolize the levels of human consciousness through which the soul ascends in seeking enlightenment. Occasionally, the *stupa* was enclosed in a massive, rock-cut cave and placed at the end of a *chaitya* (Figure 9.19), an arcaded hall not unlike the Early Christian basilica. These rock-cut reliquary shrines of early Buddhism were not places for public worship, as were Early Christian churches, but rather, zones of spiritual retreat.

Buddhism's prohibition of idolatry influenced art in that artists avoided portraying the Buddha in human form. Instead, they devised various symbols of the Buddha, such as the fig tree under which he meditated, his footprints, elephants (one of the bodily forms assumed by the Buddha), and, most important, the Wheel of Law (see Reading 32). These symbols, along

Figure 9.20 The Great Stupa, inner face of the north gate, Sanchi, India, late first century B.C.E.–early first century c.e. Sandstone, total height of gate 34 ft. Government of India, Archaeological Survey of India. Reproduced by permission of the British Library, London.

with sensuous figures of nature deities retained from Vedic tradition, make up the densely ornamented surface of the 34-foot-high *toranas* (stone gateways) that mark the entrances to the Great Stupa at Sanchi (Figure **9.20**). In contrast to the Augustinian antagonism of flesh and spirit evidenced in the *Confessions*, and Christianity's general abhorrence of carnal pleasure, Buddhism (like Hinduism) regarded sexuality and spirituality as simply two different forms of a single, fundamental cosmic energy. Hence, Buddhist art features voluptuous fertility goddesses, whose globular breasts and firm, tubelike limbs seem to swell with life (Figure **9.21**).

Mahayana Buddhism, however, glorified the Buddha as a savior and thus the image of the Buddha himself became important in popular worship. Contacts between northwest India (Gandhara) and the West influenced the emergence of a distinctly human Buddha icon inspired by Hellenistic and Roman representations of the god Apollo. Gandharan artists carved classically draped and idealized, freestanding figures of the Buddha and the *bodhisattvas* (see Figures 8.3, 8.4). They also carved scenes from the life of the Buddha, one of which depicts the Master seated among a group of monks and devotees (Figure **9.22**) in a manner that may be compared to benedictional images of Jesus among the apostles (see Figures 9.6, 9.9).

Between the fourth and sixth centuries, under the sway of the Gupta Empire, India experienced a Golden

Figure 9.21 Addorsed Shalabhanjika image from Stupa 1 at Sanchi, India, ca. 10–25 C.E. Sandstone, height 24½ × 16½ × 7½ in. Los Angeles County Museum of Art, from the Nasli and Alice Heeramaneck Collection, Museum Associates Purchase.

Figure 9.22 *Enlightenment.* Detail of frieze showing four scenes from the life of Buddha: Birth, Enlightenment, First Preaching, and Nirvana. Pakistani sculpture, Gandhara, Kushan dynasty, late second—early third century C.E. Dark gray-blue slate, height 26⅜ in., width 114⅛ in., thickness 3¹³⁄₁₆ in. Courtesy of the Freer Gallery of Art, Smithsonian Institution, Washington, D.C. (49.9).

Figure 9.23 Seated Buddha Preaching the First Sermon, from Sarnath, India, fifth century c.e. Sandstone, height 5 ft. 3in. Archaeological Museum, Sarnath. Government of India, Archaeological Survey of India.

Figure 9.24 Cave 17, Ajanta, India. Wall painting showing Simhala Adavana. Gupta sculpture, fifth century c.e. Government of India, Archaeological Survey of India.

Age in the arts as well as in the sciences. Gupta rulers commissioned Sanskrit prose and poetry that ranged from adventure stories and plays to sacred and philosophical works. Gupta mathematicians were the first to use a special sign for the numeric zero and Hindu physicans made significant advances in medicine. (As we shall see in chapter 10, the Arabs transmitted many of these innovations to the West.) In the hands of Gupta sculptors, the image of the Buddha assumed its classic form (Figure **9.23**): a cross-legged figure, seated in the position of meditation. The Buddha's oval head, framed by an elaborately ornamented halo, features a protuberance symbolizing spiritual wisdom, elongated earlobes (a reference to Siddhartha's princely origins), and a third "eye" – a symbol of spiritual vision – between the eyebrows (see Figures 8.3, 9.23). The Buddha's masklike face with downcast eyes and gentle smile denotes the state of inner repose. His hands form a *mudra* – a gesture belonging to a spiritual sign language – that indicates the Wheel of the Law, the subject of the Buddha's First Sermon. More stylized than its Gandharan predecessors, Gupta figures are typically full-bodied and smoothly modeled with details reduced to decorative linear patterns.

The Gupta period also produced some of the earliest surviving examples of Indian painting. The extraordinary frescoes found on the walls of some thirty rock-cut sanctuaries at Ajanta in central India show scenes of the lives and incarnations of the Buddha (as told in Mahayana literature), as well as stories from Indian history and legend. In the Ajanta frescoes, musicians, dancers, and lightly clad *bodhisattvas* (Figure **9.24**) rival the sensual elegance of the carved figures at Sanchi. The Ajanta frescoes are among the best-preserved and most magnificent of Indian paintings and rank with the great mosaic cycles of Early Christian and Byzantine churches, though in subject matter – and especially in their depiction of erotic love – they have no equivalent in the medieval West. They attest to the fact that in Buddhist thought, the divine and the human, the spirit and the body, are considered complementary rather than antagonistic.

Buddhist Art and Architecture in China

Between the first and third centuries, Buddhist missionaries introduced many of the basic conventions of Indian art and architecture into China. The Chinese adopted the *stupa* as a temple-shrine and place of worship, transforming its moundlike base and umbrellalike structure into a **pagoda**, or multitiered tower with many roofs. These Chinese temple-towers are characterized by sweeping curves and upturned corners similar to those used in ancient watchtowers and multistoried houses (see Figure 7.26). Favoring timber as the principal building medium, Chinese architects devised complex vaulting systems for the construction of pagodas, of which no early examples have survived (see Figures 14.19, 14.20).

The earliest Buddhist building in China whose date is known is the twelve-sided brick pagoda on Mount Sung in Honan, which served as a shrine for the nearby Buddhist monastery (Figure **9.25**). Constructed in the early sixth century, this pagoda consists of a hollow interior that may once have held a large statue of the Buddha. The pagoda, whether built in brick or painted wood, became popular throughout Southeast Asia and provided a model for all religious shrines – Taoist and Confucian – as well as for Hindu temples in medieval India (see chapter 14).

In addition to the pagoda, the Chinese produced rock-cut sanctuaries modeled on the reliquary shrines of India. These contain colossal images of the Buddha and his *bodhisattvas* (Figure **9.26**). Carved into the native sandstone, the sharply cut masklike faces and clinging draperies produce animated surface designs. The Chinese preference for abstract patterns and flowing, rhythmic lines also dominates the relief carvings found on the walls of late fifth- and sixth-century Buddhist caves (Figure **9.27**). Once painted with bright colors, the reliefs showing the Emperor Hsüan-wu and his consort bearing ritual gifts to the shrine of the Buddha may be compared with the almost contempor-

Figure 9.25 Pagoda of the Sung Yneh Temple, Mount Sung, Honan, China, 523 c.e.

Figure 9.26 The colossal Buddha with attendant Buddha, Yun Kang, China. Northern Wei monumental Buddhist sculpture, ca. 460–470 c.e. Height 46 ft. © George Holton. 1979/Photo Researchers, Inc.

Figure 9.27 The Empress as Donor with Attendants, from the chapels of Lungmen, Honan, China, ca. 502–523 c.e. Northern Wei dynasty (386–534 c.e.). Fine gray limestone with traces of color, 6 ft. 4 in. × 9 ft. 1 in. The Nelson-Atkins Museum of Art, Kansas City, Missouri (Purchase: Nelson Trust) 40–38 detail.

aneous mosaics of Justinian and Theodora in San Vitale in Ravenna (see Figures 9.13, 9.15). Less hieratic than its Byzantine counterpart, the image of the Empress as donor with attendants achieves an ornamental elegance that is as typical of Chinese relief sculpture as it is of Chinese calligraphy and painting (see chapter 14).

Sixth-century China produced an extraordinary selection of outstanding bronze altarpieces. In the example pictured in Figure **9.28**, the slender Buddha stands, his hands in the teaching *mudra*, amidst a group of *bodhisattvas* and monks. His head is framed by a pierced, flame-shaped halo from which winged angelic creatures sprout. The vitality of the design depends on a calligraphic line that twists and flutters as if blown by a gentle breeze. A comparison of this devotional object with the Gupta statue of the Buddha preaching the Wheel of the Law (see Figure 9.23) and with such Early Christian reliefs as the *Crucifixion* on the doors of Santa Sabina (see Figure 9.5) or the ivory book cover from Murano (see Figure 9.6), reveals the extent to which artists – East and West – depended on stylization and abstraction to convey divine truths that surpassed the illusions of ordinary reality.

Buddhist Music in India and China

In its origins and development, the music of India was inseparable from India's religious history. For thousands of years, Hindu priests chanted the Vedic hymns (see chapter 2). Like the ancient Greeks, Hindus identified sound and rhythm with the cosmic principle and considered music a powerful curative. Moreover, to the Hindu, music represented the marriage of physical breath and spiritual being, a union of the personal life force (Atman) and the Absolute Spirit (Brahman).

Scholars did not begin to survey Buddhist music until the early twentieth century. It seems clear, however, that Buddhist religious practices were based in India's ancient musical traditions, specifically those that involved the intoning of sacred Hindu texts. The recitation of *mantras* and the chanting of Sanskrit prayers were central acts of meditation among Buddhist monks, and the performance of such texts assumed a trancelike quality similar to that of Western plainsong. Buddhist chant was monophonic, but unlike Western church music, it was usually accompanied by percussion instruments (such as drums, bells, cymbals, and gongs) that imparted a rich polyphonic texture. Complex drumming techniques were among the most notable of Indian musical contributions.

As in India, Buddhist chant in China and Japan was performed in the monasteries. It featured the intoning of statements and responses interrupted by the sounding of percussion instruments such as bells or

Figure 9.28 Buddhist Altarpiece, sixth century C.E. Gilt bronze, height 23¼ in. The Metropolitan Museum of Art, New York, Rogers Fund, 1938.

drums. As the chant proceeded, the pace of recitation increased, causing an overlapping of voices and instruments that produced a hypnotic web of sound.[♭]

Sliding, nasal tones characterized the performance of Chinese music. Such tones were achieved by both the voice and by the instruments peculiar to Chinese culture. China's earliest and most important instrument was the **zither**, a five- or seven-stringed instrument that is plucked with a plectrum and the fingertips (see Figure 14.10). Associated with ancient religious and ceremonial music, the zither was quickly adopted by Buddhist monks. The vibrato or hum produced by plucking the strings of the zither is audible long after the instrument is touched, a phenomenon that Buddhists found comparable to the pervasive resonance of chant (and to the human breath seeking union with the One).

[♭]See Music Listening Selections at end of chapter.

SUMMARY

Between the fourth and sixth centuries, Christianity and Buddhism became world religions, each with its own set of religious symbols and its own identity. The Roman Empire was the vehicle by which Christianity rose to prominence in the West. It provided the Early Christian church with unique forms of administrative and cultural expression. A governing church hierarchy and periodic church councils worked to transform Christianity from a minor sect to an institutionalized religion. Four Latin church fathers – Augustine, Jerome, Ambrose, and Gregory – helped to formulate a uniform Christian doctrine and a distinctive liturgy. The writings of Augustine of Hippo, the most important of the Latin church fathers, were crucial to the development of the allegorical method. Christian monasticism, established in the West by Saint Benedict, played a large part in preserving and spreading the Christian message.

Christianity provided a mystical alternative to classical rationalism. The Christian promise of personal salvation encouraged intuition and faith as primary modes of experience. In the visual arts, Christianity inspired a turning away from objective representation and the world of the senses. A language of symbolism and allegory came to convey the Christian message of deliverance.

Parallel with the rise of Roman Catholicism in the West, the Eastern Orthodox church grew powerful in the East Roman or Byzantine Empire. The fifth and sixth centuries were a time of great church construction. Saint Peter's in Rome and Hagia Sophia in Constantinople typify the respective Western and Eastern church styles. During the reign of the Byzantine Emperor Justinian, some of the finest mosaics in the history of art were produced in Constantinople and Ravenna. In these mosaics, as in other examples of Early Christian art, formal abstraction replaced realism, and symbolism replaced narrative description. Christian churches provided splendid settings for the performance of the Mass, the ceremony celebrating the sacrament of Holy Communion. The principal parts of this ceremony were recited in moving, monophonic Gregorian chant.

Buddhist art and architecture flourished in India three centuries before the time of Jesus, but Buddhism spread into China and Southeast Asia only after the second century C.E. Unlike Christianity, Buddhism provided no fixed doctrine, no liturgy, and no clerical hierarchy to intermediate between human beings and God. Buddhism shared with Christianity a strong monastic component and a reverence for sacred relics. But while Early Christian churches became resplendent precincts for the public performance of the Christian liturgy, Buddhist *stupas*, rock-cut temples, and Chinese pagodas were essentially sanctuaries for private religious retreat. The Mahayana Buddhist emphasis on the role of the Buddha as the savior led to the increasing popularity of three-dimensional statues of the Buddha and the *bodhisattvas*, often shown teaching or meditating. Although music did not serve in any sacramental ceremony comparable to the Mass, in both India and China the percussive rhythms of religious chant filled Buddhist monasteries.

While personal salvation was the primary theme of Early Christianity, spiritual enlightenment was the focus of Buddhism. Nevertheless, both religions employed the arts to glorify their respective founders and their teachings, and both left legacies that are rich in symbolic meaning and artistic value.

SUGGESTIONS FOR READING

Bechert, Heinz and Richard Gombrich. *The World of Buddhism: Buddhist Monks and Nuns in Society and Culture.* New York: Facts on File, 1984.

Beckwith, John. *Early Christian and Byzantine Art.* New York: Penguin, 1980.

Chadwick, Henry. *Augustine.* New York: Oxford University Press, 1986.

Kitzinger, Ernst. *Byzantine Art in the Making.* Cambridge, Mass.: Harvard University Press, 1977.

Knowles, David. *Christian Monasticism.* New York: McGraw-Hill, 1969.

Lowrie, Walter. *Art in the Early Church.* New York: Harper, 1965.

Magoulias, H.J. *Byzantine Christianity: Emperor, Church and the West.* Detroit: Wayne State University Press, 1982.

Milburn, Robert. *Early Christian Art and Architecture.* Berkeley, Calif.: University of California Press, 1988.

Taylor, H.O. *The Classical Heritage of the Middle Ages.* New York: Harper, 1968.

Weitzmann, Kurt. *Age of Spirituality: Late Antique and Early Christian Art.* New York: Metropolitan Museum of Art, 1979.

MUSIC LISTENING SELECTIONS

Cassette I Selection 2 Gregorian Chant: "Alleluya, Vidimus Stellam," codified 590–604.

Cassete I Selection 3 Buddhist Chant: Morning Prayers, excerpt.

GLOSSARY

abbot (Latin, "father") the superior of an abbey or monastery for men; the female equivalent of a convent of nuns is called an "abbess"

a cappella choral singing without instrumental accompaniment

ambulatory a covered walkway, outdoors or indoors; (see Figures 9.7 and 13.7)

antiphonal a type of music in which two or more groups of voices or instruments alternate with one another

apse the semicircular recess at the east end of a Roman basilica or a Christian church; (see Figure 9.7)

benediction the invocation of a blessing; in art, indicated by the raised right hand with fore and middle fingers extended

canon law the ecclesiastical law that governs the Christian church

cantor the official in Judaism who sings or chants the liturgy; the official in medieval Christianity in charge of music at a cathedral, later a choir leader and soloist for the responsorial

catacomb a subterranean cemetery consisting of burial chambers and galleries with recesses for tombs

chaitya a Buddhist assembly hall, usually arcaded and incorporating a *stupa* at one end

chatra umbrellalike shapes that signify the sacred tree under which the Buddha reached *nirvana*

clerestory the upper part of the nave, whose walls contain openings for light (also "clerstory"); (see Figure 9.7)

diptych a two-leaved hinged tablet; a two-paneled altarpiece

dogma a prescribed body of doctrines concerning faith or morals, formally stated and authoritatively proclaimed by the church

ecumenical worldwide in extent; representing the whole body of churches

gallery the area between the clerestory and the nave arcade, usually adorned with mosaics in Early Christian churches; (see Figure 9.7)

Greek cross a cross in which all four arms are of equal length

iconography the visual imagery that conveys specific concepts and ideas in a work of art; also, the study of the symbolic meaning of such imagery

Latin cross a cross in which the vertical member is longer than the horizontal member it intersects

liturgy the prescribed rituals or body of rites for public worship

mantra a mystical formula of invocation or incantation common to Hinduism and Buddhism

melismatic the assignment of many notes of music to one syllable

mudra a gesture belonging to a spiritual sign language in Buddhist art and Indian dance

narthex a porch or vestibule at the main entrance of the church; (see Figure 9.7)

nave the central aisle of the church between the altar and the apse, usually demarcated from the side aisles by columns or piers; (see Figure 9.7)

neume a mark or symbol indicating the direction of the voice in the early notation of Gregorian chant

orans a gesture involving the raising of the arms in an attitude of prayer

pagoda an east Asian shrine in the shape of a tower, usually with roofs curving upward at the division of each of several stories

pendentive a concave piece of masonry that makes the transition between the angle of two walls and the base of the dome above; (see Figure 9.12)

putto (Italian, "child," plural *putti*) a nude, male child, usually winged; related to the classical Cupid (see Figure 7.2) and to Greco-Roman images of the angelic *psyche* or soul

regular clergy (Latin, *regula* = "rule") those who have taken vows to obey the rules of a monastic order; as opposed to the **secular clergy**, those ordained to serve the Christian church in the world

responsorial a type of music in which a single voice answers another voice or a chorus

sarcophagus (plural, "sarcophagi") a stone coffin

stupa a hemispherical mound that serves as a Buddhist shrine

syllabic the assignment of one note of music per syllable

torana a gateway that marks one of the four cardinal points in the stone fence surrounding a *stupa*

transept the part of a basilican-plan church that runs perpendicular to the nave; (see Figure 9.7)

zither a five- or seven-stringed instrument that is plucked with a plectrum and the fingertips; the favorite instrument of ancient China

10

Expansive Cultures: Germanic and Islamic

The motive forces that drive groups of people from one area of the world to another are few and fundamental: economic hardship, the desire to escape political or religious oppression, and outright imperialistic ambition. In the first centuries of the Christian era, two sizable groups of nomadic peoples – one Germanic, the other Arabic – moved upon the West (see Map **10.1**). The expansion of each played a significant role in the formative phase of European civilization. At the same time, each culture made major contributions to the humanistic tradition. The Germanic tribes that poured into the Roman Empire in the late fourth century introduced customs that blended with Roman and Christian traditions to forge the basic character of the medieval world. During the seventh century, the tribal peoples of the Arabian peninsula established the youngest of the world religions – Islam – which became a powerful religious and cultural force in world history. The subsequent expansion of Islam cut off Europe from the East and fixed the geographic contours of Western Christendom. Muslim communities in Spain, North Africa, and the Near East cultivated rich traditions in both the arts and sciences. Arab scholars in Baghdad (Persia) and Cordoba (Spain) (see Map 10.2) copied Greek manuscripts, creating a rich preserve of classical literature. And Arab intermediaries carried westward many of the greatest innovations of Asian and Oriental culture. These achievements had far-reaching effects on the European West, and more broadly on the humanistic tradition.

The Germanic Tribes

The Germanic peoples were a tribal folk who followed a migratory existence. Dependent on their flocks and herds, they lived in pre-urban, village communities and frequently raided and plundered nearby lands for material advantage. They settled no territorial state, nor did they produce any monumental architecture or sculpture. During the second century B.C.E., they began

to attack Roman territories. Lacking the hallmarks of civilization, including the art of writing, they impressed the Romans as inferiors and outsiders – hence the Romans called them *barbarians*.

During the fourth century, the loose confederacy of Germanic tribes was driven westward by a fierce Central Asian people known as Huns. The Germanic tribes were racially and culturally distinct from these more primitive and aggressive nomads. (East and West Goths, Franks, Vandals, Burgundians, Angles, and Saxons – to name only a few – belonged to the Germanic language family, dialects of which differed from tribe to tribe.) In the wake of the Hunnish advance, the Germanic tribes migrated to the fringes of the Roman Empire. Eastern Germanic tribes, or Ostrogoths, occupied the steppe region between the Black and Baltic seas, while Western Germanic peoples, the Visigoths, settled in territories closer to the Danube River (Map 10.1). Occasionally, these tribes entered into an uneasy alliance with Roman authorities: The Romans allowed the barbarians to settle on the borders of the empire, in exchange for which Germanic warriors afforded the Romans protection against other invaders. Antagonisms between Romans and barbarians along the Danube River, however, led to a military showdown. At the Battle of Adrianople (130 miles northwest of Constantinople) in 378, the Visigoths defeated the "invincible" Roman army, killing the East Roman Emperor Valens and dispersing his army. Almost immediately thereafter, the Visigoths swept across the Roman border, raiding the cities of the declining West, including Rome itself in 410.

The Battle of Adrianople opened the door to continuous barbarian invasion. During the fifth century, the Empire fell prey to such tribes as the Vandals, whose willful, malicious destruction of Rome in 455 gave us the English word to *vandalize*. Finally, in 476, a Germanic commander named Odoacer deposed the reigning Roman emperor and proclaimed himself head of the Roman state, an event that is traditionally taken

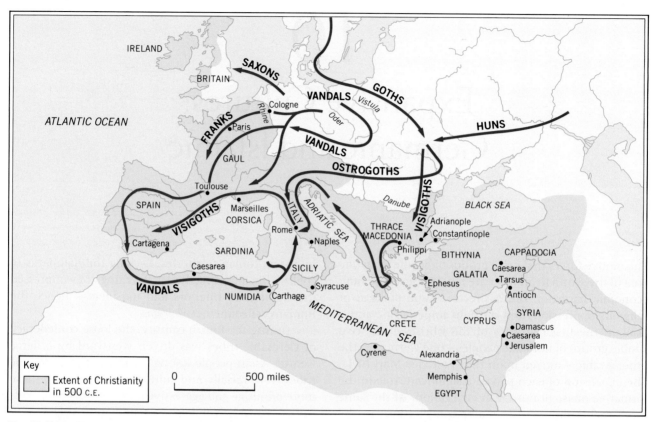

Map 10.1 The Early Christian World and the Barbarian Invasions, ca. 500 C.E.

to mark the official end of the Roman Empire. Although the Germanic tribes leveled the final assaults on an already declining empire, they did not utterly destroy that empire's vast cultural resources. The Ostrogoths embraced Christianity and sponsored literary and architectural enterprises modeled on those of Rome and Byzantium, while the Franks and the Burgundians depended on Roman models to convert their oral laws to written codes of law.

Among the Germanic tribes, as among the nomadic groups that attacked the ancient Mesopotamians, fighting was both a way of life and a highly respected skill. Minimally armed with javelins and shields, Germanic warriors fought fiercely on foot and on horseback, sometimes holding off whole Roman legions. Superb horsemen, they were equipped with spurs and foot stirrups—devices (originating in China) that firmly secured the rider in his saddle and improved his driving force. In addition to introducing to the West superior methods of fighting on horseback, the Germanic tribes imposed their own long-standing traditions on medieval Europe. Every Germanic chieftain retained a band of warriors who followed him into battle and anticipated sharing with him the spoils of victory. The bond of **fealty**, or loyalty, between warrior and chieftain and the practice of rewarding the warrior with land or the spoils of battle were basic facts of barbarian life and

became fundamental to the feudal system of the Middle Ages (see chapter 12).

At the end of the first century, the Roman historian Tacitus (see chapter 7) wrote a history of the Germanic peoples, an excerpt from which follows. Tacitus described the agrarian economy of the barbarians, their self-sufficient communities, their restless and violent habits, their traditions of fealty, and their strict social customs — some of which Tacitus found favorable in contrast to Rome's moral laxity.

READING 37

From Tacitus' *History of the Germanic Tribes*

The kings in Germany owe their election to the nobility of 1
their birth; the generals are chosen for their valor. The power of the former is not arbitrary or unlimited; the latter command more by warlike example than by their authority. To be of a prompt and daring spirit in battle, and to attack in the front of the lines, is the popular character of the chieftain: when admired for his bravery, he is sure to be obeyed . . . . They fight in clans, united by consanguinity, a family of warriors. [Those dearest to them] are near them in the field. In the heat of the engagement, the soldier hears 10
the shrieks of his wife, and the cries of his children. These are the darling witnesses of his conduct, the applauders of

his valor, at once beloved and valued. The wounded seek their mothers and wives: undismayed at the sight, the women count each honorable scar . . . . They are even hardy enough to mix with the combatants, administering refreshment and exhorting them to deeds of valor . . . .

In matters of inferior moment the chiefs decide; important questions are reserved for the whole community. Yet even in those cases where all have a voice, the business is discussed and prepared by the chiefs. The general assembly, if no sudden alarm calls the people together, has its fixed and stated periods, either at the new or full moon. This is thought the season most propitious to public affairs . . . . [When they meet to conduct business] Each man takes his seat, completely armed. Silence is proclaimed by the priests, who still retain their coercive authority. The king, or chief of the community, opens the debate: the rest are heard in their turn, according to age, nobility of descent, renown in war, or fame for eloquence. No man dictates to the assembly: he may persuade, but cannot command. When anything is advanced not agreeable to the people, they reject it with a general murmur. If the proposition pleases, they brandish their javelins. This is their highest and most honorable mark of applause: they assent in a military manner, and praise by the sound of their arms.

In this council of the state, accusations are exhibited, and capital offenses prosecuted. Pains and penalties are proportioned to the nature of the crime. For treason and desertion, the sentence is to be hanged on a tree: the coward, and such as are guilty of unnatural practices, are plunged under a hurdle into bogs and fens. In these different punishments, the point and spirit of the law is, that crimes which affect the state may be exposed to public notoriety: infamous vice cannot be too soon buried in oblivion . . . .

A German transacts no business, public or private, without being completely armed. The right of carrying arms is assumed by no person whatever, till the state has declared him duly qualified. The young candidate is introduced before the assembly, where one of the chiefs, or his father, or some near relation, provides him with a shield and javelin. This, with them, is the manly gown: the youth from that moment ranks as a citizen; till then he was considered as part of the household; he is now a member of the commonwealth . . . .

In the field of action, it is disgraceful to the prince to be surpassed in valor by his companions; and not to vie with him in martial deeds, is equally a reproach to his followers. If he dies in the field, he who survives him survives to live in infamy. All are bound to defend their leader, to succor him in the heat of action, and to make even their own actions subservient to his renown. This is the bond of union, the most sacred obligation. The chief fights for victory; the followers for their chief. If, in the course of the long peace, the people relax into sloth and indolence, it often happens that the young nobles seek a more active life in the service of other states engaged in war. The German mind cannot brook repose. The field of danger is the field of glory. Without violence and rapine, a train of dependants cannot be maintained. The chief must show his liberality, and the follower expects it. He demands, at one time this warlike horse, at another, that victorious lance drenched with the blood of the enemy. The prince's table, however inelegant, must always be plentiful: it is the only pay of his followers. War and depredation are the ways and means of the chieftain. To cultivate the earth, and wait the regular produce of the seasons, is not the maxim of a German: you will more easily persuade him to attack the enemy, and provoke honorable wounds in the field of battle. In a word, to earn by the sweat of your brow, what you might gain by the price of your blood, is, in the opinion of a German, a sluggish principle, unworthy of a soldier . . . .

The Germans, it is well known, have no regular cities; nor do they allow a continuity of houses. They dwell in separate habitations, dispersed up and down, as a grove, a meadow, or a fountain, happens to invite. They have villages, but not in our fashion, with a series of connected buildings. Every tenement stands detached, with a vacant piece of ground round it, either to prevent accidents by fire, or for want of skill in the art of building. They neither know the use of mortar nor of tiles. They build with rude materials, regardless of beauty, order, and proportion . . . .

Marriage is considered as a strict and sacred institution. In the national character there is nothing so truly commendable. To be contented with one wife, is peculiar to the Germans. They differ, in this respect, from all other savage nations. There are, indeed, a few instances of polygamy; not, however, the effect of loose desire, but occasioned by the ambition of various families, who court the alliance of the chief distinguished by the nobility of his rank and character. The bride brings no portion; she receives a dowry from her husband. In the presence of her parents and relations, he makes a tender of part of his wealth; if accepted, the match is approved. In the choice of the presents, female vanity is not consulted. There are no frivolous trinkets to adorn the future bride. The whole fortune consists of oxen, a caparisoned horse, a shield, a spear, and a sword. She in return delivers a present of arms, and, by this exchange of gifts, the marriage is concluded. This is the nuptial ceremony, this the bond of union . . . . Lest the wife should think her sex an exemption from the rigors of the severest virtue, and the toils of war, she is informed of her duty by the marriage ceremony, and thence she learns, that she is received by her husband to be his partner in toil and danger, to dare with him in war, and suffer with him in peace . . . .

In consequence of these manners, the married state is a life of affection and female constancy. The virtue of the woman is guarded from seduction; no public spectacles to seduce her; no banquets to inflame her passions; no baits of pleasure to disarm her virtue. The art of intriguing by clandestine letters is unknown to both sexes. Populous as the country is, adultery is rarely heard of: when detected, the punishment is instant, and inflicted by the husband. He cuts off the hair of his guilty wife, and having assembled her relations, expels her naked from his house, pursuing her with stripes through the village. To public loss of honor no favor is shown. She may possess beauty, youth and riches; but a husband she can never obtain. Vice is not treated by the Germans as a subject of raillery, nor is the profligacy of corrupting and being corrupted called the fashion of the age . . . .

———————◆———————

Germanic Law and Literature

Since warlike behavior was commonplace among the Germanic tribes, tribal law, as Tacitus points out, was severe, uncompromising, and directed toward publicly shaming the guilty. Among the Franks, who codified their laws around the year 500, punishments for crimes conformed – as in Hammurabi's Code – to the social standing of the guilty party. A person's guilt or innocence might be determined in trials by fire or water, practices that reflected the faith Germanic people placed in the will of gods. Some of the names of these gods came to designate days of the week; for instance, the word *Wednesday* derives from "Woden's day" and *Thursday* from "Thor's day." Germanic law was not legislated by the state, as in Roman tradition, but was, rather, a collection of customs passed orally from generation to generation. The dependence on custom among the Germanic folk influenced the development of **common law** in parts of the medieval West.

Germanic traditions, and especially the high regard for personal valor and heroism associated with a warring culture, are reflected in the epic poems of the Germanic people. The three most famous of these, *Beowulf, The Song of the Nibelungen*, and the *Song of Roland* (see chapter 11), were transmitted orally for hundreds of years before they were written down sometime between the tenth and thirteenth centuries. *Beowulf*, an adventure poem that originated among the Anglo-Saxons, was recorded in Old English; *The Song of the Nibelungen*, a product of the Burgundian tribe, in Old German; and the Frankish *Song of Roland*, in Old French. Celebrating the deeds of warrior-heroes, these epic poems have much in common with the *Iliad*, although in *Beowulf* and the *Nibelungen* fantasy mingles with adventure in a manner more reminiscent of the *Odyssey* or the Indian epic, the *Ramayana*.

Germanic Art

The arts of nomadic peoples were easily transported objects such as carpets, jewelry, and weapons. Germanic folk often buried the most lavish of these objects with their chieftains. In 1939, archeologists excavated at Sutton Hoo in southern England a seventh-century Anglo-Saxon grave that included weapons, coins, utensils, jewelry, and a small lyre. Along with the corpse of their chieftain, these treasures were packed into an eighty-nine-foot-long ship that served as a tomb. Among the extraordinary metalwork items found at Sutton Hoo were gold buckles and shoulder clasps (Figure 10.1) adorned with semiprecious stones and *cloisonné* – enamelwork produced by pouring molten colored glass between thin gold partitions (Figure 10.2). A five-pound gold belt buckle from the Sutton

Figure 10.1 Hinged shoulder clasps, Sutton Hoo treasure, first half of seventh century c.e. *Cloisonné* enamel and filigree, length 5 in. The British Museum, London. Bridgeman/Art Resource, New York.

Hoo treasure is ornamented with a dense pattern of interlaced snakes incised with a black sulfurous substance called **niello** (Figure 10.3). The **zoomorphic** (animal-shaped) motifs common to the artifacts at Sutton Hoo, as well as many of the complex techniques used in their fabrication, were absorbed from metalwork traditions belonging to ancient Persian and Scythian craftspeople. The quality of so-called "barbarian" art, as evidenced at Sutton Hoo and elsewhere, demonstrates that technical sophistication and artistic originality were by no means the monopoly of civilized societies.

The abstract, zoomorphic style of the Germanic tribes fused with the ornamental traditions of many other tribal people, including the Celts. The Celts were

Figure 10.2 *Cloisonné* enameling process. From Richard Phipps and Richard Wink, *Introduction to the Gallery.* Copyright © 1987 Wm. C. Brown Publishers, Dubuque, Iowa. All rights reserved. Reprinted by permission.

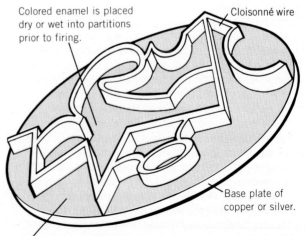

Colored enamel is placed dry or wet into partitions prior to firing.

Cloisonné wire

Base plate of copper or silver.

Base plate is enameled and permanently holds the partitions in place. They may also be soldered to the base metal before the first firing.

Figure 10.3 Buckle, Sutton Hoo treasure, first half of seventh century C.E. Gold and niello, length 5¼ in. Reproduced by courtesy of the Trustees of the British Museum, London.

Figure 10.4 "Carpet Page," Bishop Eadfrith (?), *Lindisfarne Gospels*, ca. 698–721 C.E. Vellum, 13½ × 9¾ in. Reproduced by courtesy of the Trustees of the British Museum, London.

a non-Germanic, Iron Age folk that had migrated throughout Europe between the fifth and third centuries B.C.E., settling in the British Isles before the time of Christ. The great flowering of Celtic art and literature occurred in Ireland and England following the conversion of the Celts to Christianity in the fifth century C.E. The instrument of this conversion was the British monk Saint Patrick (ca. 385–461), who is said to have baptized into Christianity more than 120,000 people and founded three hundred churches in Ireland. In the centuries thereafter, Anglo-Irish monasteries produced **illuminated manuscripts** of an extraordinary quality. The decorative style of these manuscripts is closely related to the dynamic linear ornamentation of the Sutton Hoo artifacts.

The visual masterpiece of an otherwise bleak age, the seventh-century *Lindisfarne Gospels* comes from a monastery located on an island off the east coast of England. In the pages of this extraordinary manuscript, naturalistic representation of the kind associated with classical culture has disappeared entirely. The precisely drawn Lindisfarne "carpet page" – so called for its resemblance to a woven fabric – is dominated by a magnificent **cruciform** (cross-shaped) design (Figure 10.4), but the entire spatial field writhes with knotted, ribbonlike, shapes resembling those on the Sutton Hoo belt buckle (see Figure 10.3). Looking every bit like an engraved and filigreed plaque, the carpet page combines the illusion of compositional order with a sense of labyrinthine movement. Analysis of the design shows,

Figure 10.5 Ardagh Chalice, Ireland, early eighth century C.E. Silver, gilt bronze, gold, glass, enamel. National Museum of Ireland, Dublin.

however, that one's initial impression of perfect symmetry is mistaken, for the composition depends on a complex system of mirror images and subtly varied shapes, lines, and colors. The influence of metalwork models on the art of early medieval manuscripts is a dramatic manifestation of the impulse toward the formal abstraction that characterized Germanic art.

Germanic and Celtic metalwork traditions influenced not only the style of early medieval manuscripts, but also the decoration of Christian liturgical objects such as the **paten** (Eucharistic plate) and the **chalice** (Eucharistic cup). Employed in the performance of sacred rites, these objects usually commanded the finest materials and received inordinate attention and care in execution. The Ardagh Chalice, made of silver, **gilt** (gold-surfaced) bronze, gold wire, glass, and enamel, displays the technical virtuosity of early eighth-century metalworkers in Ireland (Figure **10.5**). On the surface of the vessel, a band of interlace designs is offset by raised roundels worked in enamel and gold thread. Clearly, in the liturgical objects and illuminated manuscripts of the Early Middle Ages, the abstract, ornamental Germanic style provided Christian art with an aesthetic alternative to classical modes of representation.

Muhammad and Islam

Centuries before the time of Christ, nomadic Arabs known as *bedouins* lived in the desert peninsula of Arabia east of Egypt. At the mercy of this arid land, they traded along the caravan routes of the Near East. The Arabs were an animistic, tribal people who worshiped some three hundred different nature deities. Idols of these gods, along with the sacred Black Stone (probably an ancient meteorite), were housed in the **Kaaba**, a cubic, roofless sanctuary located in the city of Mecca. Until the sixth century C.E., the Arabs remained polytheistic and disunited, but the birth of the prophet Muhammad in 570 in Mecca changed these circumstances dramatically.

Orphaned at the age of six, Muhammad received little formal education. He traveled with his uncle as a camel driver on caravan journeys that brought him into contact with communities of Jews, Christians, and pagans. At the age of twenty-five, he married a wealthy widow fifteen years his senior. Long periods of meditation in the hills surrounding Mecca produced ecstatic visions and revelations that Muhammad interpreted as messages from the one and only Allah (the Arab word for "god"). At the age of forty, Muhammad declared himself the messenger and prophet of Allah and the last in a line of prophets descended from Abraham through Moses and Jesus. For Muhammad, the god of the Jews and that of the Christians was identical with Allah; and the religion, Islam, meaning "submission to God's will," merely completed God's revelation to the Jews and Christians.

As the Prophet of Allah, Muhammad committed to memory all of God's revelations. He then preached to his followers — called Muslims — the laws and moral injunctions of Allah. Many of Muhammad's teachings, such as the promise of resurrection, personal immortality, and the concept of Heaven and Hell, recalled Christianity, while others, such as uncompromising monotheism and strict social laws, resembled Judaism. Addressed to all people, Muhammad's religious message was simple. It rested on the Five Pillars of Faith: (1) declaration of the creed "There is no God but Allah and Muhammad is his prophet," (2) recitation of prayers five times daily, (3) charity to the poor, (4) fasting from dawn until sunset during the sacred month of Ramadan, in which Muhammad had received his divine calling, and (5) pilgrimage to the city of Mecca, Muhammad's birthplace. By God's instruction, Muhammad condemned drinking wine, eating pork, and gambling. Islam limited **polygyny** (marriage to several women at the same time) to no more than four wives, providing a man could afford them. Though Muhammad tried to raise the status of women, a Muslim wife lived for the most part at the mercy of her husband, who could end the marriage by simply renouncing her.

Although Islam would ultimately unify all of Arabia, at the outset few of Muhammad's contemporaries embraced the new faith. The Prophet thus abandoned his native city in 622 and emigrated to nearby

Medina, a journey known as the *hijra* ("migration"). After converting the population of Medina to Islam, he returned to Mecca with a force of 10,000 men, conquering the city and destroying the idols in the *Kaaba*, with the exception of the sacred Black Stone. Thereafter, Muhammad assumed a theocratic position that prompted his contemporaries to compare him to Rome's Caesars. By the time Muhammad died in 632, all of the Arabian peninsula was united in Islam. Since the history of successful missionary activity began with Muhammad's *hijra* in 622, his followers designated that date as the first year of the Muslim calendar.

The Koran

Although Muhammad himself wrote nothing, his followers memorized and recited his teachings, recording them some ten years after the Prophet's death in the Koran (literally, "recitation"), the sacred scripture of the Muslim faith. A guide to both spiritual and secular life, the Koran consists of revelations concerning the nature of God, directions for worship, and descriptions of the last judgment and resurrection, along with specific moral and social injunctions for everyday conduct. Muslims consider the Koran the eternal and absolute word of God, and centuries of Muslim leaders have governed according to its precepts. Recorded in Arabic, Muslim scriptures resemble poetry and are intended to be chanted or recited, not read silently. Committed to memory by devout Muslims, the Koran is considered untranslatable, not only because its contents are deemed sacred, but because it is impossible to capture in other languages the musical nuances of the original Arabic. So crucial to Arab culture is the Koran that it has become the main textbook for the study of the Arabic language.

READING 38

From the Koran

Chapter 76 [1] Time

In the name of Allah, most benevolent, ever-merciful.

Was there not a time in the life of man
when he was not even a mentionable thing?[2]
2. Verily We created man from a sperm yoked (to the ovum)
to bring out his real substance,
then gave him hearing and sight.
3. We surely showed him the way
that he may either be grateful or deny.

---

[1] Muhammad's followers arranged the 144 chapters of the Koran in order of length, from longest to shortest. The shorter chapters are, however, earlier in date.
[2] That is, prior to Creation.

4. We have prepared for unbelievers
chains and collars and a blazing fire.
5. Surely the devotees will drink cups
flavoured with palm blossoms
6. From a spring of which
the votaries of God will drink
and make it flow in abundance.
7. Those who fulfil their vows and fear
the Day whose evil shall be diffused far and wide,
8. And feed the needy for the love of Him,
and the orphans and the captives,
9. (Saying): "We feed you for the sake of God,
desiring neither recompense nor thanks.
10. We fear the dismal day calamitous from our Lord."
11. So God will protect them from the evil of that day,
and grant them happiness and joy,
12. And reward them for their perseverance
Paradise and silken robes,
13. Where they will recline
on couches feeling neither heat of the sun
nor intense cold.
14. The shadows will blend over them,
and low will hang the clusters of grapes.
15. Passed round will be silver flagons
and goblets made of glass,
16. And crystal clear bottles of silver,
of which they will determine the measure themselves.
17. There will they drink a cup flavoured with ginger
18. From a spring by the name of Salsabil.
19. And boys of everlasting youth will go about
attending them.
Looking at them you would think
that they were pearls dispersed.
20. When you look around, you will see
delights and great dominion.
21. On their bodies will be garments
of the finest green silk and brocade,
and they will be adorned with bracelets of silver;
and their Lord will give them a purest draught to drink.
22. "This in truth is your recompense,
and acceptance of your endeavours."

. . . .

Chapter 56 The Inevitable

In the name of Allah, most benevolent, ever-merciful.

When what is to happen comes to pass —
2. Which is bound to happen undoubtedly —
3. Degrading (some) and exalting (others);
4. When the earth is shaken up convulsively,
5. The mountains bruised and crushed,
6. Turned to dust, floating in the air,
7. You will become three categories:
8. Those of the right hand —
how (happy) will be those of the right hand!
9. Then those of the left hand —
how (unhappy) will be those of the left hand!
10. Then the foremost, how pre-excellent,
11. Who will be honoured
12. In gardens of tranquility;
13. A number of the earlier peoples,
14. And a few of later ages,

15. On couches wrought of gold,
16. Reclining face to face.
17. Youths of never-ending bloom
will pass round to them
18. Cups and decanters,
beakers full of sparkling wine,
19. Unheady, uninebriating;
20. And such fruits as they fancy,
21. Bird meats that they relish,
22. And companions
with big beautiful eyes
23. Like pearls within their shells,
24. As recompense
for all they had done.
25. They will hear no nonsense there or talk of sin,
26. Other than "Peace, peace" the salutation.
27. As for those of the right hand —
how (happy) those of the right hand —
28. They will be in (the shade)
of thornless lote
29. And acacia
covered with heaps of bloom,
30. Lengthened shadows,
31. Gushing water,
32. And fruits numberless,
33. Unending, unforbidden,
34. And maidens incomparable
35. We have formed them
in a distinctive fashion,
36. And made them virginal,
37. Loving companions matched in age,
38. For those of the right hand.

A crowd of earlier generations
40. And a crowd of the later.
41. But those of the left hand —
how (unhappy) those of the left hand —
42. Will be in the scorching wind
and boiling water,
43. Under the shadow of thick black smoke
44. Neither cool nor agreeable.
45. They were endowed with good things
46. But persisted in that greater sin,
47. And said: "What! When we are dead
and turned to dust and bones,
shall we then be raised again?
48. And so will our fathers?"
49. Say: "Indeed, the earlier and the later generations
50. Will be gathered together
on a certain day which is predetermined.
51. Then you, the erring and the deniers,
52. Will eat of the tree of Zaqqum,
53. Fill your bellies with it,
54. And drink over it scalding water,
55. Lapping it up like female camels
raging of thirst with disease."
56. Such will be their welcome
on the Day of Judgement.

. . . .

Chapter 47 Muhammad

In the name of Allah, most benevolent, ever-merciful.

Those who disbelieve
and obstruct (others) from the way of God
will have wasted their deeds.
2. But those who believe and do the right,
and believe what has been revealed to Muhammad,
which is the truth from their Lord,
will have their faults condoned by Him
and their state improved.
3. That is because those who refuse to believe
only follow what is false; but those who believe
follow the truth from their Lord.
That is how God gives men precepts of wisdom.
4. So, when you clash with the unbelievers,
smite their necks until you overpower them,
then hold them in bondage.
Then either free them graciously
or after taking a ransom,
until war shall have come to end.
If God had pleased
He could have punished them (Himself),
but He wills to test some of you through some others.
He will not allow the deeds
of those who are killed in the cause of God
to go waste.
5. He will show them the way,
and better their state,
6. And will admit them into gardens
with which he has acquainted them.
7. O you who believe, if you help (in the cause of) God
He will surely come to your aid,
and firmly plant your feet.
8. As for the unbelievers, they will suffer misfortunes,
and their deeds will be rendered ineffective.
9. That is so as they were averse
to what has been revealed by God,
and their actions will be nullified.
10. Have they not journeyed in the land
and seen the fate of those before them?
Destroyed they were utterly by God;
and a similar (fate) awaits the unbelievers.
11. This is so for God is the friend of those who believe
while the unbelievers have no friend.

. . . .

Chapter 5 The Feast

In the name of Allah, most benevolent, ever-merciful.

. . . .

8. O you who believe,
stand up as witnesses for God in all fairness,
and do not let the hatred of a people
deviate you from justice.
Be just: This is closest to piety; and beware of God. Surely
God is aware of all you do.
9. God has made a promise of forgiveness and the highest
reward
to those who believe and perform good deeds.
10. But those who disbelieve and deny Our revelations
are the people of Hell.

11. O believers, remember the favours God bestowed on you
when a people raised their hands against you
and He restrained their hands.
So fear God;
and the faithful should place their trust in God.

. . . .

O Prophet, announce
what has reached you from your Lord,
for if you do not,
you will not have delivered His message.
God will preserve you from (the mischief of) men; for God does
     not guide those
who do not believe.
68. Say to them: "O people of the Book,[3]
you have no ground (for argument)
until you follow the Torah and the Gospel
and what has been revealed
to you by your Lord."
But what has been revealed to you by your Lord
will surely increase
rebellion and unbelief in many;
so do not grieve for those who do not believe.
69. All those who believe,
and the Jews and the Sabians[4]
and the Christians,
in fact any one who believes in God and the Last Day,
and performs good deeds,
will have nothing to fear or regret.
72. They are surely infidels who say:
"God is the Christ, son of Mary."
But the Christ had only said:
"O children of Israel, worship God
who is my Lord and your Lord."
Whosoever associates a compeer with God,
will have Paradise denied to him by God,
and his abode shall be Hell;
and the sinners will have none to help them.
73. Disbelievers are they surely who say:
"God is the third of the trinity;"
but there is no god other than God the one.
And if they do not desist from saying what they say,
then indeed those among them who persist in disbelief
will suffer painful punishment.
74. Why do they not turn to God and ask His forgiveness?
God is forgiving and kind.
75. The Christ, son of Mary, was but an apostle,
and many apostles had (come and) gone before him;
and his mother was a woman of truth.
They both ate the (same) food (as men).
Behold, how We show men clear signs,
and behold, how they wander astray!
76. Tell them: "Leaving God aside, will you worship
something that has no power over your loss or gain?"
But God is all-hearing and all-knowing.
77. Tell them: "O people of the Book, do not overstep
the bounds of truth in your beliefs,
and follow not the wishes of a people who had erred before,
and led many others astray,
and wandered away from the right path."

---

[3]Jews and Christians.
[4]Semitic merchants from the Saba, a Kingdom in southern Arabia.

The Spread of Islam

To those people whose geographic heritage was a hot and arid desert, the Koran promised a shady paradise filled with flowing rivers, abundant fruit trees, and handsome youths serving cool liquids in silver goblets. But this sensuous and peaceful place of divine reward was paired with a terrifying image of Hell and an equally terrifying destiny for **infidels** (nonbelievers). For those who accepted Allah, the Koran provided a system of social justice and the guidelines for obedient worship. Moreover, it offered a universalist ethic that became the basis for an Islamic community. At the outset, Islam united the people of Arabia in a common religious and ethnic cause, a cause that took Arabs out of their desert prison. Militant expansion, allied to zealous religious struggle and war (*jihad*) propelled Muslims through Asia, Africa, and into the West. Muslim soldiers gained wealth if they survived battle – they were permitted to keep four-fifths of all booty – and Paradise if they died fighting for Allah. Generally speaking, however, early Muslims did not actively coerce those they conquered into accepting Islam. While many subject people embraced Islam out of genuine spiritual conviction, others found commercial and social advantages in conversion. Converts to Islam were exempt from paying a poll-tax levied on all non-Muslim subjects. Favorable associations between Arab merchants and members of the ruling elite (in Africa, for instance) also encouraged conversion to Islam.

Muhammad never designated a successor; hence, after his death, bitter controversies arose concerning the leadership of Islam. The divisions that followed produced major rifts within the faith that still exist today. The majority of all Muslims – the Sunnis – consider themselves the orthodox of Islam. They hold that religious rulers should be chosen by the faithful. The Shi'ites claim descent through Muhammad's cousin and son-in-law Ali and believe that only his direct descendants (one of whom was Iran's late Ayatollah Khomeini) should rule. Following Muhammad's death, leadership fell to *caliphs*, successors appointed by his followers. The first four caliphs, who ruled until 750, assumed political and religious authority, and their pursuit of *jihad* resulted in a theocratic Muslim empire. Damascus fell to Islam in 634, Persia in 636, Jerusalem in 638, and Egypt in 640. Within another seventy years, all of North Africa and Spain also lay under Arab rule (Map **10.2**).

The early history of Muslim expansion may be perceived as similar to the large-scale migrations of the Germanic tribes into the West, the major difference being that among Muslims, military and religious purpose went hand in hand. Indeed, in less than a century, Muslims had won more converts to Islam than

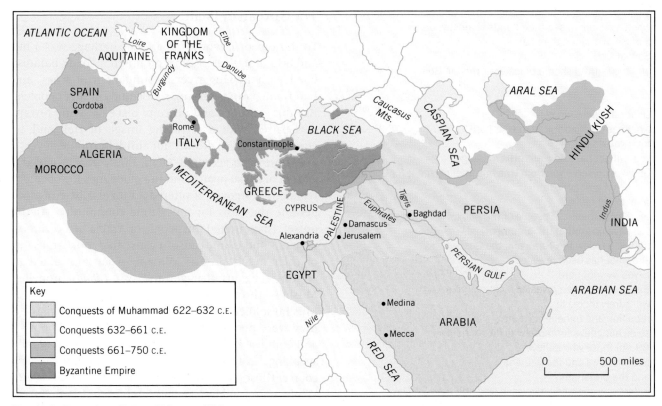

Map 10.2 Expansion of Islam 622 to ca. 750 C.E.

Christianity had gained in three hundred years. And, in most of the Asiatic and African areas conquered by Islam in its first expansion, Islam remains to this day the dominant faith. The Muslim advance upon the West encountered only two notable impasses. The first was Constantinople, where Byzantine forces equipped with "Greek fire" (an incendiary compound catapulted from ships) deterred repeated Arab attacks. The second was in southwest France near Tours, where in 732, Frankish soldiers led by Charles Martel (the grandfather of Charlemagne) turned back the Muslims, barring the progress of Islam into Europe. Nevertheless, the Arab domination of the Mediterranean Sea severed ties between East and West until at least the eleventh century, a circumstance that enforced a period of incubation for embryonic Western European culture.

Islam's success in becoming a world faith is a remarkable historical phenomenon, one that is explained in part by the fact that, at the outset, religious, political, and military goals were allied – somewhat like Christianity after the Edict of Milan. However, other factors were crucial to the success of Islam. The new faith offered rules of conduct that were easy to understand and to follow, a timely alternative, perhaps, to the growing complexity of eighth-century Christianity. In contrast with Christianity and Judaism, Islam remained free of dogma and liturgy, and unencumbered by a clerical hierarchy. Islam produced *imams* (prayer

leaders) and *mullahs* (scholars trained in Muslim law), but no priests. Millions of people found Islam egalitarian and responsive to their immediate spiritual needs. To date, Islam has suffered less alteration and is closer to its original form than any other world religion.

Islamic* Art and Architecture

Five times a day, at the call of *muezzins* (criers) usually located atop **minarets** (tall, slender towers; see Figure 9.10), Muslims interrupt their activities to kneel and pray in the direction of Mecca. The official Muslim house of worship, however, is the **mosque**, a large, columned hall in the shape of a square or rectangle. The interior space of the mosque is not, as with the Early Christian church, designed for the performance of the liturgy. Rather, it is first and foremost a place of prayer. Mosques are oriented toward Mecca, and the direction in which the Muslim prays is marked by a special wall that holds a niche or *mihrab*. To the right of the *mihrab* is a pulpit at which the Koran may be read.

The Great Mosque in Cordoba, Spain, begun in 784 and enlarged over a period of three hundred years, is one of the noblest examples of early Islamic architecture. Its interior consists of more than five hundred

---

*This term traditionally refers to those regions, both Arabic and non-Arabic, dominated by Islam.

double-tiered columns that originally supported a wooden roof (Figure 10.6). Arches consisting of contrasting light and dark wedges of marble and granite, crown a forest of ornamental pillars. The lower arches of the "piggyback" design are in the horseshoe shape that became a basic feature of Muslim architecture. In still other parts of the interior, **hexafoil** (six-leafed) arches make up a pattern of static and rhythmic forms (Figure 10.7). Within the spacious interior of the Great Mosque (now a Catholic church), arches seem to "flower" like palm fronds from column "stems." In contrast with the clarity and finality of the Early Christian church, the Great Mosque conveys a sense of infinite, unfocused space.

Islam was self-consciously resistant to image making. Like the Hebrews, Muslims condemned the worship of idols. And because Muslims deemed Allah the sole Creator, they refused to fabricate likenesses of living creatures. Hence, in Islamic religious art, where the written word takes precedence over the human form, there is almost no three-dimensional sculpture, and, with the exception of scenes of the Muslim paradise such as those found on the walls of the Great Mosque of Damascus, few pictorial cycles. But such

Figure 10.6 Interior of the Great Mosque, Cordoba, Spain, 961–976 C.E. A forest of columns in the Moorish part of the Cathedral Mosque. The Bettmann Archive.

Figure 10.7 *Mihrab* bay, Great Mosque, Cordoba, Spain, 961–976 C.E. MAS, Barcelona.

Figure 10.8 Exterior of the Great Mosque of Cordoba, Spain, begun 784 C.E. The Bettmann Archive.

Figure 10.9 Carved stucco panels from Samarra, Iraq, ninth century c.e. © Editions Citadelles and Mazenod, Paris.

Figure 10.10 Islamic bowl with inscription. Earthenware, glazed, height 7 in., diameter 18 in. The Metropolitan Museum of Art, New York, Rogers Fund, 1965.

self-imposed limitations did not prevent Muslims from creating one of the richest bodies of visual ornamentation in the history of art. The exterior of the Great Mosque, which features a bold horseshoe arch at the entrance portal, bears a delicate surface of abstract, lacework decoration consisting of popular Islamic motifs (Figure 10.8). Some are geometric, while others make use of the **arabesque**, a type of ornament featuring plant and flower forms (Figure 10.9). Equally important to Islamic art was Arabic calligraphy. In the frieze above the arches in the vestibule of the mosque at Cordoba, the Word of Allah is written in elegant gold **Kufic** (a type of script originating in the Iraqi town of Al-Kufa). Ornate surface designs executed in mosaics and glazed tiles regularly transformed the solid walls of mosques and palaces into shimmering veils of light and color.

Geometric, arabesque, and calligraphic motifs dominate Islamic frescoes, carpets, manuscripts, textiles, and ceramics. Along the rim of an earthenware bowl from the tenth century, an elegant Kufic script imparts Muhammad's injunction: "Planning before work protects one from regret; prosperity and peace" (Figure 10.10). Here, as on the pages of an early Koran (Figure 10.11), fluid, calligraphic strokes are the sole "decorative" element. In Islamic secular manuscripts— most of which date from after 1200—tales, poems, and fables are freely illustrated with human and animal representations, while calligraphy and arabesque motifs often frame the central scene (Figure 10.12).

The similarities between the Islamic arabesque and the meandering, organic style of Germanic art may be related to the fact that both Germanic and Muslim peoples were wandering folk who lived close to nature.

Both were also heirs to the ornamental vocabularies and sophisticated techniques of ancient Persian, Greek, and Egyptian art. Both Germanic and Islamic artists tended to fill up all the space of any surface, enriching it with complex, rhythmic designs that seem to expand and contract. In comparison with the art of the Germanic tribes, however, the art of Islam embraces a far wider range of media, including knotted pile carpets, glazed ceramics, and monumental religious and secular architecture. Differences also exist in subject matter: Germanic artists favored animal forms, while Islamic artists generally preferred plant and floral motifs. Perhaps most important, Islamic art lifts the beholder

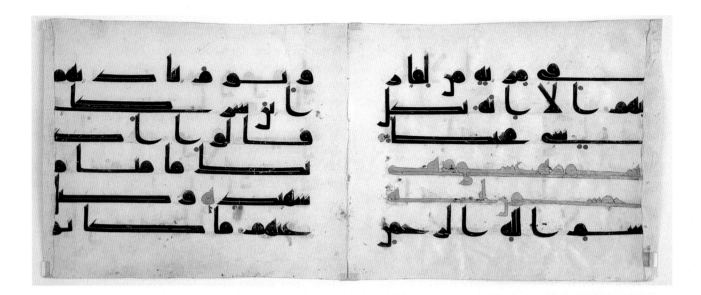

Figure 10.11 Double folio of Kufic calligraphy from the Koran. Persian manuscript, ninth to tenth centuries C.E. Ink and gold leaf on vellum, 8½ × 21 in. The Nelson-Atkins Museum of Art, Kansas City, Missouri (Purchase: Nelson Trust) 44–40/2 detail.

Figure 10.12 Shaykh Muhammad, *A Camel and Keeper Approached by his Conductor*. Persian painting, Safavid Period, Mashhad School, dated 1556–1557. Full color and gold on paper, 4⁵⁄₁₆ × 5³⁄₁₆ in. Courtesy of the Freer Gallery of Art, Smithsonian Institution, Washington, D.C. (37.21).

beyond the world of appearances to a higher, more refined, psychic order. In Islamic design, the integration of the written word, the natural motif, and the geometric pattern works to engage both the intellect and the spirit.

Music in the Islamic World

For the devout Muslim, there was no religious music other than the sounds of the chanted Koran and the *muezzin's* call to prayer. Although Muslims regarded music as a forbidden pleasure, secular music flourished in the opulent courts of Cordoba and Baghdad. And between the eighth and thirteenth centuries, Arab song mingled with the music of Persia, Syria, Egypt, and Byzantium to form a rich secular musical tradition.

The music of the Islamic world originated in the songs of the desert nomads, songs that were free in rhythm and strong in emotion. As in ancient Greece, India, and China, music in the Islamic world featured a single voice line with occasional instrumental accompaniment. Islamic music was also modal, each mode bearing association with a specific quality of emotion. The melodic line of an Arab song resembles a highly embroidered arabesque that slides and intones in ways that exploit the expressive capacity of the voice.[6] In their emphasis on ornament and variation, Arab songs may be compared with the florid surfaces of bedouin carpets or Islamic facades.

---

[6]See Music Listening Selection at end of chapter.

Figure 10.13 (a) Lute with nine strings. Spanish miniature from the *Cantigas de Santa Maria*, 1221–1289. El Escorial de Santa Maria, MS E-Eb-1-2, f. 162.
(b) Line drawing of a lute based on image from Musical Heritage.

Instrumental music was second to voice everywhere in the Islamic world, except in Persia, where a strong pre-Islamic instrumental tradition flourished. Lyres, flutes, and drums were often used to accompany the songs of bedouin camel drivers, while bells and tambourines might provide percussion for dancing. By the seventh century, however, the Arabs developed the lute (in Arabic, *ud*, meaning "wood"), a pear-shaped string instrument that was used to accompany vocal performance (Figure **10.13**). And after the eighth century, there emerged in Muslim Spain long-form orchestral compositions, consisting of five or more distinct movements, performed by string and wind instruments, percussion, and voices. It is possible that the Western tradition of orchestral music, along with the development of such instruments as oboes, trumpets, viols, and kettledrums originated among Arab musicians during the centuries of Muslim rule in Spain. Indeed, the renowned ninth-century musician, Ziryab (known for his dark complexion as "the Blackbird"), traveled from Baghdad to Cordoba to become the founder of the first conservatory of music and patriarch of Spanish musical art. Music composition and theory reached a peak during the eighth and ninth centuries, when Cordoba and Baghdad enjoyed a Golden Age in the arts. At that time, Islamic scholars wrote treatises describing musical performance and theory. They discussed the aesthetic, ethical, and medicinal functions of the modes, recommending specific types of music to relieve the distress of the sick. One Arab writer, Al-Isfahani (897–967), compiled the *Great Book of Songs*, a twenty-one-volume encyclopedia that remains our most important source of information about Arab music and poetry from its beginnings to the tenth century.

Islamic Poetry

Poetry and music were as intimately related in Islamic tradition as they were in ancient Greece and China. Pre-Islamic nomadic folk sang songs that celebrated romantic love, tribal warfare, and the affairs of daily life. As with the Greek Homer, bedouin minstrels were the "keepers" of popular poetry. The Arabic language is rich in rhyme, and a single rhyme often dominates an entire poem. No English translation can capture the lyricism of Arabic verse. Nevertheless, the sixth-century Arabic ode that follows conveys the affection and respect of a bedouin for a camel that captured his heart. Rich in descriptive imagery, it depends on vivid similes for its sensuous effect.

READING 39
Tarafa's "Praise for His Camel"

Yet I have means to fly from grief, when such pursues me,   1
   on a lean high beast, which paces swiftly by day and by
   night,
A camel sure of foot, firm and thin as the planks of a bier,
   whom I guide surely over the trodden ways, ways
   etched in earth as texture is in cloth;
A she-camel, rival of the best, swift as an ostrich. When
   she trots her hind feet fall in the marks of her forefeet
   on the beaten road.

With her white feathery tail she lashes backward and   10
   forward. Sometimes the lash falls on her rider,
   sometimes on her own dried udder, where no milk is,
   flaccid as an old bottle of leather.
Firm and polished are her haunches as two worn jambs of
   a castle gate.
The bones of her spine are supple and well-attached, and
   her neck rises solidly.

When she raises her long neck it is like the rudder of a
    boat going up the Tigris.
She carries her strong thighs well apart, as a carrier of   20
    water holds apart his buckets.
Red is the hair under her chin. Strong she is of back, long
    of stride; easily she moves her forelegs.

The marks of the girths on her sides are as the marks of
    water-courses over smooth rock.
Sometimes the marks unite and sometimes are distinct,
    like the gores in fine linen, well-cut and stitched.
Her long skull is like an anvil, and where the bones unite
    their edges are sharp as the teeth of a file.
Her cheek is smooth as paper of Syria, and her upper lip   30
    like leather of Yemen, exactly and smoothly cut.
The two polished mirrors of her eyes gleam in the caverns
    of their sockets as water gleams in rocky pools.

Her ears are sharp to hear the low voices of the night, and
    not inattentive to the loud call,
Pricked ears, that show her breeding, like those of a lone
    wild bull in the groves of Haumel.
Her upper lip is divided and her nose pierced. When she
    stretches them along the ground her pace increases.
I touch her with my whip and she quickens her step, even   40
    though it be the time when the mirage shimmers on
    the burning sands.
She walks with graceful gait, as the dancing girl walks,
    showing her master the skirts of her trailing garment.

———————————◆———————————

    In Muslim lands, the prized lyrics were those of the
Koran. However, the secular poetry of the Islamic
world formed a rich tradition that included laments
over injustice, elegies for the departed, and the celebration of the physical delights of nature. (In addition to
poetry, prose tales like those in the tenth-century
collection called *The Thousand and One Nights* were
popular sources of adventure and intrigue.) Romantic
love – both heterosexual and homosexual – became a
major theme among Arab poets, especially those who
came under the influence of Persian literature. The
eighth-century "Romance of Antar," a eulogy to a
beautiful and bewitching female, attributed to Al-
Asma'i, reflects the sensual power of the finest Islamic
lyrics. The poet's "ailment" of unrequited love, or "love
sickness," was a popular conceit among Arab bards.
Their frank examination of the psychology of love
influenced the rise of troubadour poetry and of the
romance in the Christian West (see chapter 11).

READING 40
From Al-Asma'i's "Romance of Antar"

The lovely virgin has struck my heart with the arrow of a   1
    glance, for which there is no cure.
Sometimes she wishes for a feast in the sand-hills, like a
    fawn whose eyes are full of magic.

My disease preys on me; it is in my entrails: I conceal it;
    but its very concealment discloses it.
She moves: I should say it was the branch of the tamarisk[1]
    that waves its branches to the southern breeze.
She approaches: I should say her face was truly the sun
    when its luster dazzles the beholders.   10
She walks away: I should say her face was truly the sun
    when its luster dazzles the beholders.
She gazes: I should say it was the full moon of the night
    when Orion[2] girds it with stars.
She smiles: and the pearls of her teeth sparkle, in which
    there is the cure for the sickness of lovers.
She prostrates herself in reverence towards her God;
    and the greatest of men bow down to her beauties.
O Abla! when I most despair, love for thee and all its
    weaknesses are my only hope!   20

———————————◆———————————

Scholarship in the Islamic World

Following Muhammad's dictum to "seek knowledge,"
Islam was enthusiastically receptive to the intellectual
achievements of other cultures. Arab scholars copied
and translated into Arabic Greek manuscripts (including those of Aristotle). They absorbed and preserved
much of the medical, botanical, and astrological lore of
the hellenized Near East and transmitted to the West a
rich fund of scientific and technological knowledge.
Islamic scholars were more than copyists; they made
original contributions in mathematics, medicine, op-
tics, chemistry, geography, philosophy, and astronomy, much of which did not enter the West until after
the year 1000, when Christian Crusaders directly
encountered the culture of Islam (see chapter 11).

    In the field of medicine, Islamic physicians wrote
treatises on smallpox and measles and systematized
medical learning (Figure 10.14). The vast *Canon of
Medicine* compiled by the Persian physician and philosopher Avicenna (890–1037) was a major source of
medical knowledge until well into the sixteenth century. Muslim chemists invented the process of distilla-
tion and produced a volatile liquid (and forbidden
intoxicant) called *alkuhl* (alcohol). And Muslim astronomers made advances in spherical geometry and
trigonometry that aided religious observance, which
required an accurate lunar calendar and the means of
determining the direction of Mecca from any given
location.

    Muslim philosophers, including Avicenna, were
interested in reconciling the precepts of Islam with the
ideas of Aristotle and the Neoplatonists. In the twelfth
century, Muslim commentaries on Aristotle spurred
the rise of the earliest universities in Western Europe

———————————————————————————

[1] A Mediterranean plant.
[2] A constellation of bright stars represented by the figure of a hunter with belt
and sword.

أي البسط في الطعام او من ركاب قوة نحل وصفته على هذه الصفه

ونهايا البعد ونه يؤخذ من العسل اجزا وتخلطونه بالعشار وطحونه علا الصفه الى الذهب

اللبن تشريف وتفعونه ع م م وقد تتحلفراب

فقال له ابوما لي علا هذه الصفه ويؤخذ تمع الشهد يغسل

بالما ويؤخذ ذلك الما ويرفع ه نبغى اذا اشرب هذا الشراب ان السبع

بصرف و من الناس من طنخه و من غير موافق للمرض لكثره ما ذبره من

Figure 10.14 Preparing Medicine from Honey. Leaf from an Arabic manuscript of *Materia Medica* by Dioscorides, Iraqi, thirteenth century. Colors and gilt on paper, 12⅜ × 9 in. The Metropolitan Museum of Art, New York. Cora Timken Burnett Collection of Persian Miniatures and Other Persian Art Objects, Bequest of Cora Timken Burnett, 1956 (57.51.21).

(see chapter 12). Muslim scholars passed to the West the Hindu use of the symbol for the numeric zero and replaced cumbersome Roman numerals with Arabic numbers such as those used to paginate this book. Muslims transmitted westward from China such technological wonders as paper and block printing (after the eighth century) and gunpowder (after the thirteenth century).

Between the eighth and tenth centuries, the cosmopolitan cities of the Muslim world boasted levels of wealth and culture that far exceeded those of Western Christendom or the Orient. The great centers of Muslim urban life, Cordoba in Spain and Baghdad on the Tigris River, rivaled Constantinople in learning and the arts. And even after invading Turkish nomads gained control of Baghdad during the eleventh century, the city retained undisputed cultural primacy within the civilized world until it was destroyed by the Mongols in 1258. Evidence of the longevity of Muslim culture is, moreover, confirmed by Tunisian historian Ibn Khaldun, who, in the fourteenth century, called the north African city of Cairo, "the mother of the world, the great center of Islam and the mainspring of the sciences and the crafts."

SUMMARY

The humanistic tradition is clearly the product of a wide variety of cultural ingredients. From the European perspective, the westward migrations of Germanic and Muslim peoples were intrusive episodes that threatened the safety of the West. But from a global perspective, their cultures introduced important and long-lasting customs, values, and artistic traditions. While

Germanic expansion worked to decentralize the Roman West, Germanic tribes introduced languages, laws, and patterns of warfare that persisted into the Christian Middle Ages. After the fall of Rome, the Germanic legacy mingled with the vestiges of late Roman civilization to produce a unique amalgam of Germanic, classical, and Christian cultures in the West.

In seventh-century Arabia, Islam emerged as the youngest of the great world religions. Muslims regarded Muhammad as the Prophet of Allah and sought divine instruction in the Koran. After the death of Muhammad, Islam expanded beyond the Arabian homeland. Muslim holy wars brought vast areas of land under Islamic rule. Dominating most of the Mediterranean, the Muslims isolated Western Europe from the East, forcing the West into a period of cultural incubation.

In the Dark Ages that followed the fall of Rome in the West, the Islamic world shined brightly. Muslims living in the great cities of Cordoba, Baghdad, and elsewhere made original contributions to literature, art and architecture, music, mathematics, philosophy, and medicine, most of which would have profound and far-reaching effects on European culture after the year 1000. Arab scholars made copies of Greek manuscripts and assembled a valuable corpus of medical, botanical, navigational, and mathematical knowledge. As the geographic intermediaries between Asia and Europe, the Muslims transmitted the fruits of Eastern culture to the West. To this day, Islam, with almost a billion adherents, has preserved with little change the teachings of its founder. And, in our own time, Muslim countries and their populations have assumed positions of worldwide consequence, prompting renewed attention to the Islamic heritage.

SUGGESTIONS FOR READING

Brend, Barbara. *Islamic Art*. Cambridge, Mass.: Harvard University Press, 1980.

Bruce-Mitford, Rupert. *The Sutton Hoo Ship-Burial: A Handbook*. London: British Museum, 1972.

Christopher, J.B. *The Islamic Tradition*. New York: Harper, 1972.

Drew, Katherine F., ed. *The Barbarian Invasions*. New York: Holt, 1970.

Hitti, Philip K. *Islam: A Way of Life*. Chicago: Regnery Gateway, 1970.

Lewis, Bernard, ed. *Islam and the Arab World: Faith, People, Culture*. New York: Knopf, 1976.

————. *The Muslim Discovery of Europe*. New York: Norton, 1982.

Rice, D. R. *Islamic Art*, rev. ed. New York: Praeger, 1985.

Stanton, Charles M. *Higher Learning in Islam: The Classical Period, 700 A.D. to 1300 A.D.* Lanham, Md.: Rowman & Littlefield, 1990.

GLOSSARY

arabesque a type of ornament featuring plant and flower forms

caliph the official successor to Muhammad and theocratic ruler of an Islamic state

chalice a goblet; in Christian liturgy, the Eucharistic cup

cloisonné (French, *cloison* = "fence") an enameling technique produced by pouring molten colored glass between thin metal strips secured to a metal surface; any object ornamented in this manner; (see Figure 10.2)

common law the body of unwritten law developed primarily from judicial decisions based on custom and precedent; the basis of the English legal system and that of all states in the United States with the exception of Louisiana

cruciform cross-shaped

fealty loyalty; the fidelity of the warrior to his chieftain; (see also chapter 11)

gilt gold-surfaced; covered with gold paint or gold foil

hexafoil having six leaves or arcs

hijra ("migration" or "flight") Muhammad's journey from Mecca to Medina in the year 622

illuminated manuscript a handwritten and ornamented book, parts of which (the script, illustrations, or decorative devices) might be embellished with gold or silver paint or with gold foil, hence "illuminated"

imam a Muslim prayer leader

infidel a nonbeliever

jihad (Arabic, "struggle" [to follow God's will]) the struggle to lead a virtuous life and to further the universal mission of Islam through teaching, preaching, and, when necessary, armed conflict or "holy war"

Kaaba (Arabic, "cube") a religious sanctuary in Mecca; a square temple containing the sacred Black Stone thought to have been delivered to Abraham by the angel Gabriel

Kufic a type of script originating in the Iraqi town of Al-Kufa

minaret a tall, slender tower usually attached to a mosque and surrounded by a balcony from which the *muezzin* summons Muslims to prayer

mihrab a special niche in the wall of a mosque that indicates the direction of Mecca

mosque the Muslim house of worship

muezzin a "crier" who calls the hours of Muslim prayers five times a day

mullah a Muslim trained in Islamic law and doctrine

niello a black sulfurous substance used as a decorative inlay for incised metal surfaces; the art or process of decorating metal in this manner

paten a shallow dish; in Christian liturgy, the Eucharistic plate

polygyny the marriage of one man to several women at the same time

zoomorphic animal-shaped; having the form of an animal

MUSIC LISTENING SELECTION

Cassette I Selection 4 Arabic Song: "Maqām Sika" (Egypt). Solo voice, lute, flute excerpt.

PART

II

THE MEDIEVAL WEST

The Middle Ages captures the imagination as an era of knights in shining armor, of black-hooded monks, and of castles and crusades. But while there is much about the medieval world that provides food for fantasy, there is also the dramatic reality of its impact on the evolution of Western culture. The geographic contours of modern European states and the basic political, religious, and linguistic traditions of Western Europe (to which Americans are deeply indebted) took shape during the Middle Ages. The prototypes of nation-states, cities, and universities emerged, and the Roman Catholic church reached its peak as a powerful political and spiritual institution. The feudal epic, the courtly romance, and the morality play appeared, along with the vernacular languages used in the West today. The Middle Ages generated glorious works of art, architecture, and music that still dazzle modern beholders.

Our examination of medieval Europe begins with the Age of Charlemagne in the late eighth century. Chapter 11, "Patterns of Medieval Life," compares the arts and ideas of the Early Middle Ages (ca. 500–1000), a time of relative insecurity marked by the development of feudalism and manorialism, with those of the High Middle Ages (ca. 1000–1300), a period that witnessed the revival of trade and the emergence of town life. Chapter 12, "The Christian Church and the Medieval Mind," focuses on the role of the Church in medieval life, the rise of universities, and the articulation of the Christian promise of life after death in medieval prose and poetry. Chapter 13, "The Medieval Synthesis in the Arts," explores the development of the Romanesque and Gothic styles in art and architecture and the rise of polyphonic music. It interprets the medieval synthesis as a unique combination of the arts and as a vehicle of the spiritual yearnings of an age of faith.

(opposite) Detail of Figure 11.16 Lancelot Crossing the Swordbridge; Guinevere in the Tower. From the *Romance of Lancelot*, ca. 1300. © The J. Pierpont Morgan Library, New York, 1990. MS 806 f. 166.

11
Patterns of Medieval Life

In the five centuries following the collapse of Roman civilization, a period often referred to as the Dark Ages, Western Europe faced a struggle for order and stability and a decline in literacy and the arts. During this era, more aptly termed the Early Middle Ages (ca. 500–1000), classical, Christian, and Germanic traditions fused to produce patterns of life that were at once different from those of the ancient world and crucial to the development of a vigorous new culture, that of the medieval Western world.

Charlemagne and the Carolingian Renaissance

From the time he came to the throne in 768 until his death in 814, the Frankish chieftain Charles the Great (in French, "Charlemagne") pursued the dream of restoring the Roman empire under Christian leadership. A great warrior and an able administrator, the fair-haired heir to the Frankish kingdom conquered

Map 11.1 The Empire of Charlemagne in 814 C.E.

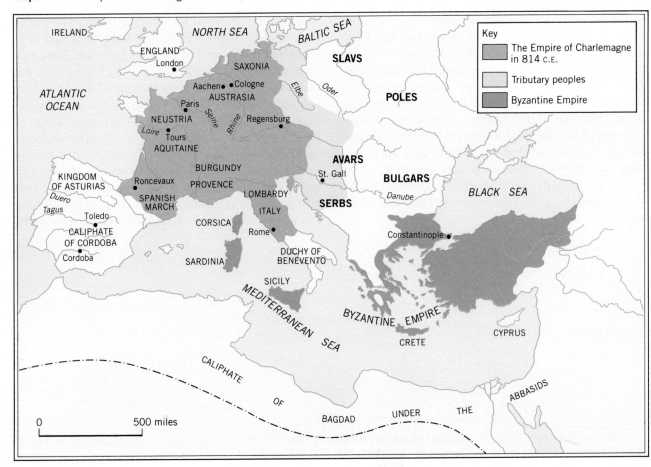

vast areas of land (Map 11.1). His holy wars – the Christian equivalent of the Muslim *jihad* – resulted in the forcible conversion of the Saxons east of the Rhine River, the Lombards of northern Italy, and the Slavic peoples along the Danube. Charlemagne's campaigns also pushed back the Muslims beyond the Pyrenees into Spain.

In the year 800, Pope Leo III crowned Charlemagne "Emperor of the Romans," thus establishing a firm relationship between church and state. But equally significant, Charlemagne's role in creating a Roman Christian or "Holy" Roman Empire cast him as the prototype of Christian kingship. During the more than thirty years in which he waged wars in the name of Christ, Charlemagne sought to control conquered lands by placing them in the hands of local administrators – on whom he bestowed the titles *count* and *duke* – and by periodically sending out royal envoys to carry his edicts abroad. He revived trade with the East, stabilized the currency of the realm, and even pursued diplomatic ties with Baghdad, whose caliph graced Charlemagne's court with the gift of an elephant.

Charlemagne's imperial mission was balanced by a passionate interest in education and the arts. Having visited the church of San Vitale in Ravenna (see chapter 9), Charles had its architectural plan and decorative program imitated in the palatine chapel at Aachen (Figure 11.1). He also revived, though on a small scale,

Figure 11.2 Equestrian statuette of Charlemagne, ninth century C.E. Bronze with traces of gilt, height 9½ in. Louvre, Paris. Cliché des Musées Nationaux. Photo: R.M.N.

the bronze-casting techniques of Roman sculptors (Figure 11.2). Though he himself could barely read and write—his sword hand was, according to his biographers, so callused that he had great difficulty forming letters – he sponsored a revival of learning and literacy. To oversee this educational program, Charlemagne invited to his court missionaries and scholars from all over Europe. He established schools at Aachen (Aix-la-Chapelle), in town centers throughout the empire, and in Benedictine monasteries such as that at Saint Gall in Switzerland, where monks and nuns copied religious manuscripts, along with texts on medicine, drama, and other secular subjects. The consequences of this **renaissance** or "rebirth" of learning are reflected in the fact that eighty percent of the oldest surviving classical Latin manuscripts exist in Carolingian copies.

Figure 11.1 Odo of Metz, Palatine Chapel of Charlemagne, Aachen, Germany, 792–805 C.E. © Deutscher Kunstverlag, Münich.

Merovingian Script

Caroline Minuscule

Figure 11.3 Comparison of Merovingian (Pre-Carolingian) Book Script and Caroline (Carolingian) Minuscule.

Carolingian copyists rejected Roman script, which lacked punctuation and spaces between words, in favor of a neat, uniform style of script known as the minuscule (Figure 11.3), the ancestor of modern typography. Carolingian artists ornamented precious books with bright colors and gold leaf or gold paint (hence the term *illuminated manuscript*). The decorative programs of many of these manuscripts reflect the union of late Roman realism and Germanic abstraction. The former is evident in the pictorial narrative that fills the capital letter in Figure 11.4, while the latter is seen in the ribbonlike pattern of the initial itself. But the Carolingian Renaissance was not limited to the copying of manuscripts. Among the most magnificent artifacts of the period were liturgical and devotional objects – often made of ivory and precious metals. Dating from the decades shortly after Charlemagne's death, the sacramental book cover for the Lindau Gospels testifies to the superior technical abilities of Carolingian goldsmiths (Figure 11.5). The surface of the lower cover, worked in silver gilt, inlaid with *cloisonné* enamel, and encrusted with precious gems, consists of an ornate Greek cross that dominates a field of writhing, interlaced creatures similar to those found in Anglo-Saxon metalwork (see Figure 10.3) and manuscripts (see Figure 10.4). At the corners of the inner rectangle are four tiny scenes showing the evangelists at their writing desks. These realistically conceived representations contrast sharply with the more stylized figural images that appear in the arms of the cross. The synthesis of Germanic, Roman, and Byzantine artistic traditions manifested in the cover of the Lindau Gospels typified the Carolingian Renaissance, the glories of which would not be matched for at least three centuries.

Figure 11.4 The Ascension from the Sacramentary of Archbishop Drogo of Metz (826–855 c.e.), ca. 842 c.e. Bibliothèque Nationale, Paris, MS Lat. 9428, f. 71v.

Figure 11.5 Back cover of Lindau Gospels, ca. 800 c.e. Silver gilt with enamel and precious stones, 13⅜ × 10⅜ in. The J. Pierpont Morgan Library, New York.

Feudal Society

When Charlemagne died in the year 814, the short-lived unity he had brought to Western Europe died with him. Although he had made the Frankish kingdom into an empire, he failed to establish any legal and administrative machinery comparable to that of imperial Rome. There was no standing army, no system of taxation, and no single code of law to unify the widely diverse population of the sprawling empire. Inevitably, following his death, the fragile stability of the Carolingian Empire was shattered by Scandinavian seafarers known as Northmen or Vikings. Charlemagne's sons and grandsons failed to repel the raids of these fierce invaders, who ravaged the northern coasts of the empire; at the same time neither were his heirs able to arrest the repeated forays of the Muslims along the Mediterranean coast. Lacking effective leadership, the Carolingian Empire disintegrated. In the mid-ninth century, Charles' three grandsons divided the empire among themselves, separating French from German-speaking territories. Increasingly, however, administration and protection fell to members of the local ruling aristocracy – heirs of the counts and dukes whom Charlemagne had appointed to administer portions of the realm, or simply those who had taken land by force. The fragmentation of the empire and the insecurity generated by the Viking invasions caused people at all social levels to attach themselves to members of a military nobility who were capable of providing protection. These circumstances enhanced the growth of a unique system of political and military organization known as **feudalism**.

Derived from Roman and Germanic traditions of rewarding warriors with the spoils of war, feudalism involved the exchange of land for military service. In return for the grant of land, known as a **fief** or *feudum* (the Germanic word for "property"), **a vassal** owed his **lord** a certain number of fighting days (usually forty) per year. The contract between lord and vassal also involved a number of other obligations, including the lord's provision of a court of justice, the vassal's contribution of ransom if his lord were captured, and the reciprocation of hospitality between the two. In an age of instability, feudalism provided a rudimentary form of local government, while answering the need for security against armed attack.

Those engaged in the feudal contract constituted roughly the upper ten percent of European society. The feudal nobility, which bore the twin responsibilities of military defense and political leadership, was a closed class of men and women whose superior status was inherited at birth. A male member of the nobility was first and foremost a mounted man-at-arms – a *chevalier* (from the French *cheval*, for "horse") or knight (from the Germanic *knecht*, a youthful servant or soldier). The medieval knight was a cavalry warrior equipped with stirrups, protected by **chain mail** (a flexible armor made of interlinked metal rings), and armed with such weapons as broadsword and shield (Figure **11.6**.).

Figure 11.6 Saladin defeats the Christians and Captures the Cross, 1187. Matthew Paris, *Historia Major*, Vol. I, before 1253. Courtesy of The Conway Library, Courtauld Institute of Art, London.

Figure 11.7 Vassal Paying Homage to his Lord. Matthew Paris, *Westminster Psalter*, English, ca. 1250. Reproduced by permission of the British Library, London.

The knight's conduct and manners in all aspects of life were guided by a strict code of behavior called **chivalry**. Chivalry demanded that the knight be courageous in battle, loyal to his lord and fellow warriors, and reverent toward women. Feudal life was marked by ceremonies and symbols almost as extensive as those of the Christian church. For instance, a vassal received his fief by an elaborate procedure known as **investiture**, in which oaths of fealty were formally exchanged (Figure **11.7**). In warfare, adversaries usually fixed the time and place of combat in advance. Medieval warfare was both a profession and a pastime, as knights entertained themselves with **jousts** (personal combat between men on horseback) or war games that imitated the trials of combat (Figure **11.8**).

Women helped to shape the chivalric society of the Middle Ages. In many parts of Europe, they inherited land, which they usually defended by means of hired soldiers. A woman controlled her fief until she married, and regained it upon becoming a widow. Men and women took great pride in their aristocratic lineage and advertised the family name by means of heraldic devices emblazoned on tunics, pennants, and shields (see Figure 11.7).

Europe was not the only place in which feudalism came to flower. Between the ninth and twelfth centuries – the period roughly equivalent to the Middle Ages in Europe – Japan's powerful aristocratic clans overthrew the imperial regents of the Heian dynasty (794–1185). The political strength of the clans depended on *samurai* (literally, "those who serve"), warriors who held land in return for military service to local landholders. Outfitted with warhorses and elaborate armor

Figure 11.8 Plaque from a casket, French, fourteenth century. Ivory, 3⅞ × ⅝ in. The Metropolitan Museum of Art, New York. Gift of J. Pierpont Morgan, 1917.

centuries, the 4,000-line poem was not written down until the early 1100s. Generation after generation of *jongleurs* (professional entertainers) wandered from court to court, chanting the story (and possibly embellishing it with episodes of folklore) to the accompaniment of a lyre. Though the music for the poem has not survived, it is likely that it consisted of a single and highly improvised line of melody. The melody was probably syllabic (one note to each syllable) and – like folk song – dependent on simple repetition. As with other works in the oral tradition (the *Epic of Gilgamesh* and the *Iliad*, for instance), the *Song of Roland* is grandiose in its dimensions and profound in its lyric power. Its rugged Old French verse describes a culture that prized the performance of heroic deeds that brought honor to the warrior, his lord, and his religion. The strong bond of loyalty between vassal and chieftain that characterized the Germanic way of life resonates in Roland's declaration of unswerving devotion to his temporal overlord, Charlemagne.

The *Song of Roland* brings to life such aspects of early medieval culture as the practice of naming one's battle gear and weapons (often considered sacred), the dependence on cavalry, the glorification of blood-and-thunder heroism, and the strong sense of comradeship among men-at-arms. Women play almost no part in the epic. The feudal contract did not exclude members of the clergy; hence a churchman like Archbishop Turpin fought, armed with a **mace** (a spike-headed club) by which he might defend himself without violating the church law that forbade a member of the clergy to shed another man's blood. Roland's willingness to die for his religious beliefs, fired by the Archbishop's promise of admission into Paradise for those who fell fighting the infidels (in this case, the Muslims), suggests that the militant fervor of Muslims was matched by that of early medieval Christians. Indeed, the *Song of Roland* captures the powerful antagonism between Christians and Muslims that dominated all of medieval history and culminated in the Christian Crusades described later in this chapter.

The descriptive language of the *Song of Roland* is stark, unembellished, and vivid: "he feels his brain gush out," reports the poet in verse 168. Such directness and simplicity lend immediacy to the action. Characters are stereotypical ("Roland's a hero, and Oliver is wise," verse 87), and groups of people are characterized with epic expansiveness: *All* Christians are good and *all* Muslims are bad. The figure of Roland epitomizes the ideals of physical courage, religious devotion, and personal loyalty. Yet, in his refusal to call for assistance from Charlemagne and his troops, who had already retreated across the Pyrenees, he exhibits a foolhardiness – perhaps a "tragic flaw" – that leads him and his warriors to their deaths.

Figure 11.9 Suit of armor belonging to Yoshihisa Matahachiro, Muromachi period, ca. 1550. Steel, blackened and gold lacquered; flame-colored silk braid, gilt bronze, stenciled deerskin, bear pelt, gilt wood, height 5 ft 6 in. The Metropolitan Museum of Art, New York, Rogers Fund, 1904 (04.4.2). Photograph by Schecter Lee.

(Figure 11.9) and trained in the arts of archery and swordsmanship, the clans of the Kamakura Shogunate (1192–1333) competed for position and power. The *samurai* upheld values similar to those of the European knight and pursued a code known as *bushido* ("the way of the warrior"): selflessness in battle, fierce loyalty to one's superior, and a disdain for death. Japanese chivalry also required a code of honor, and a ritual suicide, usually by disembowelment, if the *samurai* fell into dishonor. At court, the *samurai* cultivated a refined life-style whose fashions and tastes are described in the elegant prose of the Japanese novel (see chapter 14).

The Literature of the Feudal Nobility

The ideals of the fighting nobility in a feudal age are best exemplified in the oldest and greatest French epic poem, the *Song of Roland*. Based on an event that took place in 778 – the ambush of Charlemagne's rear guard, led by his nephew Roland as Charlemagne returned from an expedition against the Muslims in Spain – this *chanson de geste* (song of heroic deeds) captures the spirit of the Early Middle Ages. Transmitted orally for three

READING 41

From the *Song of Roland*

81

Count Oliver has climbed up on a hill;   1
From there he sees the Spanish lands below,
And Saracens[1] assembled in great force.
Their helmets gleam with gold and precious stones,
Their shields are shining, their hauberks[2] burnished gold,   5
Their long sharp spears with battle flags unfurled.
He tries to see how many men there are:
Even battalions are more than he can count.
And in his heart Oliver is dismayed;
Quick as he can, he comes down from the height,   10
And tells the Franks what they will have to fight.

82

Oliver says, "Here come the Saracens —
A greater number no man has ever seen!
The first host carries a hundred thousand shields,
Their helms are laced, their hauberks shining white,   15
From straight wood handles rise ranks of burnished spears.
You'll have a battle like none on earth before!
Frenchmen, my lords, now God give you the strength
To stand your ground, and keep us from defeat."
They say, "God's curse on those who quit the field!   20
We're yours till death — not one of us will yield."
            AOI[3]

83

Oliver says, "The pagan might is great —
It seems to me, our Franks are very few!
Roland, my friend, it's time to sound your horn;
King Charles[4] will hear, and bring his army back."   25
Roland replies, "You must think I've gone mad!
In all sweet France I'd forfeit my good name!
No! I will strike great blows with Durendal,[5]
Crimson the blade up to the hilt of gold.
To those foul pagans I promise bitter woe —   30
They all are doomed to die at Roncevaux!"[6]
            AOI

84

"Roland, my friend, let the Oliphant[7] sound!
King Charles will hear it, his host will all turn back,
His valiant barons will help us in this fight."
Roland replies, "Almighty God forbid   35
That I bring shame upon my family,
and cause sweet France to fall into disgrace!

---

[1]Another name for Muslims.
[2]Long coats of chain mail.
[3]The letters AOI have no exact meaning but probably signify a musical appendage or refrain that occurred at the end of each stanza.
[4]Charlemagne.
[5]Roland's sword.
[6]"The gate of Spain," a narrow pass in the Pyrenees where the battle takes place.
[7]A horn made from an elephant's tusk.

I'll strike that horde with my good Durendal;
My sword is ready, girded here at my side,
And soon you'll see its keen blade dripping blood.   40
The Saracens will curse the evil day
They challenged us, for we will make them pay."
            AOI

85

"Roland, my friend I pray you, sound your horn!
King Charlemagne, crossing the mountain pass,
Won't fail, I swear it, to bring back all his Franks."   45
"May God forbid!" Count Roland answers then.
"No man on earth shall have the right to say
That I for pagans sounded the Oliphant!
I will not bring my family to shame.
I'll fight this battle; my Durendal shall strike   50
A thousand blows and seven hundred more;
You'll see bright blood flow from the blade's keen steel.
We have good men; their prowess will prevail,
And not one Spaniard shall live to tell the tale."

86

Oliver says, "Never would you be blamed;   55
I've seen the pagans, the Saracens of Spain.
They fill the valleys, cover the mountain peaks;
On every hill, and every wide-spread plain,
Vast hosts assemble from that alien race;
Our company numbers but very few."   60
Roland replies, "The better, then, we'll fight!
If it please God and His angelic host,
I won't betray the glory of sweet France!
Better to die than learn to live with shame —
Charles loves us more as our keen swords win fame."   65

87

Roland's a hero, and Oliver is wise;
Both are so brave men marvel at their deeds.
When they mount chargers, take up their swords and shields,
Not death itself could drive them from the field.
They are good men; their words are fierce and proud.   70
With wrathful speed the pagans ride to war.
Oliver says, "Roland, you see them now.
They're very close, the king too far away.
You were too proud to sound the Oliphant:
If Charles were with us, we would not come to grief.   75
Look up above us, close to the Gate of Spain:
There stands the guards — who would not pity them!
To fight this battle means not to fight again."
Roland replies, "Don't speak so foolishly!
Cursed be the heart that cowers in the breast!   80
We'll hold our ground; if they will meet us here,
Our foes will find us ready with sword and spear."
            AOI

88

When Roland sees the fight will soon begin,
Lions and leopards are not so fierce as he.
Calling the Franks, he says to Oliver: 85
"Noble companion, my friend, don't talk that way!
The Emperor Charles, who left us in command

Of twenty thousand he chose to guard the pass,
Made very sure no coward's in their ranks.
In his lord's service a man must suffer pain,　　　　　90
Bitterest cold and burning heat endure;
He must be willing to lose his flesh and blood.
Strike with your lance, and I'll wield Durendal —
The king himself presented it to me —
And if I die, whoever takes my sword　　　　　　95
Can say its master has nobly served his lord."

89

Archbishop Turpin comes forward then to speak.
He spurs his horse and gallops up a hill,
Summons the Franks, and preaches in these words:
"My noble lords, Charlemagne left us here,　　　　100
And may our deaths do honor to the king!
Now you must help defend our holy Faith!
Before your eyes you see the Saracens.
Confess your sins, ask God to pardon you;
I'll grant you absolution to save your souls.　　　　105
Your deaths would be a holy martyrdom,
And you'll have places in highest Paradise."
The French dismount; they kneel upon the ground.
Then the archbishop, blessing them in God's name,
Told them, for penance, to strike when battle came.　　110

. . . .

91

At Roncevaux Count Roland passes by,
Riding his charger, swift-running Veillantif.[8]
He's armed for battle, splendid in shining mail.
As he parades, he brandishes his lance.
Turning the point straight up against the sky,　　　115
And from the spearhead a banner flies, pure white,
With long gold fringes that beat against his hands.
Fair to behold, he laughs, serene and gay.
Now close behind him comes Oliver, his friend,
With all the Frenchmen cheering their mighty lord.　　120
Fiercely his eyes confront the Saracens;
Humbly and gently he gazes at the Franks,
Speaking to them with gallant courtesy:
"Barons, my lords, softly now, keep the pace!
Here come the pagans looking for martyrdom.　　　125
We'll have such plunder before the day is out,
As no French king has ever won before!"
And at this moment the armies join in war.

　　　　　　　　　　　　　　　　　　　AOI

161

The pagans flee, furious and enraged,
Trying their best to get away in Spain.　　　　　　130
Count Roland lacks the means to chase them now,
For he has lost his war-horse Veillantif;
Against his will he has to go on foot.
He went to give Archbishop Turpin help,
Unlaced his helmet, removed it from his head,　　　135
And then took off the hauberk of light mail;
The under-tunic he cut into long strips

---

[8]Roland's horse.

With which he stanched the largest of his wounds.
Then lifting Turpin, carried him in his arms
To soft green grass, and gently laid him down.　　　140
In a low voice Roland made this request:
"My noble lord, I pray you, give me leave,
For our companions, the men we held so dear,
Must not be left abandoned now in death.
I want to go and seek out every one,　　　　　　145
Carry them here, and place them at your feet."
Said the archbishop, "I grant it willingly.
The field belongs, thank God, to you and me."

162

Alone, Count Roland walks through the battlefield,
Searching the valleys, searching the mountain heights.　150
He found the bodies of Ivon and Ivoire,
And then he found the Gascon Engelier.
Gerin he found, and Gerier his friend,
He found Aton and then Count Bérengier,
Proud Anseïs he found, and then Samson,　　　　155
Gérard the Old, the Count of Roussillon.
He took these barons, and carried every one
Back to the place where the archbishop was,
And then he put them in ranks at Turpin's knees.
Seeing them, Turpin cannot restrain his tears;　　　160
Raising his hand, he blesses all the dead.
And then he says, "You've come to grief, my lords!
Now in His glory, may God receive your souls,
Among bright flowers set you in Paradise!
It's my turn now; death keeps me in such pain,　　　165
Never again will I see Charlemagne."

163

Roland goes back to search the field once more,
And his companion he finds there, Oliver.
Lifting him in his arms he holds him close,
Brings him to Turpin as quickly as he can,　　　　170
Beside the others places him on a shield;
Turpin absolves him, signing him with the cross,
And then they yield to pity and to grief.
Count Roland says, "Brother in arms, fair friend,
You were the son of Renier, the duke　　　　　175
Who held the land where Runers valley lies.
For breaking lances, for shattering thick shields,
Bringing the proud to terror and defeat,
For giving counsel, defending what is right,
In all the world there is no better knight."　　　　180

164

When Roland sees that all his peers are dead,
And Oliver whom he so dearly loved,
He feels such sorrow that he begins to weep;
Drained of all color, his face turns ashen pale,
His grief is more than any man could bear,　　　　185
He falls down, fainting whether he will or no.
Says the archbishop, "Baron, you've come to woe."

. . . .

168

Now Roland knows that death is very near.
His ears give way, he feels his brain gush out.

He prays that God will summon all his peers; 190
Then, for himself, he prays to Gabriel.
Taking the horn, to keep it from all shame,
With Durendal clasped in his other hand,
He goes on, farther than a good cross-bow shot,
West into Spain, crossing a fallow field. 195
Up on a hilltop, under two lofty trees.
Four marble blocks are standing on the grass.
But when he comes there, Count Roland faints once more,
He falls down backward; now he is at death's door.

. . . .

174

Count Roland feels the very grip of death 200
Which from his head is reaching for his heart.
He hurries then to go beneath a pine;
In the green grass he lies down on his face,
Placing beneath him the sword and Oliphant;
He turns his head to look toward pagan Spain. 205
He does these things in order to be sure
King Charles will say, and with him all the Franks,
The noble count conquered until he died.
He makes confession, for all his sins laments.
Offers his glove to God in penitence. 210

AOI

◆

The Norman Conquest and the Arts

During the tenth century, the Viking seafarers who had terrorized Charlemagne's lands settled in northwest France. Within one hundred years, these aggressive Northmen, or Normans, as they came to be called, made Normandy one of the strongest fiefs in France. In 1066 under the leadership of William of Normandy, some five thousand men crossed the English Channel; at the Battle of Hastings, William defeated the Anglo-Saxon Duke Harold and seized the throne of England. The Norman Conquest had enormous consequences for the histories of England and France, for it marked the transfer of power in England from Anglo-Saxon rulers to Norman noblemen who were already vassals of the king of France. The Normans brought feudalism to England. To raise money, William ordered a detailed census of all property in the realm, the Domesday Survey, which laid the basis for the collection of taxes. The King controlled all aspects of government with the aid of the *Curia Regis*, a royal court and council consisting of his feudal barons. Under the Norman kings, England would become one of Europe's leading medieval states.

The Normans led the way in the construction of stone churches and castles. Atop hills and at such vulnerable sites as Dover on the southeast coast of England, Norman kings erected austere castle-fortresses (Figure **11.10**). The castle featured a **keep** (square tower) containing a dungeon, a main hall, and a chapel, and incorporated a central open space with workshops and storehouses (Figure **11.11**). The enclosing stone walls were usually surmounted by turrets with **crenellations** that provided archers with protection in defensive combat. A **moat** (a trench filled with water) often surrounded the castle walls to deter enemy invasion. The brilliance of Norman achievement in architecture, apparent in their fortresses and in some of the earliest Romanesque churches (see chapter 13), lies in the use of stone to replace earlier timber fortifications and in the clarity with which the form of the building reflects its function.

One of the most famous Norman artifacts is the Bayeux Tapestry, a visual record of the conquest of England by William of Normandy. This eleventh-century embroidered wallhanging, named for the city in northwestern France where it was sewn and where it is still displayed today, documents the history and folklore of the Normans with the same energetic spirit that animates the *Song of Roland*. Sewn into the linen cloth, which measures some twenty inches wide and 231 feet long, are lively pictorial representations of the incidents leading up to and including the Battle of Hastings (Figure **11.12**). Above and alongside the images are Latin captions that serve to identify characters, places, and events. The inscription above the scene in Figure 11.12 reads, "Here the English and French have fallen together in battle." In the margin below the spectacle appear fallen soldiers, weapons, and a bodiless head. The seventy-nine scenes progress in the manner of a parchment scroll or a cartoon comic strip. Rendered in only eight colors of wool yarn, the ambitious narrative includes 626 figures, 190 horses, and over five hundred other animals. Since embroidery was almost exclusively a female occupation, it is likely that the Bayeux Tapestry was the work of women – although women are depicted only four times throughout the entire piece.

The *Song of Roland* and the Bayeux Tapestry have much in common: Both are epic in theme and robust in style. Both consist of sweeping narratives whose episodes are irregular rather than uniform in length. Like the stereotypical (and almost exclusively male) characters in the *chanson*, the figures of the Tapestry are delineated by means of ideographic gestures and simplified physical features; the Normans, for instance, are distinguished by the shaved backs of their heads. Weapons and armor in both epic and embroidery are described with loving detail. Indeed, in the Bayeux Tapestry, scenes of combat provide a veritable encyclopedia of medieval battle gear: kite-shaped shields, conical iron helmets, hauberks, short bows, double-edged swords, battle axes, and lances. Both the *Song of Roland* and the Bayeux Tapestry offer a vivid record of feudal life in all its heroic splendor.

Figure 11.10 Dover Castle, England, twelfth century.
Photo: Ministry of Public Building and Works, London, England.
NMR 1224/119 © Royal Commission on the Historical Monuments of England.

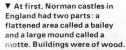

▼ At first, Norman castles in England had two parts: a flattened area called a bailey and a large mound called a motte. Buildings were of wood.

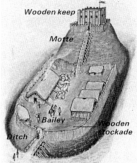

Wooden keep

Motte

Bailey

Ditch *Wooden stockade*

▼ Later castles were built of stone. There was no motte, for the heavy keep had to stand on flat, firm earth that would not collapse.

Keep

Bailey

Figure 11.11 Development of the Norman Castle. From Patrick Rook, *The Normans*. Macdonald Education Ltd., 1977.

Figure 11.12 The Battle Rages. Detail from the Bayeux Tapestry, ca. 1070–1080. Wool embroidery on linen, height approx. 20 in., entire length 231 ft. Town Hall, Bayeux, with special authorization of the Village of Bayeux, France. © Arch. Phot. Paris/S.P.A.D.E.M.

The Lives of Medieval Serfs

Although the feudal class monopolized land and power within medieval society, this elite group represented only a tiny percentage of that society's total population. The vast majority of that population – more than ninety percent – were unfree peasants or **serfs**, who, along with freemen, farmed the soil. Medieval serfs lived quite differently from their noble landlords. Bound to large farms or manors, they, like the farmers of the old Roman *latifundia*, provided food in exchange for military protection furnished by the nobility. They owned no property. They were forbidden to leave the land, though neither could they be evicted. Their bondage to the soil assured them the protection of feudal lords, who, in an age lacking effective central authority, were the sole sources of political authority.

During the Middle Ages, the reciprocal obligations of serfs and lords and the serf's continuing tenure on the land became firmly fixed. At least until the eleventh century, the interdependence between the two classes was beneficial to both; serfs needed protection, and lords, whose position as gentlemen-warriors excluded them from menial toil, needed food. For upper and lower classes alike, the individual's place in medieval society was inherited and bound by tradition.

The medieval fief usually included one or more manors. The typical manor consisted of farmlands, woodland, and pasture, and included a common mill, wine press, and oven (Figure **11.13**). Serfs cultivated the major crops of oats and rye on strips of arable land. In addition to the food they produced from fields reserved for the lord, they owed the lord a percentage – usually a third – of their own agricultural yield. They also performed services in the form of labor. In the medieval world, manor was isolated from manor, and a subsistence economy similar to that of the Neolithic village prevailed. The annual round of peasant labor, beset by a continuing war with the elements, was harsh and demanding. Nevertheless, during the Early Middle Ages, serfs made considerable progress in the production of farm technology and agricultural practices. They invented the heavy-wheeled plow and the tandem harness, developed wind and water mills, recovered land by dredging swamps and clearing forests, and offset soil exhaustion by devising systems of crop rotation, such as the "three-field system," which left one-third of the land fallow to allow it to recover its fertility. Such innovations eventually contributed to the production of a food surplus, which in turn stimulated the revival of trade.

The average medieval manor comprised fifteen to twenty families, while a large manor of five thousand acres might contain some fifty families. The lord usually appointed the local priest, provided a local court of justice, and governed the manor from a fortified residence or castle. Between the eighth and tenth centuries, such residences were simple wooden structures, but by the twelfth century, elaborate stone manor houses with crenellated walls and towers became commonplace. On long winter nights, the lord's castle might be the scene of reveling and entertainment by *jongleurs* singing epic tales like the *Song of Roland* (Reading 41).

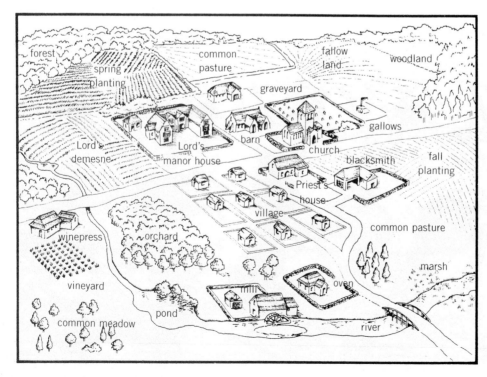

Figure 11.13 The Medieval Manor.

Figure 11.14 Carpenters' Guild Signature window. Detail of a stained glass window, Chartres Cathedral, France, early thirteenth century. Photo: Sonia Halliday, Weston Turville.

Figure 11.15 Women and Men Reaping. Detail from the *Luttrell Psalter*, English, ca. 1340. Reproduced by permission of the British Library, London, Add. MS. 42130 f. 172.

The day-to-day life of the medieval serf was difficult. Many serfs lived at a subsistence level not unlike that of Neolithic folk. They were subject to perennial toil and constant privations, including those of famine and disease. Most could neither read nor write. Unfortunately, art and literature leave us little insight into the lives and values of the lower classes of medieval society. Occasionally, however, in the sculp-

tures of laboring peasants found on medieval cathedrals, in stained glass windows (Figure 11.14), and in medieval manuscripts (Figure 11.15), we find visual representations of lower-class life. And although these examples may provide an idealized version of reality conceived by those who directed such programs of illustration, this visual evidence constitutes a valuable resource for our understanding of the Middle Ages.

The Christian Crusades

During the eleventh century, numerous circumstances contributed to a change in the character of medieval life. The Normans effectively pushed the Muslims out of the Mediterranean Sea, and as the Normans and other marauders began to settle down, Europeans enjoyed a greater degree of security. At the same time, rising agricultural productivity and surplus stimulated a revival of trade. The Christian Crusades of the eleventh to thirteenth centuries were directly related to these changes. They were both a cause of economic revitalization and a symptom of the increased freedom and new mobility of Western Europeans during the High Middle Ages (ca. 1000–1300).

The Crusades began in an effort to rescue Jerusalem from Muslim Turks who were threatening the Byzantine Empire and denying Christian pilgrims access to the Holy Land. At the request of the Byzantine Emperor, the Roman Catholic church launched a series of military expeditions designed to regain territories dominated by the Turks. The first Crusade, called by Pope Urban II in 1095, began in the spirit of a Holy War but unlike the Muslim *jihad*, the intention was to recover land, not to convert pagans. Thousands of people, both laymen and clergy, "took up the Cross" and marched overland through Europe to the Byzantine East (Map **11.2**). It soon became apparent, however, that the material benefits of the Crusades outweighed the spiritual ones, especially since the campaigns provided economic and military opportunities for the younger sons of the nobility. While the eldest son of an upper-class family inherited his father's fief under the principle of **primogeniture**, his younger brothers were left to seek their own fortunes. The Crusades stirred the ambitions of these disenfranchised young men. Equally ambitious were the Italian city-states. Eager to expand their commercial activities, they encouraged the Crusaders to become middlemen in trade between Italy and the East. On the eve of the fourth Crusade in 1204, Venetian profit seekers persuaded the Crusaders to sack Constantinople and capture trade ports in the Aegean in the interest of Venetian trade. Moral inhibitions failed to restrain the vampires of greed, and the Christian Crusades deteriorated into a contest for personal profit.

Map 11.2 The Major Crusades, 1096–1204.

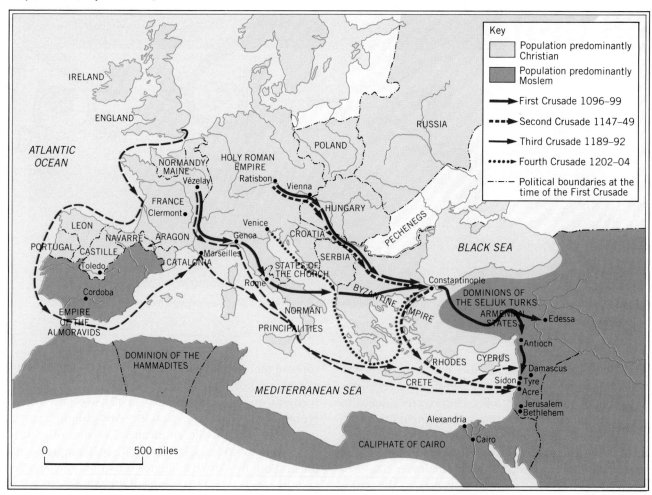

Aside from such economic advantages as those enjoyed by individual Crusaders and the Italian city-states, the gains made by the Crusades were slight. In the first of the four major expeditions, the Crusaders did retake some important cities, including Jerusalem. But by 1291, all recaptured lands were lost again to the Muslims. Indeed, in over two hundred years of fighting, the Christian Crusaders did not secure any territory permanently, nor did they stop the westward advance of the Turks; Constantinople finally fell in 1453 to a later wave of Muslim Turks.

Despite their failure as religious ventures, the Crusades had enormous consequences for the West: The revival of trade between East and West enhanced European commercial life, encouraging the rise of towns and bringing great wealth to the cities of Venice, Genoa, and Pisa in Italy. Then too, in the absence or death of crusading noblemen, feudal lords (including emperors and kings) seized every opportunity to establish greater authority over the lands within their domains, thus consolidating and centralizing political power in the embryonic nation-states of England and France. Finally, renewed contact with Byzantium promoted an atmosphere of commercial and cultural receptivity that had not existed since Roman times. Luxury goods, such as saffron, citrus, silks, and damasks, entered Western Europe, as did sacred relics associated with the lives of Jesus, Mary, and the Christian saints. And, to the delight of the literate, Arabic translations of Greek manuscripts poured into France, along with all genres of Islamic literature (see chapter 10).

The Medieval Romance and the Code of Courtly Love

The Crusades inspired the writing of chronicles that were an admixture of historical fact, Christian lore, and stirring fiction. As such histories had broad appeal in an age of increasing upper-class literacy, they came to be written in the everyday language of the lay-person — the vernacular — rather than in Latin. The Crusades also contributed to the birth of the **medieval romance**, a fictitious tale of love and adventure that became the most popular form of literary entertainment in the West between the years 1200 and 1500. The medieval romance first appeared in twelfth-century France in the form of rhymed verse, but later romances were written in prose. While romances were probably recited before a small, courtly audience rather than read individually, the development of the form coincided with the rise of a European "textual culture," that is, a culture dependent on written language rather than on oral tradition. In this textual culture, vernacular languages gained importance for intimate kinds of literature, while Latin remained the official language of church and state.

The "spice" of the typical medieval romance was an illicit relationship or forbidden liaison between a man and woman of the upper class. During the Middle Ages, marriage among members of the nobility was usually an alliance formed in the interest of securing land. Indeed, noble families might arrange marriages for offspring who were still in the cradle. Under such circumstances, romantic love was more likely to flourish outside of marriage. An adulterous affair between Lancelot, a knight of King Arthur's court, and Guinevere, the king's wife, is central to the popular twelfth-century verse romance *Lancelot*. Written in vernacular French by Chrétien de Troyes (?–ca. 1183), *Lancelot* belongs to a cycle of stories associated with a semilegendary sixth-century Welsh chieftain named Arthur. This lively romance, a portion of which appears (in prose translation) in the following pages, is filled with bloody combat, supernatural events, and, of course, episodes of courtly love.

The so-called code of courtly love, popularized in twelfth-century manuals of conduct for European aristocrats, held that love (whether requited or unrequited) had a purifying and ennobling influence on the lover. To love was to suffer; witness, in the excerpt below, Queen Guinevere's distress upon hearing the false report of Lancelot's death. Courtly love was also associated with a variety of distressing physical symptoms, such as an inability to eat or sleep. The tenets of courtly love required that a knight prove his love for his lady by performing daring and often impossible deeds; he must even be willing to die for her. In these features, the medieval romance is far removed from the rugged, bellicose spirit of earlier medieval works like the *Song of Roland*. Indeed, *Lancelot* dramatizes the feminization of the chivalric ideal. As we saw in the *Song of Roland*, early medieval culture was characterized by heroic idealism and personal loyalty between men. The medieval romance, however, redefined these qualities in the direction of sentiment and sensuality. Lancelot fights not for his country, nor even for his lord, but to win the love of his mistress. His prowess is not exercised, as with Roland, on a field of battle, but as individual combat undertaken in the courtyard of his host. While Roland is motivated by the ideal of glory in battle, Lancelot is driven by his love for Guinevere.

The code of courtly love that prevailed during the twelfth and thirteen centuries contributed to shaping the romantic perception of women as objects, particularly objects of reward for the performance of extraordinary deeds. For although courtly love elevated the woman (and her prototype, the Virgin Mary) as worthy of adoration, it defined her exclusively in terms of the interests of men. Nevertheless, the medieval romance, which flattered and exalted the aristocratic lady as an object of desire, was directed toward a primarily female audience. A product of the aristocratic (and male) imagination, the lady of the medieval romance had no counterpart in the lower classes of society, where women worked side by side with men in the fields (see Figure 11.15) and in a variety of trades, including textiles, beer making, and inn-keeping. Despite its artificiality, however, the theme of courtly love and the romance itself had a significant influence on Western literary tradition. In that tradition, even into modern times, writers have tended to treat love more as a mode of spiritual purification or as an emotional affliction than as a condition of true affection and sympathy between the sexes.

READING 42

From Chrétien de Troyes' *Lancelot*

[*Gawain and Lancelot, knights of King Arthur's court, set out in quest of Queen Guinevere. In the forest, they meet a damsel, who tells them of the Queen's whereabouts.*]

Then the damsel relates to them the following story: 1
"In truth, my lords, Meleagant, a tall and powerful knight, son of the King of Gorre, has taken her off into the kingdom whence no foreigner returns, but where he must perforce remain in servitude and banishment." Then they ask her: "Damsel, where is this country? Where can we find the way thither?" She replies: "That you shall quickly learn; but you may be sure that you will meet with many obstacles and difficult passages, for it is not easy to enter there except with the permission of the king, whose 10 name is Bademagu; however, it is possible to enter by two very perilous paths and by two very difficult passage-ways. One is called 'the water-bridge,' because the bridge is under water, and there is the same amount of water beneath it as above it, so that the bridge is exactly in the middle; and it is only a foot and a half in width and in thickness. This choice is certainly to be avoided, and yet it is the less dangerous of the two . . . . The other bridge is still more impracticable and much more perilous, never having been crossed by man. It is just like a sharp sword, 20 and therefore all the people call it 'the sword-bridge.' Now I have told you all the truth I know . . . ."

[*They reach the sword-bridge.*]

At the end of this very difficult bridge they dismount from their steeds and gaze at the wicked-looking stream, which is as swift and raging, as black and turgid, as fierce and terrible as if it were the devil's stream; and it is so dangerous and bottomless that anything falling into it would be as completely lost as if it fell into the salt sea. And the bridge, which spans it, is different from any other bridge; for there never was such a one as this. If any one 30 asks of me the truth, there never was such a bad bridge, nor one whose flooring was so bad. The bridge across the cold stream consisted of a polished, gleaming sword; but the sword was stout and stiff, and was as long as two lances. At each end there was a tree-trunk in which the

sword was firmly fixed. No one need fear to fall because of its breaking or bending, for its excellence was such that it could support a great weight . . . [Lancelot] prepares, as best he may, to cross the stream, and he does a very marvellous thing in removing the armor from his feet and 40 hands. He will be in a sorry state when he reaches the other side [Figure **11.16**]. He is going to support himself with his bare hands and feet upon the sword, which was sharper than a scythe, for he had not kept on his feet either sole or upper[1] or hose. But he felt no fear of wounds upon his hands or feet; he preferred to maim himself rather than to fall from the bridge and be plunged in the water from which he could never escape. In accordance with this determination, he passes over with great pain and agony, being wounded in the hands, knees, and feet. But even 50 this suffering is sweet to him: for Love, who conducts and leads him on, assuages and relieves the pain. Creeping on his hands, feet, and knees, he proceeds until he reaches the other side . . . .

[*Lancelot confronts the Queen's captors: King Bademagu's son, Meleagant, refuses to make peace with Lancelot and promptly challenges him to battle.*]

. . . Very early, before prime[2] had yet been sounded, both of the knights fully armed were led to the place, mounted upon two horses equally protected. Meleagant was very graceful, alert, and shapely; the hauberk with its fine meshes, the helmet, and the shield hanging from his neck — all these became him well . . . . Then the 60 combatants without delay make all the people stand aside; then they clash the shields with their elbows, and thrust their arms into the straps, and spur at each other so violently that each sends his lance two arms' length through his opponent's shield, causing the lance to split and splinter like a flying spark. And the horses meet head on, clashing breast to breast, and the shields and helmets crash with such a noise that it seems like a mighty thunder-clap; not a breast-strap, girth, rein or surcingle[3] remains unbroken, and the saddle-bows, though strong, 70 are broken to pieces. The combatants felt no shame in falling to earth, in view of their mishaps, but they quickly spring to their feet, and without waste of threatening words rush at each other more fiercely than two wild boars, and deal great blows with their swords of steel like men whose hate is violent. Repeatedly they trim the helmets and shining hauberks so fiercely that after the sword the blood spurts out. They furnished an excellent battle, indeed, as they stunned and wounded each other with their heavy, wicked blows. Many fierce, hard, long bouts 80 they sustained with equal honor, so that the onlookers could discern no advantage on either side. But it was inevitable that he who had crossed the bridge should be much weakened by his wounded hands. The people who sided with him were much dismayed, for they notice that his strokes are growing weaker, and they fear he will get the worst of it; it seemed to them that he was weakening, while Meleagant was triumphing, and they began to

---

[1] Parts of the shoe or boot.
[2] The second of the Canonical Hours, around 6 A.M. The devout recited special devotional prayers at each of the Canonical Hours: lauds, prime, terce, sext, none, vespers, and compline.
[3] A band passing around a horse's body to bind the saddle.

Figure 11.16 Lancelot Crossing the Swordbridge; Guinevere in the Tower. From the *Romance of Lancelot*, ca. 1300. © The J. Pierpont Morgan Library, New York, 1990. MS. 806 f. 166.

murmur all around. But up at the window of the tower there was a wise maiden who thought within herself that 90 the knight had not undertaken the battle either on her account or for the sake of the common herd who had gathered about the list, but that his only incentive had been the Queen; and she thought that, if he knew that she was at the window seeing and watching him, his strength and courage would increase . . . . Then she came to the Queen and said: "Lady, for God's sake and your own as well as ours, I beseech you to tell me, if you know, the name of yonder knight, to the end that it may be of some help to him." "Damsel," the Queen replies, "you have 100 asked me a question in which I see no hate or evil, but rather good intent; the name of the knight, I know, is Lancelot of the Lake." "God, how happy and glad at heart I am!" the damsel says. Then she leans forward and calls to him by name so loudly that all the people hear: "Lancelot, turn about and see who is here taking note of thee!"

When Lancelot heard his name, he was not slow to turn around: he turns and sees seated up there at the window of the tower her whom he desired most in the world to see. 110 From the moment he caught sight of her, he did not turn or take his eyes and face from her, defending himself with backhand blows . . . . Lancelot's strength and courage grow, partly because he has love's aid, and partly because he never hated any one so much as him with whom he is engaged. Love and mortal hate, so fierce that never before was such hate seen, make him so fiery and bold that Meleagant ceases to treat it as a jest and begins to stand in awe of him, for he had never met or known so doughty a knight, nor had any knight ever wounded or injured him as 120 this one does . . . .

[*Lancelot spares Meleagant but thereafter is taken prisoner. Rumor reaches the Queen that Lancelot is dead.*]

The news of this spread until it reached the Queen, who was sitting at meat. She almost killed herself on hearing the false report about Lancelot, but she supposes it to be true, and therefore she is in such dismay that she almost loses the power to speak; but, because of those present, she forces herself to say: "In truth, I am sorry for his death, and it is no wonder that I grieve, for he came into this country for my sake, and therefore I should mourn for

him." Then she says to herself, so that the others should 130 not hear, that no one need ask her to drink or eat, if it is true that he is dead, in whose life she found her own. Then grieving she rises from the table, and makes her lament, but so that no one hears or notices her. She is so beside herself that she repeatedly grasps her throat with the desire to kill herself; but first she confesses to herself, and repents with self-reproach, blaming and censuring herself, for the wrong she had done him, who, as she knew, had always been hers, and would still be hers, if he were alive . . . . "Alas how much better I should feel, and how much 140 comfort I should take, if only once before he died I had held him in my arms! What? Yes, certainly, quite unclad, in order the better to enjoy him. If he is dead, I am very wicked not to destroy myself. Why? Can it harm my lover for me to live on after he is dead, if I take no pleasure in anything but in the woe I bear for him? In giving myself up to grief after his death, the very woes I court would be sweet to me, if he were only still alive. It is wrong for a woman to wish to die rather than to suffer for her lover's sake. It is certainly sweet for me to mourn him long. I would rather be 150 beaten alive than die and be at rest."

[*Once freed, Lancelot makes his way to the castle and Guinevere agrees to meet with him secretly.*]

Lancelot . . . was so impatient for the night to come that his restlessness made the day seem longer than a hundred ordinary days or than an entire year. If night had only come, he would gladly have gone to the trysting place. Dark and sombre night at last won its struggle with the day, and wrapped it up in its covering, and laid it away beneath its cloak. When he saw the light of day obscured, he pretended to be tired and worn, and said that, in view of his protracted vigils, he needed rest. You, who have ever done 160 the same, may well understand and guess that he pretends to be tired and goes to bed in order to deceive the people of the house; but he cared nothing about his bed, nor would he have sought rest there for anything, for he could not have done so and would not have dared, and furthermore he would not have cared to possess the courage or the power to do so. Soon he softly rose, and was pleased to find that no moon or star was shining, and that in the house there was no candle, lamp or lantern burning. Thus he went out and looked about, but there was no one on the 170 watch for him, for all thought that he would sleep in his bed all night. Without escort or company he quickly went out into the garden, meeting no one on the way, and he was so fortunate as to find that a part of the garden-wall had recently fallen down. Through this break he passes quickly and proceeds to the window, where he stands, taking good care not to cough or sneeze, until the Queen arrives clad in a very white chemise. She wore no cloak or coat, but had thrown over her a short cape of scarlet cloth and shrew-mouse fur. As soon as Lancelot saw the Queen leaning on 180 the window-sill behind the great iron bars, he honored her with a gentle salute. She promptly returned his greeting, for he was desirous of her, and she of him. Their talk and conversation are not of vulgar, tiresome affairs. They draw close to one another, until each holds the other's hand. But they are so distressed at not being able to come together more completely, that they curse the iron bars. Then Lancelot asserts that, with the Queen's consent, he will come inside to be with her, and that the bars cannot keep him out. And the Queen replies: "Do you not see how the 190 bars are stiff to bend and hard to break? You could never so twist, pull or drag at them as to dislodge one of them." "Lady," says he, "have no fear of that. It would take more than these bars to keep me out . . . ."

Then the Queen retires, and he prepares to loosen the window. Seizing the bars, he pulls and wrenches them until he makes them bend and drags them from their places. But the iron was so sharp that the end of his little finger was cut to the nerve, and the first joint of the next finger was torn; but he who is intent upon something else 200 paid no heed to any of his wounds or to the blood which trickled down. Though the window is not low, Lancelot gets through it quickly and easily . . . then he comes to the bed of the Queen, whom he adores and before whom he kneels, holding her more dear than the relic of any saint. And the Queen extends her arms to him and, embracing him, presses him tightly against her bosom, drawing him into the bed beside her and showing him every possible satisfaction: her love and her heart go out to him. It is love that prompts her to treat him so; and if she feels great love 210 for him, he feels a hundred thousand times as much for her. For there is no love at all in other hearts compared with what there is in his; in his heart love was so completely embodied that it was niggardly toward all other hearts. Now Lancelot possesses all he wants, when the Queen voluntarily seeks his company and love, and when he holds her in his arms, and she holds him in hers. Their sport is so agreeable and sweet, as they kiss and fondle each other, that in truth such a marvellous joy comes over them as was never heard or known. But their joy will not be revealed by 220 me, for in a story it has no place. Yet, the most choice and delightful satisfaction was precisely that of which our story must not speak. That night Lancelot's joy and pleasure was very great. But, to his sorrow, day comes when he must leave his mistress' side. It cost him such pain to leave her that he suffered a real martyr's agony. His heart now stays where the Queen remains; he has not the power to lead it away, for it finds such pleasure in the Queen that it has no desire to leave her: so his body goes, and his heart remains; . . .

The Cult of the Virgin Mary

From the earliest years of its formation as a religion, Christianity exalted the Virgin Mary as an object of veneration; but beginning in the twelfth century, Mary's roles as Mother of God, Queen of Heaven, and principal intercessor between Jesus and the humble Christian received great attention in literature, music, and art (Figures 11.17, 13.24, 13.30). In the High Middle Ages, the impulse that led to the veneration of Mary seems to have colored the veneration of women in general – especially in literature and song (see "The Motet," chapter 13). Lancelot's worship of Guinevere and his repeated references to her "saintliness" illustrate the confusion of sensual and spiritual passions that characterized the culture of the High Middle Ages. The fact that Lancelot uses the terminology of religious veneration to flatter an unfaithful wife reflects the interdependence of spiritual and secular forms of love that some scholars identify as the "religion of love." However one explains the paradoxes of this phenomenon, Lancelot remains representative of the climate of shifting values and the degeneration of feudal ideals, especially those of honor and loyalty among gentleman warriors.

Figure 11.17 Yolande de Soissons before an Image of the Virgin and Child. From a French Psalter, late thirteenth century. The J. Pierpont Morgan Library, New York, MS 729, f. 232v.

The Poetry of the Troubadours

During the Early Middle Ages, few men and women could read or write. But by the eleventh century, literacy was spreading beyond the cathedral schools and monasteries. The popularity of such forms of vernacular literature as lyric poetry, the chronicle, and the romance gives evidence of the increasing lay literacy among upper-class men and women. To enter- tain the French nobility, *trouvères* (in the North) and *troubadours* (in the South) composed and performed poems devoted to courtly love, chivalry, religion, and politics. *Minnesingers* provided a similar kind of enter- tainment at German-speaking courts, while *meistersin- gers*, masters of the guilds of poets and musicians, flourished somewhat later in German towns. Unlike the minstrels of old, troubadours were usually men and women of noble birth. Their poems, like the *chansons* of

Figure 11.18 Medieval Lovers, "Herr Konrad von Altretten." From the *Manesse Codex*, Zürich, ca. 1315–1330. Universitätsbibliothek, Heidelberg, Germany, MS Pal. germ. 848, f. 84. Rheinisches Köln Bildarchiv, Cologne, Germany.

the Early Middle Ages, were monophonic and syllabic, but they were more expressive in content and more delicate in style than the earlier secular songs. Often, troubadours (or the professional musicians who recited their poems) accompanied themselves on a lyre or a lute (see Figure 10.13). Many of the 2,600 extant troubadour poems exalt the passionate affection of a gentleman for a lady, or, as in those written by the dozen or so identifiable female troubadours, the reverse (Figure **11.18**).

Influenced by Islamic verse, such as that found in chapter 10, troubadour poems generally manifest a positive, even joyous, response to physical nature and the world of the senses. An eleventh-century poem by William IX, Duke of Aquitaine and one of the first troubadours, compares the anticipation of sexual fulfillment with the coming of spring. It opens with these high-spirited words:

> In the sweetness of the new season
> when woods burst forth and birds
> sing, each in its own voice
> to the lyrics of a new song,
> *then* should one seize
> the pleasures one most desires.

In a more melancholic vein, the mid-twelfth-century poet Bernart de Ventadour adopted the popular theme of unrequited love for the poem "When I Behold the Lark."[♭] Occasionally, troubadour verse gives evidence of hostility between upper and lower social classes. Such is the case with the second of the poems reprinted here, in which the troubadour Peire Cardenal levels a fierce attack on social inequity and upper-class greed.

READING 43

Bernart de Ventadour's "When I Behold the Lark"

When I behold the lark arise   1
with wings of gold for heaven's height,
to drop at last from flooded skies,
lost in its fullness of delight,
such sweetness spreads upon the day   5
I envy those who share the glee.
My heart's so filled with love's dismay
I wait its breaking suddenly.
I thought in love's ways I was wise,
yet little do I know aright.   10
I praised a woman as love's prize
and she gives nothing to requite.
My heart, my life she took in theft,
she took the world away from me,
and now my plundered self is left   15
only desire and misery.

[♭]See Music Listening Selection at end of chapter.

Her rule I'm forced to recognize
since all my broken joys took flight.
I looked within her lifted eyes,
that mirror sweet with treacherous might: 20
O mirror, here I weep and dream
of depths once glimpsed and now denied.
I'm lost in you as in the stream
comely Narcissus looked and died.

Now trust in indignation dies   25
and womanhood I henceforth slight.
I find that all her worths are lies.
I thought her something made of light.
And no one comes to plead for me
with her who darkens all my days.   30
Woman I doubt and now I see
that she like all the rest betrays.

Aye, pity women all despise.
Come face the truth and do not fight.
The smallest kindness she denies,   35
yet who but she should soothe my plight?
So gentle and so fair is she,
it's hard for others to believe.
She, who could save, in cruelty
watches her wasting lover grieve.   40

My love has failed and powerless lies;
devotion bears for me no right.
She laughs to hear my deepest sighs —
then silently I'll leave her sight.
I cast my love of her away.   45
She struck and I accept the blow.
She will not speak and I must stray
in exile. Where, I do not know.

Tristan, I've made an end, I say.
I'm going — where, I do not know.   50
My song is dying, and away
all love and joy I cast, and go.

Peire Cardenal's "Lonely the Rich Need Never Be"

Lonely the rich need never be,   1
they have such constant company.
For Wickedness in front we see,
behind, all round, and far and wide.
The giant called Cupidity   5
is always hulking at their side.
Injustice waves the flag, and he
is led along by Pride . . .

If a poor man has snitched a bit of rag,
he goes with downcast head and frightened eye.   10
But when the rich thief fills his greedy bag,
he marches on with head still held as high.
The poor man's hanged, he stole a rotten bridle.
The man who hanged him stole the horse. O fie.
To hang poor thieves the rich thieves still aren't idle. 15
That kind of justice arrow-swift will fly . . .

The rich are charitable? Yes,
as Cain who slew his brother Abel.
They're thieves, no wolves as merciless.
They're liars, like a whoreshop-babel.   20

O stick their ribs, O stick their souls!
No truth comes bubbling from the holes,
but lies. Their greedy hearts, abhorrent,
are rabid as a mountain-torrent . . .

With loving-kindness how they quicken,   25
what hoards of charity they spread.
If all the stones were loaves of bread,
if all the streams with wine should thicken,
the hills turn bacon or boiled chicken,
they'd give no extra crumb. That's flat,   30
   Some people are like that.

―――――――◆―――――――

The Rise of Medieval Towns

Observing the plight of the poor at the hands of the rich, Peire Cardenal condemned a universal condition, but his poem discloses a new social consciousness associated with economic change. During the High Middle Ages, a class of people "midway" between serfs and landlords – the middle class – was emerging. Many factors, including increased agricultural production and the reopening of trade routes, encouraged the rise of the middle class. During the eleventh century, merchants (often younger sons of noble families) engaged in commercial enterprises that promoted the growth of local markets. Usually established near highways or rivers, trade markets became an essential part of manorial life. The permanent market (or *fauberg*) provided the basis for the medieval town – an urban center that attracted farmers and artisans who might buy freedom from their lord or simply run away from the manor. "City air makes a man free" was the cry of those who had discovered the urban alternative to manorial life.

In the newly established towns, the middle class pursued profit from commercial exchange. Merchants and craftspeople in like occupations formed **guilds** for the mutual protection of buyers and sellers. The guilds regulated prices, fixed wages, established standards of quality in the production of goods, and provided training for newcomers in each profession. During the eleventh and twelfth centuries, urban dwellers purchased charters of self-government from lords in whose fiefs their towns were situated. Such charters allowed townspeople (in French, *bourgeois*; in German, *burghers*) to establish municipal governments and regulate their own economic activities. Such commercial centers as Milan, Florence, and Venice became completely self-governing city-states similar to those of ancient Greece and Rome. The Flemish cities of Bruges and Antwerp exported fine linen and wool to England and to towns along the Baltic Sea. The spirit of urban revival was manifested in the construction of defensive stone walls that protected the townspeople, as at Carcassonne in south-western France (Figure **11.19**) and in the building of cathedrals and guildhalls that flanked the open marketplace. Although by the twelfth century, town dwellers constituted less than fifteen percent of the total European population, the middle class continued to expand and ultimately came to dominate Western society.

Middle-class values differed considerably from those of the feudal nobility. Whereas warfare and chivalry preoccupied the nobility, financial prosperity and profit were the principal concerns of the middle

Figure 11.19 Walled City of Carcassonne, France, twelfth to thirteenth centuries.
Arch. Phot. Paris/S.P.A.D.E.M.

class. In European cities, there evolved a lively vernacular literature expressive of middle-class concerns. It included humorous narrative tales (*fabliaux*) and poems (*dits*) describing urban occupations, domestic conflict, and street and tavern life (Figure **11.20**). These popular genres, which feature such stereotypes as the miserly husband and the lecherous monk, slyly reflect many of the social tensions and sexual prejudices of the day. A favorite theme of medieval *fabliaux* and *dits* was the antifemale diatribe, a denunciation of women as bitter as Juvenal's (see chapter 7), and one that was rooted in a long tradition of misogyny, the hatred of women. While medieval romances generally cast the female in the role of Mary, Mother of God, *fabliaux* and *dits* often described all women as descended from the sinful and seductive Eve. The hostile attitude toward womankind, intensified perhaps by women's increasing participation in some of the commercial activities traditionally dominated by men, is readily apparent in the following late-thirteenth-century *dit*, in which woman is pictured as aggressive, immoral, and unfaithful.

Figure 11.20 Young Lady Shopping for Belts and Purses. From the *Manesse Codex*, Zürich, ca. 1315–1333. Universitätsbibliothek, Heidelberg, Germany, MS Pal. germ. f. 64. Rheinisches Köln Bildarchiv, Cologne, Germany.

READING 44

From *The Vices of Women*

She's like a roadside watering hole,	1
Attracting each and every soul;	
She's a bargain, without peer,	
Always slugging she'll persevere;	
She's a tavern-keeper who	5
Rips off each who passes through;	
She's a hell-mouth that is cursed	
With an all-consuming thirst.	
Woman shuns fidelity,	
Gives evil counsel readily;	10
Woman's deaf to what she's saying,	
All her chatter's foolish braying;	
She's more artful than the devil	
And she's equally unfaithful;	
Woman's a creature with a fickle heart,	15
She's close to you now, tomorrow she'll part.	

· · · · · · · · · · · ·

———————————◆———————————

Appended to the poem was a popular medieval proverb:

> He who takes a wife trades peace for strife,
> Long weariness, despair, oppress his life,
> A heavy load, a barrel full of chatter,
> Uncorkable, her gossip makes a clatter,
> Now, ever since I took a wife,
> Calamity has marred my life.

SUMMARY

The Carolingian Empire was the cultural oasis of the Early Middle Ages. By converting much of Western Europe to Christianity and by encouraging education and the arts, Charlemagne made a lasting contribution to the humanistic tradition. Early medieval life was feudal and agrarian. The practice of exchanging land for military service evolved among members of the nobility. Feudalism provided local protection during the period of instability that followed the disintegration of Charlemagne's empire. The characteristic works of the early Middle Ages — the *Song of Roland*, the Norman castle, and the Bayeux Tapestry — all describe a heroic age that glorified warfare, male prowess, and the conquest of land. Manorialism, the economic basis for medieval society, offered the lower classes protection in exchange for food production, but left in its wake little tangible evidence of the lives and values of those who constituted the majority of the population.

The Christian Crusades, the definitive expression of Christian-Muslim hostility, brought changes to European economic and cultural life, even as they reflected the new mobility of the High Middle Ages. In vernacular literature, sentiment and sensuousness replaced the early medieval ideals of heroism and chivalry. Romantic love, a medieval invention, dominated both the vernacular romance and troubadour poetry.

The revival of trade and the rise of towns encouraged the birth of the middle class, whose ambitions were distinctly materialistic and profit oriented. The values of merchants and craftspeople differed from those of the feudal nobility, for whom land provided the basis of wealth, and chivalry dictated manners and morals. Vernacular tales and poems often satirized inequality between classes and antagonism between sexes. Whereas medieval romances generally pictured their heroines as figures of the Virgin Mary, *fabliaux* and *dits* condemned women as the daughters of Eve. The changes that occurred in secular life between the years 750 and 1300 reflect the shift from a feudal society marked by heroic idealism to an urban society distinguished by complex interactions between male and female, lord and vassal, farmer and merchant.

GLOSSARY

chain mail a flexible medieval armor made of interlinked metal rings

chanson de geste (French, "song of heroic deeds") an epic poem of the early Middle Ages

chivalry a code of behavior practiced by upper-class men and women of medieval society

crenellations tooth-like battlements surmounting a wall and used for defensive combat

feudalism the system of political organization prevailing in Europe between the ninth and fifteenth centuries and having as its basis the exchange of land for military defense

fief in feudal society land or property given to a warrior in return for military service

guild an association of merchants or craftspeople organized according to like occupation

investiture the procedure by which a feudal lord granted a vassal control over a fief

jongleur a professional entertainer who wandered from court to court in medieval Europe

joust a form of personal combat, usually with lances on horseback, between men-at-arms

keep a square tower, the strongest and most secure part of the medieval castle; (see Figure 11.11)

lord any member of the feudal nobility who invested a vassal with a fief

mace a heavy, spike-headed club used as a weapon in medieval combat

medieval romance a tale of adventure that supplanted the older *chanson de geste* and that deals with knights, kings, and ladies acting under the impulse of love, religious faith, or the desire for adventure

moat a wide trench, usually filled with water, surrounding a fortified place, such as a castle; (see Figure 11.11)

primogeniture the principle by which a fief was passed from father to oldest son

renaissance (French, "rebirth") a revival of the learning of former and especially classical culture

samurai (Japanese, "those who serve") the warrior aristocracy of Japan

serf an unfree peasant

vassal any member of the feudal nobility who vowed to serve a lord in exchange for control of a fief

SUGGESTIONS FOR READING

Brooke, Christopher. *The Structure of Medieval Society*. New York: McGraw-Hill, 1971.

Duby, George. *Love and Marriage in the Middle Ages*, trans. Jane Dunnett. Chicago: University of Chicago Press, 1994.

Erickson, Carolly. *The Medieval Vision, Essays in History and Perception*. New York: Oxford University Press, 1976.

———. *Life in a Medieval City*. New York: Harper, 1981.

Gies, Frances and J. Gies. *Life in a Medieval Village*. New York: Harper, 1991.

Gies, Joseph and F. Gies. *Women in the Middle Ages*. New York: Barnes and Noble, 1980.

Herlihy, David. *Opera Muliera, Women and Work in Medieval Europe*. New York: McGraw-Hill, 1990.

Lewis, Archibald R. *Knights and Samurai: Feudalism in Northern France and Japan*. London: Temple Smith, 1974.

Macauley, David. *Castle*. Boston: Houghton Mifflin, 1982.

Riche, Pierre. *Daily Life in the World of Charlemagne*, trans. J. MacNamara. Philadelphia: University of Pennsylvania Press, 1978.

Stephenson, Carl. *Medieval Feudalism*. Ithaca: Cornell University Press, 1973.

Strayer, J. R. *Western Europe in the Middle Ages*. Glenview, Ill.: Scott-Foresman, 1982.

Trever-Roper, Hugh. *The Rise of Christian Europe*. New York: Harcourt, 1965.

MUSIC LISTENING SELECTION

Cassette I Selection 5 Bernart de Ventadour, "Can vei la lauzeta mover" ("When I Behold the Lark"), ca. 1150, excerpt.

12

The Christian Church
and the Medieval Mind

For a thousand years after the fall of Rome (ca. 500–1500), the Catholic Church was the primary source of spiritual authority and religious leadership in the European West. In 1054, disagreements between Rome and Constantinople over doctrinal and liturgical matters resulted in a permanent breach in the Church. Both the Catholic Church and the Eastern or Greek Orthodox Church, however, shared the view that the terrestrial world mirrored a divine order that was sustained through the ministry of God's representatives on earth. Church doctrine and liturgy gave coherence and meaning to everyday life. More important, the Church offered the sole means by which the medieval Christian might achieve life everlasting.

The Church and the Promise of Salvation

The promise of personal immortality was central to the medieval worldview. That promise must be understood in the context of the profound and universal fact of death, or nonbeing, and of the human inability to imagine the condition of nonbeing. In both the physical and the intellectual sense, death represents humankind's ultimate vulnerability. Almost all religious belief systems in history offer the promise of personal immortality – the ultimate act of controlling (even defying) nature.

With the exception of the purest forms of Hinduism and Buddhism, which anticipate the extinction of the Self, most world religions have met the human fear of death with an ideology (a body of doctrine supported by myth and symbols) that promises the survival of some aspect of the Self in a life hereafter. The nature of that hereafter usually depends on the moral status of the believer – that is, his or her conduct on earth.

Christianity addressed the question of personal extinction more effectively than any other world religion. The Christian immortality ideology* provided a system by which medieval Christians achieved final victory over death. Through the **sacraments**, a set of sacred acts that impart **grace** (the free and unearned favor of God), medieval Christians were assured of the soul's redemption from sin and its eternal life in a world to come. The seven sacraments – the number fixed by the Fourth Lateran Council of 1215 – touched every significant phase of human life: At birth, baptism purified the recipient of Original Sin; confirmation admitted the baptized to full church privileges; ordination invested those entering the clergy with priestly authority; matrimony blessed the union of man and woman; penance acknowledged repentance of sins and offered absolution; Eucharist – the central and most important of the sacraments – joined human beings to God by means of the blood and body of Jesus; and finally, just prior to death, extreme unction provided final absolution from sins.

By way of sacraments, the Church participated in virtually every major aspect of the individual's life, enforcing a set of values that determined the collective spirituality of Christendom. Since only church officials could administer the sacraments, the clergy held a "monopoly" on personal salvation. Medieval Christians thus looked to representatives of the mother church as shepherds guiding the members of their flock on their long and hazardous journey through life. Their conduct on earth determined whether their souls went to heaven, hell, or purgatory (the place of purification from sins). But only by way of the clergy might they receive the gifts of grace that made salvation possible.

---

*The phrase is from Ernest Becker, *The Denial of Death* (New York: The Free Press, 1973).

Medieval Literature and the Promise of Salvation

The Christian immortality ideology shaped all forms of medieval expression. However, three works stand out as definitive of that ideology: a papal sermon, an allegorical drama, and an epic poem. The first of these, the classic medieval sermon entitled *On the Misery of the Human Condition*, was written by one of Christendom's most influential popes, Innocent III (d. 1216). Innocent's sermon is a compelling description of the natural sinfulness of humankind and a scathing condemnation of the "vile and filthy [human] condition." Warning of the "nearness of death," it is also a *memento mori*, a device by which listeners in a predominantly oral culture might "remember death" and thus prepare themselves for its inevitable arrival. Innocent's portrayal of the decay of the human body reflects the medieval disdain for the world of matter, a major theme in most medieval didactic literature. During the late Middle Ages, especially after the onslaught of the bubonic plague (see chapter 15), the motif of the body as "food for worms" – one of Innocent's most vivid images – became particularly popular in gruesomely forthright tomb sculptures (Figure 12.1).

Innocent's vivid account of the Christian Hell transforms the concept of corruption into an image of eternal punishment for unabsolved sinners – a favorite subject matter for medieval artists (Figure 12.2). The

Figure 12.2 The Mouth of Hell. From the Psalter of Henry of Blois, Bishop of Winchester, English, twelfth century. Reproduced by permission of the British Library, London, MS Cotton Nero. C. IV, f. 39.

contrast that Innocent draws between physical death and spiritual life has its visual counterpart in the representations of the Last Judgment depicted in medieval manuscripts and on Romanesque and Gothic church portals (see Figure 13.9).

Figure 12.1 Detail of *transi* (effigy of the dead): Francois de la Sarra. Tomb, La Sarraz, Switzerland, ca. 1390. Photo: De Jongh, Lausanne. © Musée de l'Elysée, Lausanne, Switzerland.

READING 45

From Pope Innocent III's *On the Misery of the Human Condition*

Of the Miserable Entrance upon the Human Condition

. . . Man was formed of dust, slime, and ashes: what is   1
even more vile, of the filthiest seed. He was conceived
from the itch of the flesh, in the heat of passion and the
stench of lust, and worse yet, with the stain of sin. He was
born to toil, dread, and trouble; and more wretched still,
was born only to die. He commits depraved acts by which
he offends God, his neighbor, and himself; shameful acts
by which he defiles his name, his person, and his
conscience; and vain acts by which he ignores all things
important, useful and necessary. He will become fuel for   10
those fires which are forever hot and burn forever bright;
food for the worm which forever nibbles and digests; a
mass of rottenness which will forever stink and reek . . . .

On the Nearness of Death

A man's last day is always the first in importance, but his first day is never considered his last. Yet it is fitting to live always on this principle, that one should act as if in the moment of death. For it is written: "Remember that death is not slow."[1] Time passes, death draws near. In the eyes of the dying man a thousand years are as yesterday, which is past. The future is forever being born, the present forever 20 dying and what is past is utterly dead. We are forever dying while we are alive; we only cease to die when we cease to live. Therefore it is better to die to life than to live waiting for death, for mortal life is but a living death . . . .

On the Putrefaction of the Dead Body

. . . Man is conceived of blood made rotten by the heat of lust; and in the end worms, like mourners, stand about his corpse. In life he produced lice and tapeworms; in death he will produce worms and flies. In life he produced dung and vomit; in death he produces rottenness and stench. In life he fattened one man; in death he fattens a multitude of 30 worms. What then is more foul than a human corpse? What is more horrible than a dead man? He whose embrace was pure delight in life will be a gruesome sight in death.

Of what advantage, then, are riches, food, and honors? For riches will not free us from death, neither food protect us from the worm nor honors from the stench. That man who but now sat in glory upon a throne is now looked down on in the grave; the dandy who once glittered in his palace lies now naked and vile in his tomb; and he who supped once on delicacies in his hall is now in his sepulcher food 40 for worms . . . .

That Nothing Can Help the Damned

. . . O strict judgment! — not only of actions, but "of every idle word that men shall speak, they shall render an account";[2] payment with the usurer's interest will be exacted to the last penny. "Who hath showed you to flee from the wrath to come?"[3]

"The Son of Man shall send his angels and they shall gather out of his kingdom all scandals, and them that work iniquity, and they will bind them as bundles to be burnt, and shall cast them into the furnace of fire. There shall be 50 weeping and gnashing of teeth,"[4] there shall be groaning and wailing, shrieking and flailing of arms and screaming, screeching and shouting; there shall be fear and trembling, toil and trouble, holocaust and dreadful stench, and everywhere darkness and anguish; there shall be asperity, cruelty, calamity, poverty, distress and utter wretchedness; they will feel an oblivion of loneliness and namelessness; there shall be twistings and piercings, bitterness, terror, hunger and thirst, cold and hot, brimstone and fire burning, forever and ever world without 60 end . . . .

————————◆————————

[1] Ecclesiastes 14:12
[2] Matthew 12:36
[3] Luke 3:7
[4] Matthew 13:41–42

The Medieval Morality Play

While medieval churches rang with sermons like those preached by Innocent III, town squares (often immediately adjacent to a cathedral) became open-air theaters for the dramatization of Christian history and legend. To these urban spaces, people flocked to see plays that might last from sunrise to sunset. The **mystery play** dramatized biblical history from the fall of Lucifer to the Last Judgment, while the **miracle play** enacted stories from the life of Christ, the Virgin, or the saints. The **morality play**, the last to evolve among the three types of medieval plays, dealt with such themes as the conflict between good and evil and the fall of humankind. Usually performed by members of the craft guilds and produced on **pageants** (roofed wagon-stages) that were rolled into the town square, medieval plays were a popular form of local entertainment, as well as a source of religious and moral instruction.

Just as ancient Greek drama originated in religious ritual, so medieval drama had its roots in the performance of Church liturgy. The Catholic Mass, the principal rite of Christian worship, admitted all of the trappings of theater: colorful costumes, symbolic props, solemn processions, dramatic gestures, and ceremonial music. Most likely, the gradual dramatization of church liturgy (see chapter 13) influenced the rise of mystery and miracle plays. The morality play, however, had its precedents in allegorical poetry and in sermons like those of Innocent III. In keeping with most medieval literature, the morality play featured allegory, a literary device encountered in Plato's *Republic* (see chapter 5) and in Augustine's *City of God* (see chapter 9) that depends on symbolic representation to capture the essence of a person, thing, or idea. The characters of the morality play are personifications of abstract qualities and universal conditions. In the play *Everyman*, for instance, the main character represents all Christian souls, Fellowship stands for friends, Goods for worldly possessions, and so forth.

Although *Everyman* has survived only in fifteenth-century Dutch and English editions, plays similar to it originated considerably earlier. The most popular of all medieval morality plays, *Everyman* symbolically recreates the pilgrimage of the Christian soul to its ultimate destiny. The play opens with the Messenger who expounds on the transitory nature of human life. The subsequent conversation between Death and God, somewhat reminiscent of that between Satan and God in the Book of Job (see chapter 2), shows God to be an angry, petulant deity who regards human beings as "drowned in sin." If left to their own devices, he opines, "they will become much worse than beasts."

As the action unfolds, Everyman discovers that Death has come for him. He soon discovers that his best friends, his kin, his worldly possessions, indeed, all that he so treasured in life, will not accompany him to the grave. Knowledge, Wits, Beauty, and Discretion may point the way to redemption, but they cannot save him. Ultimately, only Good-Deeds will accompany him to confront judgment by "eternal God." *Everyman* is essentially a moral allegory that illustrates the Christian immortality ideology; but typical of its time, it is also an exposition on the importance of the Catholic Church in helping the medieval Christian achieve salvation. Indeed, as Five-Wits observes, only the clergy can dispense the "blessed sacraments" that are the "keys" to Paradise. Like Pope Innocent's sermon, *Everyman* teaches that all things contributing to worldly pleasure are ultimately valueless, that life is transient, and that sin can be mitigated solely by salvation earned through grace as dispensed by the Church.

READING 46

From *Everyman*

Characters

Messenger	Cousin	Strength
God (Adonai)	Goods	Discretion
Death	Good-Deeds	Five-Wits
Everyman	Knowledge	Angel
Fellowship	Confession	Doctor
Kindred	Beauty	

HERE BEGINNETH A TREATISE HOW THE HIGH FATHER OF HEAVEN SENDETH DEATH TO SUMMON EVERY CREATURE TO COME AND GIVE ACCOUNT OF THEIR LIVES IN THIS WORLD AND IS IN MANNER OF A MORAL PLAY.

MESSENGER: I pray you all give your audience,   1
And hear this matter with reverence,
By figure a moral play —
The *Summoning of Everyman* called it is,
That of our lives and ending shows
How transitory we be all day.[1]
This matter is wondrous precious,
But the intent of it is more gracious,
And sweet to bear away.
The story saith — Man, in the beginning,   10
Look well, and take good heed to the ending,
Be you never so gay!
Ye think sin in the beginning full sweet,
Which in the end causeth thy soul to weep,
When the body lieth in clay.
Here shall you see how *Fellowship* and *Jollity*,
Both *Strength*, *Pleasure*, and *Beauty*,
Will fade from thee as flower in May.
For ye shall hear, how our heaven king
Calleth *Everyman* to a general reckoning: 20
Give audience, and hear what he doth say.

GOD: I perceive here in my majesty,
How that all creatures be to me unkind,[2]
Living without dread in worldly prosperity:
Of ghostly sight the people be so blind,
Drowned in sin, they know me not for their God:
In worldly riches is all their mind,
They fear not my right wiseness, the sharp rod:
My law that I shewed, when I for them died,
They forget clean, and shedding of my blood red: 30
I hanged between two, it cannot be denied:
To get them life I suffered to be dead:
I healed their feet, with thorns hurt was my head:
I could do no more than I did truly,
And now I see the people do clean forsake me,
They use the seven deadly sins damnable;
As pride, covetise, wrath, and lechery,
Now in the world be made commendable;
And thus they leave of angels the heavenly company;
Everyman liveth so after his own pleasure,   40
And yet of their life they be nothing sure:
I see the more that I them forbear
The worse they be from year to year;
All that liveth appaireth[3] fast,
Therefore I will in all the haste
Having a reckoning of Everyman's person
For and[4] I leave the people thus alone
In their life and wicked tempests,
Verily they will become much worse than beasts;
For now one would by envy another up eat;   50
Charity they all do clean forget.
I hoped well that Everyman
In my glory should make his mansion,
And thereto I had them all elect;
But now I see, like traitors deject,
They thank me not for the pleasure that I to them meant
Nor yet for their being that I them have lent;
I proffered the people great multitude of mercy,
And few there be that asketh it heartily;
They be so combered with worldly riches,   60
That needs of them I must do justice,
On Everyman living without fear.
Where art thou, Death, thou mighty messenger?
DEATH: Almighty God, I am here at your will,
Your commandment to fulfil.
GOD: Go thou to Everyman,
And show him in my name
A pilgrimage he must on him take,
Which he in no wise may escape:
And that he bring with him a sure reckoning   70
Without delay or any tarrying.
DEATH: Lord, I will in the world go run over all,
And cruelly outsearch both great and small;
Every man will I beset that liveth beastly
Out of God's laws, and dreadeth not folly:
He that loveth riches I will strike with my dart,
His sight to blind, and from heaven to depart,
Except that alms be his good friend,
In hell for to dwell, world without end.
Lo, yonder I see Everyman walking;   80
Full little he thinketh on my coming;

---

[1] Always.   [2] Ungrateful.   [3] Decays.   [4] If.

His mind is on fleshly lusts and his treasure,
And great pain it shall cause him to endure
Before the Lord Heaven King.
Everyman, stand still; whither art thou going
Thus gaily? Hast my Maker forgot?
    EVERYMAN: Why askst thou?
Wouldest thou wete?[5]
    DEATH: Yea, sir, I will show you;
In great haste I am sent to thee   90
From God out of his majesty.
    EVERYMAN: What, sent to me?
    DEATH: Yea, certainly.
Though thou have forget him here,
He thinketh on thee in the heavenly sphere,
As, or we depart, thou shalt know.
    EVERYMAN: What desireth God of me?
    DEATH: That shall I show thee;
A reckoning he will needs have
Without any longer respite.   100
    EVERYMAN: To give a reckoning longer leisure I crave;
This blind matter troubleth my wit.
    DEATH: On thee thou must take a long journey:
Therefore thy book of count with thee thou bring:
    For turn again thou can not by no way.
And look thou be sure of thy reckoning:
For before God thou shalt answer, and show
Thy many bad deeds and good but a few;
How thou hast spent thy life, and in what wise,
Before the chief lord of paradise.   110
Have ado that we were in that way,
For, wete thou well, thou shalt make none attournay.[6]
    EVERYMAN: Full unready I am such reckoning to give.
I know thee not: what messenger art thou?
    DEATH: I am Death, that no man dreadeth.
For every man I rest[7] and no man spareth;
For it is God's commandment
That all to me should be obedient.
    EVERYMAN: O Death, thou comest when I had thee least in
        mind,
In thy power it lieth me to save,   120
Yet of my good[s] will I give thee, if ye will be kind,
Yea, a thousand pound shalt thou have,
And defer this matter till another day.
    DEATH: Everyman, it may not be by no way;
I set not by gold, silver, nor riches,
Ne by pope, emperor, king, duke, ne princes,
For and I would receive gifts great,
All the world I might get;
But my custom is clean contrary.
I give thee no respite: come hence, and not tarry.   130
    EVERYMAN: Alas, shall I have no longer respite?
I may say Death giveth no warning:
To think on thee, it maketh my heart sick,
For all unready is my book of reckoning.
But twelve year and I might have abiding,
My counting book I would make so clear,
That my reckoning I should not need to fear.
Wherefore, Death, I pray thee, for God's mercy.
Spare me till I be provided of remedy.

DEATH: Thee availeth not to cry, weep, and pray: 140
But haste thee lightly that you were gone the journey.
And prove thy friends if thou can.
For, wete thou well, the tide abideth no man,
And in the world each living creature
For Adam's sin must die of nature.
    EVERYMAN: Death, if I should this pilgrimage take,
And my reckoning surely make,
Show me, for saint charity,
Should I not come again shortly?
    DEATH: No, Everyman; and thou be once there,   150
Thou mayst never more come here,
Trust me verily.
    EVERYMAN: O gracious God, in the high seat celestial,
Have mercy on me in this most need;
Shall I have no company from this vale terrestrial
Of mine acquaintance that way me to lead?
    DEATH: Yea, if any be so hardy,
That would go with thee and bear thee company.
Hie thee that you were gone[8] to God's magnificence,
Thy reckoning to give before his presence.   160
What, weenest[9] thou thy life is given thee,
And thy worldly goods also?
    EVERYMAN: I had wend[10] so, verily.
    DEATH: Nay, nay; it was but lent thee;
For as soon as thou art go,
another awhile shall have it, and then go therefro
Even as thou has done.
Everyman, thou art mad; thou hast thy wits five,
And here on earth will not amend thy life,
For suddenly I do come.   170
    EVERYMAN: O wretched caitiff, wither shall I flee,
That I might scape this endless sorrow!
Now, gentle Death, spare me till to-morrow,
That I may amend me
With good advisement.
    DEATH: Nay, thereto I will not consent,
Nor no man will I respite,
But to the heart suddenly I shall smite
Without any advisement.
And now out of thy sight I will me nie;   180
See thou make thee ready shortly,
For thou mayst say this is the day
That no man living may scape away.
    EVERYMAN: Alas, I may well weep with sighs deep,
Now have I no manner of company
To help me in my journey, and me to keep;
And also my writing is full unready.
How shall I do now for to excuse me?
I would to God I had never be gete![11]
To my soul a full great profit it had be;   190
For now I fear pains huge and great.
The time passeth; Lord, help that all wrought;
For though I mourn it availeth nought.
The day passeth, and is almost a-go;
I wot not well what for to do.
To whom were I best my complaint to make?
What, and I[12] to Fellowship thereof spake,
And showed him of this sudden chance?

---

[5] Know.
[6] Mediator.
[7] Arrest.

[8] Hurry and go.
[9] Do you suppose.
[10] Supposed.

[11] Been born.
[12] What if.

For in him is all mine affiance;[13]
We have in the world so many a day   200
Be on good friends in sport and play.
I see him yonder, certainly;
I trust that he will bear me company;
Therefore to him will I speak to ease my sorrow.
Well met, good Fellowship, and good morrow!
    FELLOWSHIP: Everyman, good morrow by this day.
Sir, why lookest thou so piteously?
If any thing be amiss, I pray thee, me say,
That I may help to remedy.
    EVERYMAN: Yea, good Fellowship, yea.   210
I am in great jeopardy.
    FELLOWSHIP: My true friend, show to me your mind;
I will not forsake thee, unto my life's end,
In the way of good company.
    EVERYMAN: That was well spoken, and lovingly.
    FELLOWSHIP: Sir, I must needs know your heaviness;
I have pity to see you in any distress;
If any have ye wronged he shall revenged be,
Though I on the ground be slain for thee —
Thou that I know before that I should die.   220
    EVERYMAN: Verily, Fellowship, gramercy.
    FELLOWSHIP: Tush! by thy thanks I set not a straw;
Show me your grief, and say no more.
    EVERYMAN: If I my heart should to you break,
And then you to turn your mind from me,
And would not me comfort, when you hear me speak,
Then should I ten times sorrier be.
    FELLOWSHIP: Sir, I say as I will do in deed.
    EVERYMAN: Then be you a good friend at need:
I have found you true here before.   230
    FELLOWSHIP: And so ye shall evermore;
For, infaith, and thou go to Hell,
I will not forsake thee by the way!
    EVERYMAN: Ye speak like a good friend: I believe you well;
I shall deserve it,[14] and I may.
    FELLOWSHIP: I speak of no deserving, by this day.
For he that will say and nothing do
Is not worthy with good company to go;
Therefore show me the grief of your mind,
As to your friend most loving and kind.   240
    EVERYMAN: I shall show you how it is;
Commanded I am to go a journey,
A long way, hard and dangerous,
And give a strait count without delay
Before the high judge Adonai.[15]
Wherefore I pray you, bear me company,
As ye have promised, in this journey.
    FELLOWSHIP: That is matter indeed! Promise is duty,
But, and I should take such a voyage on me,
I know it well, it should be to my pain: 250
Also it make me afeard, certain.
But let us take counsel here as well as we can,
For your words would fear[16] a strong man.
    EVERYMAN: Why, ye said, if I had need,
Ye would me never forsake, quick nor dead,
Though it were to Hell truly.
    FELLOWSHIP: So I said, certainly,

But such pleasures be set aside, thee sooth to say:
And also, if we took such a journey,
When should we come again?   260
    EVERYMAN: Nay, never again till the day of doom.
    FELLOWSHIP: In faith, then will not I come there!
Who hath you these tidings brought?
    EVERYMAN: Indeed, Death was with me here.
    FELLOWSHIP: Now, by God that all hath bought,
If Death were the messenger,
For no man that is living today
I will not go that loath journey —
Not for the father that begat me!
    EVERYMAN: Ye promised other wise, pardie.[17]   270
    FELLOWSHIP: I wot well I say so truly
And yet if thou wilt eat, and drink, and make good cheer,
Or haunt to women, the lusty company,
I would not forsake you, while the day is clear,
Trust me verily!
    EVERYMAN: Yea, thereto ye would be ready;
To go to mirth, solace, and play
Your mind will sooner apply
Than to bear me company in my long journey.
    FELLOWSHIP: Now, in good faith, I will not that way.   280
But and thou wilt murder, or any man kill,
In that I will help thee with a good will!
    EVERYMAN: O that is a simple advice indeed!
Gentle fellow: help me in my necessity;
We have loved long, and now I need,
And now, gentle Fellowship, remember me.
    FELLOWSHIP: Whether ye have loved me or no,
By Saint John, I will not with thee go.
    EVERYMAN: Yet I pray thee, take the labour, and do
        so much for me
To bring me forward, for saint charity,   290
And comfort me till I come without the town.
    FELLOWSHIP: Nay, and thou would give me a new gown,
I will not a foot with thee go;
But and you had tarried I would not have left thee so.
And as now, God speed thee in thy journey,
For from thee I will depart as fast as I may.
    EVERYMAN: Whither away, Fellowship? Will you forsake
        me?
    FELLOWSHIP: Yea, by my fay,[18] to God I betake thee.
    EVERYMAN: Farewell, good Fellowship; for this my heart is
        sore;
Adieu for ever, I shall see thee no more.   300
    FELLOWSHIP: In faith, Everyman, farewell not at the end;
For you I will remember that parting is mourning.
    EVERYMAN: Alack! shall we thus depart indeed?
Our Lady, help, without any more comfort,
Lo, Fellowship forsaketh me in my most need:
For help in this world whither shall I resort?
Fellowship herebefore with me would merry make;
And now little sorrow for me doth he take.
It is said, in prosperity men friends may find,
Which in adversity be full unkind.   310
Now whither for succour shall I flee,
[since] Fellowship hath forsaken me?
To my kinsmen I will truly,

---

[13] Trust.   [15] God.
[14] Repay.   [16] Terrify.

[17] By God.
[18] Faith.

Praying them to help me in my necessity:
I believe that they will do so,
For kind will creep where it may not go,
Where be ye now, my friends and kinsmen?
    KINDRED: Here be we now at your commandment.
Cousin, I pray you show us your intent
In any wise, and not spare.   320
    COUSIN: Yea, Everyman, and to us declare
If ye be disposed to go any whither,
For wete you well, we will live and die together.
    KINDRED: In wealth and woe we will with you hold,
For over his kin a man may be bold.
    EVERYMAN: Gramercy, my friends and kinsmen kind.
Now shall I show you the grief of my mind:
I was commanded by a messenger,
That is an high king's chief officer;
He bade me go a pilgrimage to my pain,   330
And I know well I shall never come again;
Also I must give a reckoning straight,
For I have a great enemy, that hath me in wait,
Which intendeth me for to hinder.
    KINDRED: What account is that which ye must render?
That would I know.
    EVERYMAN: Of all my works I must show
How I have lived and my days spent;
Also of ill deeds, that I have used
In my time, sith life was me lent;   340
And of all virtues that I have refused.
Therefore I pray you go thither with me,
To help to make mine account, for saint charity.
    COUSIN: What, to go thither? Is that the matter?
Nay, Everyman, I had liefer[19] fast bread and water
All this five year and more.
    EVERYMAN: Alas, that ever I was bore![20]
For now shall I never be merry
If that you forsake me.
    KINDRED: Ah, sir, what, ye be a merry man!   350
Take good heart to you, and make no moan.
But one thing I warn you, by Saint Anne,
As for me, ye shall go alone.
    EVERYMAN: My Cousin, will you not with me go?
    COUSIN: No, by our Lady; I have the cramp in my toe.
Trust not to me, for, so God me speed,
I will deceive you in your most need.
    KINDRED: It availeth not us to tice.[21]
Ye shall have my maid with all my heart;
She loveth to go to feasts, there to be nice,   360
And to dance, and abroad to start:
I will give her leave to help you in that journey,
If that you and she may agree.
    EVERYMAN: Now show me the very effect of your mind.
Will you go with me, or abide behind?
    KINDRED: Abide behind? Yea, that I will and I may!
Therefore farewell until another day.
    EVERYMAN: How should I be merry or glad?
For fair promises to me make,
But when I have most need, they me forsake.   370
I am deceived; that maketh me sad.
    COUSIN: Cousin Everyman, farewell now,

For verily I will not go with you;
Also of mine own an unready reckoning
I have to account: therefore I make tarrying.
Now, God keep thee, for now I go.
    EVERYMAN: Ah, Jesus, is all come hereto?
Lo, fair words maketh fools feign;
They promise and nothing will do certain.
My kinsmen promised me faithfully   380
For to abide with me steadfastly,
And now fast away do they flee:
Even so Fellowship promised me.
What friend were best me of to provide?
I lose my time here longer to abide.
Yet in my mind a thing there is: —
All my life I have loved riches;
If that my goods now help me might,
He would make my heart full light.
I will speak to him in this distress. —   390
Where art thou, my Goods and riches?
    GOODS: Who calleth me? Everyman? What haste thou
        hast!
I lie here in corners, trussed and piled so high,
And in chests I am locked so fast,
Also sacked in bags, thou mayst see with thine eye,
I cannot stir; in packs low I lie,
What would ye have, lightly me say.[22]
    EVERYMAN: Come hither, Good, in all the haste thou may,
For of counsel I must desire thee.
    GOODS: Sir, and ye in the world have trouble or adversity. 400
That can I help you to remedy shortly.
    EVERYMAN: It is another disease that grieveth me;
In this world it is not, I tell thee so.
I am sent for another way to go,
To give a straight account general
Before the highest Jupiter of all;
And all my life I have had joy and pleasure in thee.
Therefore I pray thee go with me,
For, peradventure, thou mayst before God Almighty
My reckoning help to clean and purify;   410
For it is said ever among,
That money maketh all right that is wrong.
    GOODS: Nay, Everyman, I sing another song.
I follow no man in such voyages;
For and I went with thee
Thou shouldst fare much the worse for me;
For because on me thou did set thy mind,
Thy reckoning I have made blotted and blind
That thine account thou cannot make truly;
And that has thou for the love of me.   420
    EVERYMAN: That would grieve me full sore,
When I should come to that fearful answer.
Up, let us go thither together.
    GOODS: Nay, no so, I am too brittle, I may not endure:
I will follow no man one foot, be ye sure.
    EVERYMAN: Alas, I have thee loved, and had great pleasure
All my life-days on good and treasure.
    GOODS: That is to thy damnation without lesing,
For my love is contrary to the love everlasting
But if thou had me loved moderately during,   430

---

[19] Rather.
[20] Born.
[21] It is useless to try to entice us.

---

[22] Quickly tell me.

As, to the poor give part of me,
Then shouldst thou not in this dolour be,[23]
Nor in this great sorrow and care.
    EVERYMAN: Lo, now was I deceived or I was ware,
And all I may wyte[24] my spending of time.
    GOODS: What, weenest thou that I am thine?
    EVERYMAN: I had wend so.
    GOODS: Nay, Everyman, I say no;
As for a while I was lent thee,
A season thou hast had me in prosperity   440
My condition is man's soul to kill;
If I save one, a thousand I do spill;[25]
Weenest thou that I will follow thee?
Nay, from this world, not verily.
    EVERYMAN: I had wend otherwise.
    GOODS: Therefore to thy soul Good is a thief;
For when thou art dead, this is my guise
Another to deceive in the same wise
As I have done thee, and all to his soul's reprief.[26]
    EVERYMAN: O false Good, cursed thou be!   450
Thou traitor to God, that has deceived me,
And caught me in thy snare.
    GOODS: Marry,[27] thou brought thyself in care,
Whereof I am glad,
I must needs laugh, I cannot be sad.
    EVERYMAN: Ah, Goods, thou has had long my heartly love;
I gave thee that which should be the Lord's above.
But wilt thou not go with me in deed?
I pray thee truth to say.
    GOODS: No, so God me speed,   460
Therefore farewell, and have good day.
    EVERYMAN: O, to whom shall I make moan
For to go with me in that heavy journey?
First Fellowship said he would with me gone;
His words were very pleasant and gay,
But afterward he left me alone.
Then spake I to my kinsmen all in despair,
And also they gave me words fair,
They lacked no fair speaking,
But all forsake me in the ending.   470
Then went I to my Goods that I loved best,
In hope to have comfort, but there had I least:
For my Goods sharply did me tell
That he bringeth many into hell.
Then of myself I was ashamed;
And so I am worthy to be blamed;
Thus may I well myself hate,
Of whom shall I now counsel take?
I think that I shall never speed
Till that I go to my Good-Deed,   480
But alas, she is so weak,
That she can neither go nor speak,
Yet will I venture on her now. —
My Good-Deeds, where be you?
    GOOD-DEEDS: Here I lie cold on the ground,
Thy sins hath me sore bound,
That I cannot stir.
    EVERYMAN: O, Good-Deeds, I stand in fear;
I must you pray of counsel,

For help now should come right well.   490
    GOOD-DEEDS: Everyman, I have understanding
That ye be summoned account to make
Before Messias, of Jerusalem King;
And you by me[28] that journey what[29] you will I take.
    EVERYMAN: Therefore I come to you, my moan to make;
I pray you, that ye will go with me.
    GOOD-DEEDS: I would full fain,[30] but I cannot stand verily.
    EVERYMAN: Why, is there anything on you fall?
    GOOD-DEEDS: Yea, sir, I may think you of all;
If ye had perfectly cheered me,   500
Your book of account now full ready had be.
Look, the books of your works and deeds eke;[31]
Oh, see how they lie under the feet,
To your soul's heaviness.
    EVERYMAN: Our Lord Jesus, help me!
For one letter here I can not see.
    GOOD-DEEDS: There is a blind reckoning in time of
      distress!
    EVERYMAN: Good-Deeds, I pray you, help me in this need,
Or else I am for ever damned indeed;
Therefore help me to make reckoning   510
Before the redeemer of all thing,
That king is, and was, and ever shall.
    GOOD-DEEDS: Everyman, I am sorry of your fall,
And fain would I help you, and I were able.
    EVERYMAN: Good-Deeds, your counsel I pray you give me.
    GOOD-DEEDS: That shall I do verily;
Though that on my feet I may not go,
I have a sister, that shall with you also,
Called Knowledge, which shall with you abide,
To help you to make that dreadful reckoning.   520

[*Knowledge guides Everyman to Confession, Discretion,
Strength, Beauty, and Five-Wits, who direct him to receive
the sacrament of Extreme Unction.*]

    KNOWLEDGE: Everyman, hearken what I say;
Go to priesthood, I you advise,
And receive of him in any wise
The holy sacrament and ointment together;
Then shortly see ye turn again hither;
We will all abide you here.
    FIVE-WITS: Yea, Everyman, hie[32] you that ye ready were,
There is no emperor, king, duke, ne baron,
That of God hath commission,
As hath the least priest in the world being;   530
For of the blessed sacraments pure and benign,
He beareth the keys and thereof hath the cure
For man's redemption, it is ever sure;
Which God for our soul's medicine
Gave us out of his heart with great pine;[33]
Here in this transitory life, for thee and me
The blessed sacraments seven there be.
Baptism, confirmation, with priesthood good,
And the sacrament of God's precious flesh and blood,
Marriage, the holy extreme unction, and penance;   540
These seven be good to have in remembrance,
Gracious sacraments of high divinity.
    EVERYMAN: Fain would I receive that holy body

---

[23] Be in distress.
[24] Blame.
[25] Ruin.
[26] Shame.
[27] The Virgin Mary! (An interjection of surprise or agreement.)
[28] If you do as I advise.
[29] With.
[30] Be willing.
[31] Also.
[32] Hasten.
[33] Suffering.

And meekly to my ghostly father I will go.
    FIVE-WITS: Everyman, that is the best that ye can do:
God will you to salvation bring,
For priesthood exceedeth all other thing;
To us Holy Scripture they do teach,
And converteth man from sin heaven to reach;
God hath to them more power given,   550
Than to any angel that is in heaven;
With five words he may consecrate
God's body in flesh and blood to make,
And handleth his maker between his hands;
The priest bindeth and unbindeth all bands,
Both in earth and in heaven;
Thou ministers all the sacraments seven;
Though we kissed thy feet thou were worthy;
Thou art surgeon that cureth sin deadly:
No remedy we find under God   560
But all only priesthood.
Everyman, God gave priest that dignity,
And setteth them in his stead among us to be;
Thus be they above angels in degree.
    KNOWLEDGE: If priests be good it is so surely;
But when Jesus hanged on the cross with great smart
There he gave, out of his blessed heart,
The same sacrament in great torment:
He sold them not to us, that Lord Omnipotent.
Therefore Saint Peter the apostle doth say   570
That Jesu's curse hath all they
Which God their Savior do buy or sell,
Or they for any money do take or tell.
Sinful priests giveth the sinners example bad;
Their children sitteth by other men's fires, I have heard;
And some haunteth women's company,
With unclean life, as lusts of lechery:
These be with sin made blind.
    FIVE-WITS: I trust to God no such may we find;
Therefore let us priesthood honour,   580
And follow their doctrine for our souls' succour;
We be their sheep, and they shepherds be
By whom we all be kept in surety.
Peace, for yonder I see Everyman come,
Which hath made true satisfaction.
    GOOD-DEEDS: Methinketh it is he indeed.
    EVERYMAN: Now Jesu be our alder speed.[34]
I have received the sacrament for my redemption,
And then mine extreme unction:
Blessed be all they that counselled me to take it!   590
And now, friends, let us go without longer respite;
I thank God that ye have tarried so long.
Now set each of you on this rood[35] your hand,
And shortly follow me:
I go before, there I would be; God be our guide.

[*All but Good-Deeds then abandon Everyman.*]

    EVERYMAN: Methinketh, alas, that I must be gone
To make my reckoning and my debts pay,
For I see my time is nigh spent away.
Take example, all ye that this do hear or see,

How they that I loved best do forsake me,   600
Except my Good-Deeds that bideth truly.
    GOOD-DEEDS: All earthly things is but vanity:
Beauty, Strength, and Discretion, do man forsake,
Foolish friends and kinsmen, that fair spake,
All fleeth save Good-Deeds, and that am I.
    EVERYMAN: Have mercy on me, God most mighty;
And stand by me, thou Mother and Maid, holy Mary.
    GOOD-DEEDS: Fear not, I will speak for thee.
    EVERYMAN: Here I cry God mercy.
    GOOD-DEEDS: Short our end, and minish our pain;   610
Let us go and never come again.
    EVERYMAN: Into thy hands, Lord, my soul I commend;
Receive it, Lord, that it be not lost;
As thou me boughtest, so me defend,
And save me from the fiend's boast,
That I may appear with that blessed host
That shall be saved at the day of doom.
In mannus tuas – of might's most
For ever – *commendo spiritum meum.*[36]
    KNOWLEDGE: Now hath he suffered that we all shall   620
    endure:
The Good-Deeds shall make all sure.
Now hath he made ending;
Methinketh that I hear angels sing
And make great joy and melody,
Where Everyman's soul received shall be.
    ANGEL: Come, excellent elect spouse to Jesu:[37]
Hereabove thou shalt go
Because of thy singular virtue:
Now the soul is taken the body fro;
Thy reckoning is crystal-clear.   630
Now shalt thou into the heavenly sphere,
Unto the which all ye shall come
That liveth well before the day of doom.
    DOCTOR: This moral men may have in mind;
Ye hearers, take it of worth, old and young,
And forsake pride, for he deceiveth you in the end,
And remember Beauty, Five-Wits, Strength, and
    Discretion,
They all at the last do Everyman forsake,
Save his Good-Deeds, there doth he take.
But beware, and they be small   640
Before God, he hath not help at all.
None excuse may be there for Everyman:
Alas, how shall he do then?
For after death amends may no man make,
For then mercy and pity do him forsake.
If his reckoning be not clear when he do come,
God will say – *ite maledicti in ignem aeternum.*[38]
And he that hath his account whole and sound,
High in heaven he shall be crowned;
Unto which place God brings us all thither   650
That we may live body and soul together.
Thereto help the Trinity,
Amen, say ye, for saint Charity
THUS ENDETH THIS MORALL PLAY OF EVERYMAN.

———————◆———————

---

[34] Speed in help of all.
[35] Cross.

[36] Into your hands I commend my spirit.
[37] Bride of Christ, a term symbolizing the soul's union with God.
[38] Be damned to the eternal fire.

Dante's Divine Comedy

The medieval view of life on earth as a vale of tears was balanced by the triumphant belief in the divine promise of deliverance and eternal bliss. By far the most profound and imaginative statement of these ideas is the epic poem known as the *Commedia Divina* or *Divine Comedy*. Begun in the year 1312 by the Florentine poet Dante Alighieri (1265–1321), it records, on the literal level, the poet's adventure-packed journey through the realm of the dead (Figure 12.3). On a symbolic level, the poem describes the spiritual pilgrimage of the Christian soul from sin (Hell), through purification (Purgatory), to salvation (Paradise) (Figure 12.4). The *Divine Comedy* sums up the intellectual achievements of the Middle Ages: It brings to life with epic grandeur both the Christian immortality ideology and the medieval perception of nature as the mirror of God's plan.

Every aspect of Dante's *Commedia* carries symbolic meaning. For instance, Dante is accompanied through Hell by the Roman poet Virgil, who stands for human reason. Dante deeply admired Virgil's epic poem, the *Aeneid*, and was familiar with the hero's journey to the underworld included in the sixth book of the poem. As Dante's guide, Virgil may travel only as far as the top of Mount Purgatory, for while human reason serves as the pilgrim's initial guide to salvation, it cannot penetrate the divine mysteries of the Christian faith. In Paradise, Dante is escorted by Beatrice, the symbol of Divine Wisdom, modeled on a Florentine woman who had been, throughout the poet's life, the object of his devotion. Dante structured the *Commedia* according to a strict moral hierarchy. The three parts of the poem correspond to the Aristotelian divisions of the human psyche: reason, will, and love. They also represent the potential moral conditions of the Christian soul: perversity, repentance, and grace.

Sacred numerology – especially the number 3, symbolic of the Trinity – permeates the design of the *Commedia*. The poem is divided into three canticles (books); each canticle has thirty-three **cantos**, to which Dante added one introductory canto to total a sublime one hundred (the number symbolizing plenitude and perfection); and each canto consists of stanzas composed in *terza rima*, that is, interlocking lines that rhyme as follows: a/b/a, b/c/b, c/d/c, and so on. There are three guides to escort Dante, three divisions of Hell and Purgatory, three main rivers in Hell, and so on. Three squared (9) are the regions of sinners in the Inferno, the circles of penitents in Purgatory, and the spheres of Heaven. The elaborate numerology of the *Commedia* is matched by a multileveled symbolism that draws into

Figure 12.3 Domenico di Michelino, *Dante and His Poem*, 1465. Fresco in Florence Cathedral, Italy. Dante, with an open copy of the *Comedy*, points to Hell with his right hand. The mount of Purgatory with its seven terraces is behind him. Florence's cathedral (with its newly finished dome) represents Paradise on the poet's left. Alinari/Art Resource, New York.

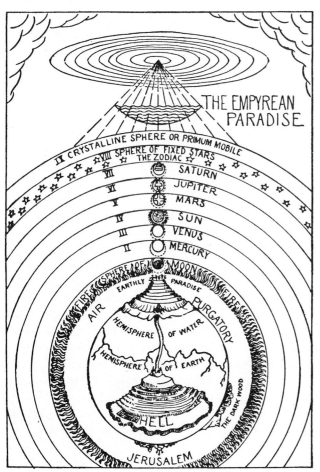

Figure 12.4 Plan of Dante's Universe.

with joy (Heaven). Later admirers added the adjective "divine" to the title, not simply to describe its religious character, but also in praise of the music of its lyrics and the artistry of its composition.

The most lively of the canticles, and the one that best manifests Dante's talent for creating realistic images with words, is the Inferno, the first book of the *Commedia*. With grim moral logic, the sinners are each assigned to one of the nine rings in Hell (Figure **12.5**), where they are punished according to the nature of their sins: The violent are immersed for eternity in boiling blood and the gluttons wallow like pigs in their own excrement. By the law of symbolic retribution, the sinners are punished not *for* but *by* their sins. Those condemned for sins of passion – the least grave of sins – inhabit the conical rings at the top of Hell, while those who have committed sins of the will lie farther down. Those guilty of sins of the intellect are imprisoned still lower, deep within the pit ruled by Satan (Figure **12.6**).

Figure 12.5 Plan of Dante's Inferno.

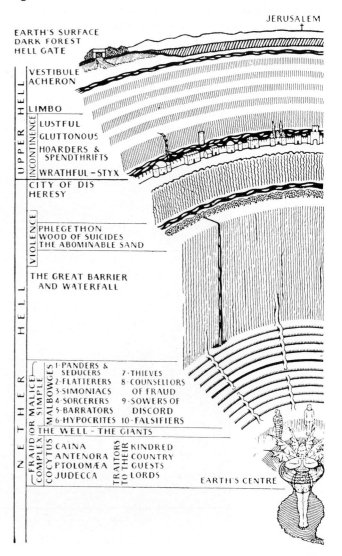

relationship theological, scientific, and historical information based in ancient and medieval sources. Given this wealth of symbolism, it is remarkable that the language of the poem is so sharply realistic. And while the characters in the *Commedia*, like those in *Everyman*, serve an allegorical function, they are, at the same time, convincing flesh-and-blood creatures. Dante employs real people, some drawn from history and legend, others drawn from his own era – the inhabitants of the bustling urban centers of Italy through which Dante had wandered for nineteen years after being exiled for political reasons from his native Florence. By giving the poem a realistic, literal level and an allegorical level, Dante aims to show that though the poem is set in the next world, it has a significance in this world.

Well versed in both classical and Christian literature, Dante had written Latin treatises on political theory and on the origins and development of language. But for the poem that constituted his epic masterpiece, he rejected the Latin of churchmen and scholars and wrote in his native Italian, the language of everyday speech. Dante called his poem a comedy because the piece begins with affliction (Hell) and ends

Figure 12.6 Satan eating and excreting the souls of the damned in Hell. Louvre, Paris. Photo: Roger Viollet, Paris.

Thus, Dante's Hell proclaims a moral hierarchy and a divinely graded system in which the damned assume their proper destiny.

In the last canto of the Inferno, Dante describes the ninth circle of Hell, the very bottom of the infernal pit. Lodged in ice up to his chest, a three-faced Satan beats his six batlike wings to create a chilling wind – the setting provides sharp contrast with the flaming regions of Upper Hell. Surrounding Satan, whom Dante calls "the Emperor of the Universe of Pain," those guilty of treachery – the most foul of all sins, according to Dante – are imprisoned in the ice, "like straws in glass." Satan, weeping tears "mixed with bloody froth and pus," chews with "rake-like teeth" on the bodies of the three most infamous traitors of Christian and classical history respectively: Judas, Brutus, and Cassius. The mood of darkness and brooding despair that pervades the Inferno reflects the medieval view of Hell as a condition of the soul farthest from the light of God. Neverthe- less, the last canto of the Inferno ends with Dante and Virgil climbing from the frozen pit "into the shining world," a motif of ascent that pervades the second and third canticles.

Satan's domain stands in grim contrast with the blissful and brilliant experience of God enjoyed by those in Paradise. Light, the least material of natural elements, is a prime image in Dante's evocation of Heaven, and light imagery – as central to the *Commedia* as it is to Saint Ambrose's hymn (see chapter 9) – pervades Dante's vision of God's mystery and majesty. The last eight stanzas of Canto 33 of Paradise (reproduced here) are the culminating phase of that vision. In the perfect shape of the circle, as in a cathedral rose window, Dante sees the image of humankind absorbed into the sub- stance of God. And as that wheel of love turns, the poet discovers the redemptive radiance of God.

It is impossible to recreate the grandeur of the *Commedia* by means of a single (or even a few) cantos, especially since, translated into English, a great deal of the richness of the original Tuscan dialect is lost. Nevertheless, some of the majesty of Dante's poem may be conveyed by the excerpts reproduced herein.

READING 47

From Dante's *Divine Comedy*

The Dark Wood of Error (*Inferno*, Canto 1)

Midway in our life's journey, I went astray
    from the straight road and woke to find myself
    alone in a dark wood. How shall I say   3

what wood that was! I never saw so drear,
    so rank, so arduous a wilderness!
    Its very memory gives a shape to fear.   6

Death could scarce be more bitter than that place!
    But since it came to good, I will recount
    all that I found revealed there by God's grace.   9

How I came to it I cannot rightly say,
    so drugged and loose with sleep had I become
    when I first wandered there from the True Way.   12

But at the far end of the valley of evil
    whose maze had sapped my very heart with fear!
    I found myself before a little hill   15

and lifted up my eyes. Its shoulders glowed
    already with the sweet rays of that planet
    whose virtue leads men straight on every road,   18

and the shining strengthened me against the fright
    whose agony had wracked the lake of my heart
    through all the terrors of that piteous night.   21

Just as a swimmer, who with his last breath
    flounders ashore from perilous seas, might turn
    to memorize the wide water of his death —   24

so did I turn, my soul still fugitive
    from death's surviving image, to stare down
    that pass that none had ever left alive.   27

And there I lay to rest from my heart's race
    till calm and breath returned to me. Then rose
    and pushed up that dead slope at such a pace   30

each footfall rose above the last. And lo!
    almost at the beginning of the rise
    I faced a spotted Leopard, all tremor and flow   33

and gaudy pelt. And it would not pass, but stood
    so blocking my every turn that time and again
    I was on the verge of turning back to the wood.   36

This fell at the first widening of the dawn
    as the sun was climbing Aries with those stars
    that rode with him to light the new creation.   39

Thus the holy hour and the sweet season
    of commemoration did much to arm my fear
    of that bright murderous beast with their good omen.   42

Yet not so much but what I shook with dread
    at sight of a great Lion that broke upon me
    raging with hunger, its enormous head   45

held high as if to strike a mortal terror
    into the very air. And down his track,
    a She-Wolf drove upon me, a starved horror   48

ravening and wasted beyond all belief.
    She seemed a rack for avarice, gaunt and craving.
    Oh many the souls she has brought to endless grief!   51

She brought such heaviness upon my spirit
    at sight of her savagery and desperation,
    I died from every hope of that high summit.   54

And like a miser — eager in acquisition
    but desperate in self-reproach when Fortune's wheel
    turns to the hour of his loss — all tears and attrition   57

I wavered back; and still the beast pursued,
    forcing herself against me bit by bit
    till I slid back into the sunless wood.   60

And as I fell to my soul's ruin, a presence
    gathered before me on the discolored air,
    the figure of one who seemed hoarse from long silence.   63

At sight of him in that friendless waste I cried:
    "Have pity on me, whatever thing you are,
    whether shade or living man." And it replied: 66

"Not man, though man I once was, and my blood
    was Lombard, both my parents Mantuan.
    I was born, though late, *sub Julio*, and bred   69

in Rome under Augustus in the noon
    of the false and lying gods. I was a poet
    and sang of old Anchises' noble son   72

who came to Rome after the burning of Troy.
    But you — why do *you* return to these distresses
    instead of climbing that shining Mount of Joy   75

which is the seat and first cause of man's bliss?"
    "And are you then that Virgil and that fountain
    of purest speech?" My voice grew tremulous: 78

"Glory and light of poets! now may that zeal
    and love's apprenticeship that I poured out
    on your heroic verses serve me well!   81

For you are my true master and first author,
    the sole maker from whom I drew the breath
    of that sweet style whose measures have brought me
        honor.   84

See there, immortal sage, the beast I flee.
    For my soul's salvation, I beg you, guard me from her,
    for she has struck a mortal tremor through me."   87

And he replied, seeing my soul in tears:
    "He must go by another way who would escape
    this wilderness, for that mad beast that fleers   90

before you there, suffers no man to pass.
    She tracks down all, kills all, and knows no glut,
    but, feeding, she grows hungrier than she was.   93

She mates with any beast, and will mate with more
    before the Greyhound comes to hunt her down.
    He will not feed on lands nor loot, but honor   96

and love and wisdom will make straight his way.
    He will rise between Feltro and Feltro, and in him
    shall be the resurrection and new day   99

of that sad Italy for which Nisus died,
  and Turnus, and Euryalus, and the maid Camilla.
  He shall hunt her through every nation of sick pride   102

till she is driven back forever to Hell
  whence Envy first released her on the world.
  Therefore, for your own good, I think it well   105

you follow me and I will be your guide
  and lead you forth through an eternal place.
  There you shall see the ancient spirits tried   108

in endless pain, and hear their lamentation
  as each bemoans the second death of souls.
  Next you shall see upon a burning mountain   111

souls in fire and yet content in fire,
  knowing that whensoever it may be
  they yet will mount into the blessed choir.   114

To which, if it is still your wish to climb,
  a worthier spirit shall be sent to guide you.
  With her shall I leave you, for the King of Time,   117

who reigns on high, forbids me to come there
  since, living, I rebelled against his law.
  He rules the waters and the land and air   120

and there holds court, his city and his throne.
  Oh blessed are they he chooses!" And I to him:
  "Poet, by that God to you unknown,   123

lead me this way. Beyond this present ill
  and worse to dread, lead me to Peter's gate
  and be my guide through the sad halls of Hell."   126

And he then: "Follow." And he moved ahead
in silence, and I followed where he led.

Notes to *Inferno* (Canto 1)

line 1 *midway in our life's journey:* The biblical life span is three-score years and ten. The action opens in Dante's thirty-fifth year, i.e., 1300 c.e.

line 17 *that planet:* The sun. Ptolemaic astronomers considered it a planet. It is also symbolic of God as He who lights man's way.

line 31 *each footfall rose above the last:* The literal rendering would be: "So that the fixed foot was ever the lower." "Fixed" has often been translated "right" and an ingenious reasoning can support that reading, but a simpler explanation offers itself and seems more competent: Dante is saying that he climbed with such zeal and haste that every footfall carried him above the last despite the steepness of the climb. At a slow pace, on the other hand, the rear foot might be brought up only as far as the forward foot. This device of selecting a minute but exactly-centered detail to convey the whole of a larger action is one of the central characteristics of Dante's style.
The Three Beasts: These three beasts undoubtedly are taken from *Jeremiah* v, 6. Many additional and incidental interpretations have been advanced for them, but the central interpretation must remain as noted. They foreshadow the three divisions of Hell (incontinence, violence, and fraud) which Virgil explains at length in Canto XI, 16–111. I am not at all sure but what the She-Wolf is better interpreted as Fraud and the Leopard as Incontinence. Good arguments can be offered either way.

line 38–9 *Aries . . . that rode with him to light the new creation:* The medieval tradition had it that the sun was in Aries at the time of the Creation. The significance of the astronomical and religious conjunction is an important part of Dante's intended allegory. It is just before dawn of Good Friday 1300 c.e. when he awakens in the Dark Wood. Thus his new life begins under Aries, the sign of creation, at dawn (rebirth) and in the Easter season (resurrection). Moreover the moon is full and the sun is in the equinox, conditions that did not fall together on any Friday of 1300. Dante is obviously constructing poetically the perfect Easter as a symbol of his new awakening.

line 69 *sub Julio:* In the reign of Julius Ceasar.

line 95 *The Greyhound . . . Feltro and Feltro:* Almost certainly refers to Can Grande della Scala (1290–1329), great Italian leader born in Verona, which lies between the towns of Feltre and Montefeltro.

line 100–101 *Nisus, Turnus, Euryalus, Camilla:* All were killed in the war between the Trojans and the Latians when, according to legend, Aeneas led the survivors of Troy into Italy. Nisus and Euryalus (*Aeneid* IX) were Trojan comrades-in-arms who died together. Camilla (*Aeneid* XI) was the daughter of the Latian king and one of the warrior women. She was killed in a horse charge against the Trojans after displaying great gallantry. Turnus (*Aeneid* XII) was killed by Aeneas in a duel.

line 110 *the second death:* Damnation. "This is the second death, even the lake of fire." (*Revelation* xx, 14)

line 118 *forbids me to come there since, living, etc.:* Salvation is only through Christ in Dante's theology. Virgil lived and died before the establishment of Christ's teachings in Rome, and cannot therefore enter Heaven.

line 125 *Peter's gate:* The gate of Purgatory. (See *Purgatorio* IX, 76 ff.) The gate is guarded by an angel with a gleaming sword. The angel is Peter's vicar (Peter, the first Pope, symbolized all Popes; i.e., Christ's vicar on earth) and is entrusted with the two great keys.

Some commentators argue that this is the gate of Paradise, but Dante mentions no gate beyond this one in his ascent to Heaven. It should be remembered, too, that those who pass the gate of Purgatory have effectively entered Heaven.

The three great gates that figure in the entire journey are: the gate of Hell (Canto III, 1–11), the gate of Dis (Canto VIII, 79–113, and Canto IX, 86–87), and the gate of Purgatory, as above.

The Ninth Circle of Hell (*Inferno*, Canto 34)

"On march the banners of the King of Hell,"
  my Master said. "Toward us. Look straight ahead:
  can you make him out at the core of the frozen shell?"   3

Like a whirling windmill seen afar at twilight,
  or when a mist has risen from the ground —
  just such an engine rose upon my sight   6

stirring up such a wild and bitter wind
  I cowered for shelter at my Master's back
  there being no other windbreak I could find.   9

I stood now where the souls of the last class
  (with fear my verses tell it) were covered wholly:
  they shone below the ice like straws in glass.   12

Some lie stretched out; others are fixed in place
  upright, some on their heads, some on their
  soles; another, like a bow, bends foot to face.   15

When we had gone so far across the ice
  that it pleased my Guide to show me the foul creature
  which once had worn the grace of Paradise,   18

he made me stop, and, stepping aside, he said:
  "Now see the face of Dis! This is the place
  where you must arm your soul against all dread."   21

Do not ask, Reader, how my blood ran cold
  and my voice choked up with fear. I cannot write it:
  this is a terror that cannot be told.   24

I did not die, and yet I lost life's breath:
  imagine for yourself what I became,
  deprived at once of both my life and death.   27

The Emperor of the Universe of Pain
    jutted his upper chest above the ice;
    and I am closer in size to the great mountain   30

the Titans make around the central pit,
    than they to his arms. Now starting from this part,
    imagine the whole that corresponds to it.   33

If he was once as beautiful as now
    he is hideous, and still turned on his Maker,
    well may he be the source of every woe!   36

With what a sense of awe I saw his head
    towering above me! for it had three faces:
    one was in front, and it was fiery red,   39

the other two, as weirdly wonderful,
    merged with it from the middle of each shoulder
    to the point where all converged at the top of the skull;   42

the right was something between white and bile;
    the left was about the color that one finds
    on those who live along the banks of the Nile.   45

Under each head two wings rose terribly,
    their span proportioned to so gross a bird:
    I never saw such sails upon the sea.   48

They were not feathers — their texture and their form
    were like a bat's wings — and he beat them so
    that three winds blew from him in one great storm: 51

it is these winds that freeze all Cocytus.
    He wept from his six eyes, and down three chins
    the tears ran mixed with bloody froth and pus.   54

In every mouth he worked a broken sinner
    between his rake-like teeth. Thus he kept three
    in eternal pain at his eternal dinner.   57

For the one in front the biting seemed to play
    no part at all compared to the ripping: at times
    the whole skin of his back was flayed away.   60

"That soul that suffers most," explained the Guide,
    "is Judas Iscariot, he who kicks his legs
    on the fiery chin and has his head inside.   63

Of the other two, who have their heads thrust forward
    the one who dangles down from the black face
    is Brutus: note how he writhes without a word.   66

And there, with the huge sinewy arms, is the soul
    of Cassius. But the night is coming on
    and we must go, for we have seen the whole."   69

Then, as he bade, I clasped his neck, and he,
    watching for a moment when the wings
    were opened wide, reached over dexterously   72

and seized the shaggy coat of the king demon;
    then grappling matted hair and frozen crusts
    from one tuft to another, clambered down.   75

When we had reached the joint where the great thigh
    merges into the swelling of the haunch,
    my Guide and Master, straining terribly,   78

turned his head to where his feet had been
    and began to grip the hair as if he were climbing;
    so that I thought we moved toward Hell again.   81

"Hold fast!" my Guide said, and his breath came shrill
    with labor and exhaustion. "There is no way
    but by such stairs to rise above such evil."   84

At last he climbed out through an opening
    in the central rock, and he seated me on the rim;
    then joined me with a nimble backward spring.   87

I looked up, thinking to see Lucifer
    as I had left him, and I saw instead
    his legs projecting high into the air.   90

Now let all those whose dull minds are still vexed
    by failure to understand what point it was
    I had passed through, judge if I was perplexed.   93

"Get up. Up on your feet," my Master said.
    "The sun already mounts to middle tierce,
    and a long road and hard climbing lie ahead."   96

It was no hall of state we had found there,
    but a natural animal pit hollowed from rock
    with a broken floor and a close and sunless air.   99

"Before I tear myself from the Abyss,"
    I said when I had risen, "O my Master,
    explain to me my error in all this: 102

where is the ice? and Lucifer — how has he
    been turned from top to bottom: and how can the sun
    have gone from night to day so suddenly?"   105

And he to me: "You imagine you are still
    on the other side of the center where I grasped
    the shaggy flank of the Great Worm of Evil   108

which bores through the world — you *were* while I climbed down,
    but when I turned myself about, you passed
    the point to which all gravities are drawn.   111

You are under the other hemisphere where you stand;
    the sky above us is the half opposed
    to that which canopies the great dry land.   114

Under the mid-point of that other sky
    the Man who was born sinless and who lived
    beyond all blemish, came to suffer and die.   117

You have your feet upon a little sphere
    which forms the other face of the Judecca.
    There it is evening when it is morning here.   120

And this gross Fiend and Image of all Evil
    who made a stairway for us with his hide
    is pinched and prisoned in the ice-pack still.   123

On this side he plunged down from heaven's height,
    and the land that spread here once hid in the sea
    and fled North to our hemisphere for fright;   126

and it may be that moved by that same fear,
    the one peak that still rises on this side
    fled upward leaving this great cavern here."   129

Down there, beginning at the further bound
    of Beelzebub's dim tomb, there is a space
    not known by sight, but only by the sound   132

of a little stream descending through the hollow
    it has eroded from the massive stone
    in its endlessly entwining lazy flow.   135

My Guide and I crossed over and began
    to mount that little known and lightless road
    to ascend into the shining world again.   138

He first, I second, without thought of rest
    we climbed the dark until we reached the point
    where a round opening brought in sight the blest   141

and beauteous shining of the Heavenly cars.
And we walked out once more beneath the Stars.

Notes to *Inferno* (Canto 34)

line 1 *On march the banners of the King:* The hymn (*Vexilla regis prodeunt*) was written in the sixth century by Venantius Fortunatus, Bishop of Poitiers. The original celebrates the Holy Cross, and is part of the service for Good Friday to be sung at the moment of uncovering the cross.

line 17 *the foul creature:* Satan.

line 38 *three faces:* Numerous interpretations of these three faces exist. What is essential to all explanation is that they be seen as perversions of the qualities of the Trinity.

line 54 *bloody froth and pus:* The gore of the sinners he chews which is mixed with his slaver.

line 62 *Judas:* Note how closely his punishment is patterned on that of the Simoniacs (Canto XIX).

line 67 *huge and sinewy arms:* The Cassius who betrayed Caesar was more generally described in terms of Shakespeare's "lean and hungry look." Another Cassius is described by Cicero (*Catiline* III) as huge and sinewy. Dante probably confused the two.

line 68 *the night is coming on:* It is now Saturday evening.

line 82 *his breath came shrill:* CF. Canto XXIII, 85, where the fact that Dante breathes indicates to the Hypocrites that he is alive. Virgil's breathing is certainly a contradiction.

line 95 *middle tierce:* In the canonical day tierce is the period from about six to nine A.M. Middle tierce, therefore, is seven-thirty. In going through the center point, they have gone from night to day. They have moved ahead twelve hours.

line 128 *the one peak:* The Mount of Purgatory.

line 129 *this great cavern:* The natural animal pit of line 98. It is also "Beelzebub's dim tomb," line 131.

line 133 *a little stream:* Lethe. In classical mythology, the river of forgetfulness, from which souls drank before being born. In Dante's symbolism it flows down from Purgatory, where it has washed away the memory of sin from the souls who are undergoing purification. That memory it delivers to Hell, which draws all sin to itself.

line 143 *Stars:* As part of his total symbolism Dante ends each of the three divisions of the *Commedia* with this word. Every conclusion of the upward soul is toward the stars, God's shining symbols of hope and virtue. It is just before dawn of Easter Sunday that the Poets emerge — a further symbolism.

From The Vision of God (*Paradise*, Canto 33)

O Light Eternal fixed in Itself alone,
    by Itself alone understood, which from Itself
    loves and glows, self-knowing and self-known;   126

that second aureole which shone forth in Thee,
    conceived as a reflection of the first —
    or which appeared so to my scrutiny —   129

seemed in Itself of Its own coloration
    to be painted with man's image. I fixed my eyes
    on that alone in rapturous contemplation.   132

Like a geometer wholly dedicated
    to squaring the circle, but who cannot find,
    think as he may, the principle indicated —   135

so did I study the supernal face.
    I yearned to know just how our image merges
    into that circle, and how it there finds place;   138

but mine were not the wings for such a flight.
    Yet, as I wished, the truth I wished for came
    cleaving my mind in a great flash of light.   141

Here my powers rest from their high fantasy,
    but already I could feel my being turned —
    instinct and intellect balanced equally   144

as in a wheel whose motion nothing jars —
by the Love that moves the Sun and the other stars.

Notes to *Paradise* (Canto 33)

lines 130–144 *seemed in Itself of Its own coloration . . . instinct and intellect balanced equally.* The central metaphor of the entire *Comedy* is the image of God and the final triumphant in Godding of the elected soul returning to its Maker. On the mystery of that image, the metaphoric symphony of the *Comedy* comes to rest.

In the second aspect of Trinal-unity, in the circle reflected from the first, Dante thinks he sees the image of mankind woven into the very substance and coloration of God. He turns the entire attention of his soul to that mystery, as a geometer might seek to shut out every other thought and dedicate himself to squaring the circle. In *Il Convivio* II, 14, Dante asserted that the circle could not be squared, but that impossibility had not yet been firmly demonstrated in Dante's time and mathematicians still worked at the problem. Note, however, that Dante assumes the impossibility of squaring the circle as a weak mortal example of mortal impossibility. How much more impossible, he implies, to resolve the mystery of God, study as man will.

The mystery remains beyond Dante's mortal power. Yet, there in Heaven, in a moment of grace, God revealed the truth to him in a flash of light — revealed it, that is, to the God-enlarged power of Dante's emparadised soul. On Dante's return to the mortal life, the details of that revelation vanished from his mind but the force of the revelation survives in its power on Dante's feelings.

So ends the vision of the *Comedy* and yet the vision endures, for ever since that revelation, Dante tells us, he feels his soul turning ever as one with the perfect motion of God's love.

---◆---

The Power and Prestige of the Medieval Church

During the High Middle Ages, the Catholic Church exercised great power and authority not only as a religious force, but also as a political institution. The papacy took strong measures to ensure the independence of the Church from secular interference, especially that of the emerging European states. In 1022, for instance, the Church formed the College of Cardinals as the sole agency responsible for the election of popes. Medieval pontiffs functioned much like secular monarchs, governing a huge and complex bureaucracy that incorporated financial, judicial, and disciplinary branches. The Curia, the papal council and highest church court, headed a vast network of ecclesiastical courts, while the Camera (the papal treasury) handled financial matters. The Church was enormously wealthy in the medieval period. Over the centuries, Christians had donated and bequeathed to Christendom so many thousands of acres of land that by the end of the twelfth century, the Catholic Church was the largest single landholder in Western Europe.

Among lay Christians of every rank the Church commanded religious obedience. It enforced religious conformity by means of such spiritual penalties as **excommunication** (exclusion from the sacraments) and **interdict**, the excommunication of an entire city or state – used to dissuade secular rulers from opposing papal policy. In spite of these spiritual weapons, **heresy** (the denial of the revealed truths of the Christian faith) spread rapidly within the increasingly cosmopolitan centers of twelfth-century Europe. Such anticlerical groups as the Waldensians, followers of the French thirteenth-century reformer Peter Waldo, denounced the growing worldliness of the Church. Waldo proposed that lay Christians administer the sacraments and that the Bible – sole source of religious authority – should be translated into the vernacular.

Condemning such views as threats to civil and religious order, the Church launched antiheretical crusades that were almost as violent as those advanced against the Muslims. Further, in 1233, the pope established the Inquisition, a special court designed to stamp our heresy. The Inquisition brought to trial those individuals whom local townspeople denounced as heretics. The accused were deprived of legal counsel and were usually tried in secret. Inquisitors might use physical torture to obtain confession, for the Church considered injury to the body preferable to the eternal damnation of the soul. If the Inquisition failed to restore accused heretics to the faith, it might impose such penalties as exile or excommunication, or, it might turn over the defendants to the state to be hanged or burned at the stake – the preferred punishment for female heretics. With the same energy that the Church persecuted heretics, it acted as a civilizing agent. It preserved order by enforcing periods in which warfare was prohibited. It assumed moral and financial responsibility for the poor, the sick, and the homeless; and it provided for the organization of hospitals, refuges, orphanages, and other charitable institutions.

The power and prestige of the Church was enhanced by the outstanding talents of some popes as diplomats, canon lawyers, and administrators. Under the leadership of the lawyer/pope Innocent III, the papacy emerged as the most powerful political institution in Western Europe. Pope Innocent enlarged the body of canon law and refined the bureaucratic machinery of the Church. He used his authority to influence secular rulers and frequently intervened in the political, financial, and personal affairs of heads of state. At the Fourth Lateran Council (1215), he endorsed the establishment of the Franciscans, a monastic order that would revive the humane candor and devotional simplicity of the Sermon on the Mount.

The Franciscans followed the example of one of the most remarkable personalities of the Middle Ages: Francis of Assisi (ca. 1181–1226). The son of a wealthy Italian cloth merchant, Francis renounced worldly comforts and dedicated himself to a life of preaching and service to the poor. In imitation of the apostles, he practiced absolute poverty and begged for his food and lodging as he traveled from town to town. His affection for all forms of life inspired a wave of humanitarianism that swept through late thirteenth-century music and the visual arts (Figure **12.7**). During the same century, the followers of the well-educated Spanish priest Saint Dominic (ca. 1170–1221) founded a second mendicant ("begging") order. Deeply committed to the study of theology, the Dominicans educated many renowned preachers and scholars, including Thomas Aquinas, discussed later in this chapter. The Franciscan and Dominican friars ("brothers") and their female counterparts, the Poor Clares and the Dominican nuns, earned long-lasting respect and acclaim for educating the young, fighting heresy, and ministering to the sick and needy (Figure **12.8**).

Figure 12.7 Giotto, *Sermon to the Birds*, ca. 1290. Fresco in the Upper Church, Assisi, Italy. Alinari/Art Resource, New York.

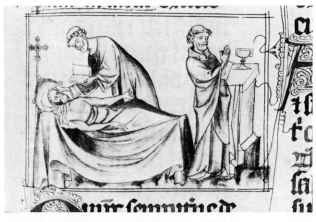

Figure 12.8 *Mass for one who is close to death*. Franciscan Missal, French, early fourteenth century. Bodleian Library, Oxford, MS Douce 313, f. 39S.

The Conflict Between Church and State

As secular rulers grew in power among the burgeoning nation-states of medieval Europe, the early medieval alliance between church and state deteriorated. The attempts of kings and emperors to win the allegiance of their subjects — especially those in the newly formed towns — and to enlarge their financial resources often interfered with papal ambitions and church decree. When, for example, King Philip IV ("the Fair") of France (1268–1314) attempted to tax the clergy as citizens of the French realm, Pope Boniface VIII (ca. 1234–1302) protested, threatening to excommunicate and depose the king. In the dispute that followed, Pope Boniface issued the edict *Unam Sanctum* ("One [and] Holy [Church]"), the boldest assertion of spiritual authority ever published. The edict rested upon the centuries-old papal claim that the Church held primacy over the state, since, while the Church governed the souls of all Christians, the state governed only their bodies. Although in the ensuing struggle between popes and kings, the latter emerged victorious, *Unam Sanctum* remained the classic justification for Church supremacy in both temporal and spiritual realms.

The Medieval University

Of the many lasting contributions of the Middle Ages to modern Western society — including trial by jury and the Catholic church itself — one of the most significant was the university. Education in medieval Europe was almost exclusively a religious enterprise, and monastic schools had monopolized learning for many centuries. By the twelfth century, however, spurred by the resurgence of economic activity and the rise of towns, education shifted from monastic and parish schools to cathedral schools located in the new urban centers of Western Europe. Growing out of these schools, groups of students and teachers formed guilds for higher learning; the Latin word *universitas* describes a guild of learners and teachers.

In medieval Europe, as in our own day, universities were arenas for intellectual inquiry and debate. At Bologna, Paris, Oxford, and Cambridge, to name but four among some eighty universities founded in the Middle Ages, the best minds of Europe grappled with the compelling ideas of their day, often testing those ideas against the teachings of the Church. The universities offered a basic liberal arts curriculum divided into two parts: the *trivium*, consisting of grammar, logic, and rhetoric; and the *quadrivium*, which included arithmetic, geometry, astronomy, and music. Programs in professional disciplines, such as medicine, theology, and law, were also available. Textbooks — that is, handwritten manuscripts — were expensive and difficult to obtain, therefore, teaching took the form of oral instruction, and students took copious notes based on class lectures (Figure 12.9). Exams for the bachelor of arts (B.A.) degree, usually taken upon completion of a three- to five-year course of study, were oral. Beyond the B.A. degree, one might pursue additional study leading to mastery of a specialized field. The master of arts (M.A.) degree qualified the student to teach theology or practice law or medicine. Still another four years of study were usually required for the doctoral candidate, whose efforts culminated in his defense of a thesis before a board of learned masters. (Tradition required the successful candidate to honor his examiners with a banquet.)

Among the first universities was the university founded at Bologna in northern Italy in 1159. Bologna was a center for the study of law. Its curriculum was run by students who hired professors to teach courses in law and other fields. University students brought pressure on townsfolk to maintain reasonable prices for food and lodging. They controlled the salaries and teaching schedules of their professors, requiring a teacher to obtain permission from his students for even a single day's absence and docking his "salary" if he was tardy. In contrast to the student-run university at Bologna, the university in Paris was a guild of teachers organized primarily for instruction in theology. This university, which grew out of the cathedral school of Notre Dame, became independent of church control by a royal charter issued in the year 1200. Its respected degree in theology drew an international student body that made Paris the intellectual melting pot of the medieval West.

Until the thirteenth century, men and women of the upper class received basically the same kinds of formal education. But with the rise of the university women were excluded from receiving a higher education, much the same as they were forbidden from

Figure 12.9 University Lecture from a medieval edition of Aristotle's *Ethics*, German, fourteenth century. Manuscript illumination. Staatliche Museum, Berlin.

entering the priesthood. Ranging between the ages of seventeen and forty, students often held minor orders in the Church, and the intellectual enterprise of the most famous of the theologically trained schoolmen or scholastics, as they came to be called, inspired an important movement in medieval intellectual life known as Scholasticism.

Medieval Scholasticism

Before the twelfth century, intellectuals (as well as ordinary men and women) considered Scripture and the writings of the church fathers the major repositories of knowledge. Faith in these established sources superseded any mode of rational inquiry and preempted the empirical examination of the physical world. Indeed, most intellectuals upheld the Augustinian credo that faith preceded reason. They maintained that since both

faith and reason derived from God, the two could never stand in contradiction. When, in the late twelfth century, Arabic copies of the writings of Aristotle filtered into the West from Muslim Spain and the Near East, along with Arab commentaries on Aristotle, a new intellectual challenge confronted churchmen and scholars. How were they to reconcile Aristotle's rational and dispassionate views of physical reality with the supernatural truths of the Christian faith? The Church's initial reaction was to ban Aristotle's works (with the exception of the *Logic*, which had long been available in the West), but by the early thirteenth century, all of the writings of the venerated Greek philosopher were in the hands of medieval schoolmen. For the next hundred years, these scholars engaged in an effort to reconcile the two primary modes of knowledge: faith and reason, the first as defended by theology, the second as exalted in Greek philosophy.

Even before the full body of Aristotle's works were available, a brilliant logician and popular teacher at the University of Paris, Peter Abelard (1079–1142), had inaugurated a rationalist approach to Church dogma. In his treatise *Sic et Non* (*Yes and No*), written several years before the high tide of Aristotelian influence, Abelard put into practice one of the principal devices of the scholastic method, that of balancing opposing points of view. *Sic et Non* presented 150 conflicting opinions on important religious matters from such sources as the Old Testament, the Greek philosophers, the Latin Fathers, and the decrees of the Church. Abelard's methodical compilation of Hebrew, classical, and Christian thought was an expression of the scholastic inclination to collect and reconcile vast amounts of information. This impulse toward synthesis – the combination of independent parts to form a coherent whole – also inspired the many *compendia* (collections), *specula* ("mirrors" of knowledge), and *summa* (comprehensive treatises) that were written during the twelfth and thirteenth centuries.

The greatest of the scholastics and the most influential teacher of his time was the Dominican theologian Thomas Aquinas (ca. 1225–1274). Aquinas lectured and wrote on a wide variety of theological and biblical subjects, but his major contribution was the *Summa Theologica*, a vast compendium of virtually all of the major theological issues of the High Middle Ages. In this unfinished work, which exceeded Abelard's *Sic et Non* in both size and conception, Aquinas posed 631 questions ranging from the nature of God to the ethics of money lending. The comprehensiveness of Aquinas' program is suggested by the following list of queries drawn arbitrarily from the *Summa*:

> Whether God exists
> Whether God is the highest good
> Whether God is infinite
> Whether God wills evil
> Whether there is a trinity in God
> Whether it belongs to God alone to create
> Whether good can be the cause of evil
> Whether angels assume bodies
> Whether woman should have been made in the first production of things
> Whether woman should have been made from man
> Whether the soul is composed of matter and form
> Whether man has free choice
> Whether paradise is a corporeal place
> Whether there is eternal law
> Whether man can merit eternal life without grace
> Whether it is lawful to sell a thing for more than it is worth

In dealing with each question, Aquinas followed Abelard's method of marshalling opinions that seemed to oppose or contradict each other. But where Abelard had merely mediated, Aquinas offered carefully reasoned answers; he brought to bear all the intellectual ammunition of his time in an effort to prove that the truths of reason (those proceeding from the senses and from the exercise of logic) were compatible with the truths of revelation (those that had been divinely revealed). Aquinas begins by posing an initial question – for instance, "Whether woman should have been made in the first production of things"; then he offers objections or negations of the proposition, followed by positive responses drawn from a variety of authoritative sources – mainly biblical and patristic writings. The exposition of these "seeming opposites" is followed by Aquinas' own opinion, a synthesis that invariably resolves the contradictions. Finally, Aquinas answers the original objections to the question, with a definitive, concluding statement.

In the following excerpt, Aquinas deals with the question of whether and to what purpose God created women, whom some medieval churchmen regarded as the "daughters of Eve" (see chapter 11) and hence the source of humankind's depravity. Following Aristotle, Aquinas concludes that though inferior to man in "the discernment of reason," woman was created as man's helpmate in reproducing the species. Even this brief examination of the *Summa Theologica* reveals its majestic intellectual sweep and its hierarchic rigor – two of the principal characteristics of medieval expression.

READING 48

From Aquinas' *Summa Theologica*

Whether Woman Should Have Been Made in the First Production of Things?
We proceed thus to the First Article:

Objection 1. It would seem that woman should not have been made in the first production of things. For the Philosopher[1] says that the *female is a misbegotten male*. But nothing misbegotten or defective should have been in the first production of things. Therefore woman should not have been made at that first production.

Objection 2. Further, subjection and limitation were a result of sin, for to the woman was it said after sin (*Gen.* iii. 16): *Thou shalt be under the man's power;* and Gregory[2] says that, *Where there is no sin, there is no inequality*. But woman is naturally of less strength and dignity than man, *for the agent is always more honorable than the patient*, as Augustine says. Therefore woman should not have been made in the first production of things before sin.

1

10

---

[1]Aristotle.
[2]Gregory the Great (chapter 9).

Objection 3. Further, occasions of sin should be cut off. But God foresaw that woman would be an occasion of sin to man. Therefore He should not have made woman.

On the contrary, It is written (*Gen.* ii. 18): *It is not good for man to be alone; let us make him a helper like to himself.*

I answer that, It was necessary for woman to be made, as the Scripture says, as a *helper* to man; not, indeed, as a helpmate in other works, as some say, since man can be more efficiently helped by another man in other works: but as a helper in the work of generation . . . . Among perfect animals, the active power of generation belongs to the male sex, and the passive power to the female. And as among animals there is a vital operation nobler than generation, to which their life is principally directed, so it happens that the male sex is not found in continual union with the female in perfect animals, but only at the time of coition; so that we may consider that by coition the male and female are one, as in plants they are always united, even though in some cases one of them preponderates, and in some the other. But man is further ordered to a still nobler work of life, and that is intellectual operation. Therefore there was greater reason for the distinction of these two powers in man; so that the female should be produced separately from the male, and yet that they should be carnally united for generation. Therefore directly after the formation of woman, it was said: *And they shall be two in one flesh* (*Gen.* ii. 24).

Reply Objection 1. As regards the individual nature, woman is defective and misbegotten, for the active power in the male seed tends to the production of a perfect likeness according to the masculine sex; while the production of woman comes from defect in the active power, or from some material indisposition, or even from some external influence, such as that of a south wind, which is moist, as the Philosopher observes. On the other hand, as regards universal human nature, woman is not misbegotten, but is included in nature's intention as directed to the work of generation. Now the universal intention of nature depends on God, Who is the universal Author of nature. Therefore, in producing nature, God formed not only the male but also the female.

Reply Objection 2. Subjection is twofold. One is servile, by virtue of which a superior makes use of a subject for his own benefit; and this kind of subjection began after sin. There is another kind of subjection, which is called economic or civil, whereby the superior makes use of his subjects for their own benefit and good; and this kind of subjection existed even before sin. For the good of order would have been wanting in the human family if some were not governed by others wiser than themselves. So by such a kind of subjection woman is naturally subject to man, because in man the discernment of reason predominates. Nor is inequality among men excluded by the state of innocence, as we shall prove.

Reply Objection 3. If God had deprived the world of all those things which proved an occasion of sin, the universe would have been imperfect. Nor was it fitting for the common good to be destroyed in order that individual evil might be avoided; especially as God is so powerful that He can direct any evil to a good end.

———————◆———————

The scholastics aimed at producing a synthesis of Christian and classical learning, but the motivation for and the substance of their efforts were still largely religious. Despite their attention to Aristotle's writings and their respect for his methods of inquiry, medieval scholastics created no system of knowledge that completely dispensed with supernatural assumptions of faith. Nevertheless, the scholastics were the humanists of the medieval world; they held that the human being, the noblest of God's creatures, was the link between the created universe and divine intelligence. They believed that human reason was the handmaiden of faith, and that reason – though incapable of transcending revelation – was humankind's noblest means of understanding God's divine plan.

SUMMARY

The Catholic Church was the dominant political, spiritual, and cultural force of the European Middle Ages. As spiritual caretaker of the Christian soul, the Church guided medieval men and women through the rites of passage in anticipation of personal immortality. The Christian immortality ideology taught that life on earth was woeful and transient and that, depending on their conduct on earth, Christian souls would reap reward or punishment in an eternal hereafter. These concepts dominated medieval literary and artistic expression.

Medieval sermons and morality plays warned Christians of the perpetual struggle between good and evil and reminded them of the need to prepare for death. As the allegorical play *Everyman* illustrates, the medieval mind interpreted reality in symbolic and hierarchic terms: Everything in God's universe held a predesigned place and the place of each was fixed and unchanging. The literary work that best reflects the spirit of the late Middle Ages is Dante's *Commedia,* an epic poem that offers a sublime moral and intellectual vision of the Christian universe.

Wealthy and powerful, the medieval Church governed vast lands, a complex bureaucracy, and a large body of secular and regular clergymen. By means of excommunication, interdict, and the Inquisition, the Church challenged the rising tide of heresy and enforced a climate of conformity and stability. And despite the challenge of increasingly powerful secular rulers among the European states, the Church maintained a position of political dominance in the West until the sixteenth century.

With the rise of universities in twelfth-century Bologna, Paris, and elsewhere, intellectual life flourished. Inspired by the writings of Aristotle, schoolmen tried to synthesize the fundamental precepts of Christianity with the teachings of the Greek and Arab philosophers. Abelard and Aquinas, both of whom taught at the University of Paris, were proponents of Scholasticism, an intellectual movement aimed at reconciling faith and reason. The scholastics considered the truths of reason subordinate to the truths of revelation. Among medieval schoolmen, as among less learned Christians, matters concerning the eternal destiny of the soul and the fulfillment of God's design took precedence over the pursuit of finite knowledge.

SUGGESTIONS FOR READING

Adams, Henry. *Mont-Saint-Michel and Chartres*. Garden City, N.Y.: Doubleday, 1959.

Daly, Lowrie J. *The Medieval University: 1200–1400*. New York: Sheed and Ward, 1961.

Duby, George. *The Age of the Cathedrals: Art and Society: 980–1420*, trans. E. Levieux and B. Thompson. Chicago: University of Chicago Press, 1981.

Heer, Frederick. *The Medieval World*. New York: New American Library, 1963.

LeGoff, Jacques. *The Medieval Imagination*, trans. A. Goldhammer. Chicago: University of Chicago Press, 1992.

Oakley, Francis. *The Medieval Experience: Foundations of Western Cultural Singularity*. New York: Scribner, 1974.

Rowling, Margorie. *Life in Medieval Times*. New York: Putnam's, 1968.

Sayers, Dorothy L. *Introductory Papers on Dante*. New York: Harper, 1954.

Vittorini, Domenico. *The Age of Dante*. New York: Citadel, 1964.

GLOSSARY

canto one of the main divisions of a long poem

excommunication ecclesiastical censure that excludes the individual from receiving the sacraments

grace the free, unearned favor of God

heresy the denial of the revealed truths or orthodox doctrine by a baptized member of the Church; an opinion or doctrine contrary to church dogma

interdict the excommunication of an entire city, district, or state

memento mori (Latin, "remember death") a warning of the nearness of death and the need to prepare for one's own death

miracle play a type of medieval play that dramatized the lives and especially the miracles performed by Christ, the Virgin Mary, or the saints

morality play a type of medieval play that dramatized moral themes, such as the conflict between good and evil

mystery play a type of medieval play originating in church liturgy and dramatizing biblical history from the fall of Satan to the Last Judgment

pageant a roofed wagon-stage on which medieval plays and spectacles were performed

sacrament a sacred act or pledge; in Christianity, a visible sign instituted by Jesus Christ to confer grace

13

The Medieval Synthesis
in the Arts

If the Catholic Church was the major source of moral and spiritual instruction in the West, it was also the wellspring of artistic productivity and the patron of some of the most glorious works of art ever created. The great monastic complexes and majestic cathedrals, the spirited sculptures and radiant stained glass windows, the richly illuminated manuscripts, and the polyphonic Masses and motets – all reflect the irrepressible religious vitality of an age of faith. Although each one of these genres is distinct from every other, each functioned in close relation to the next to form a grand synthesis. The medieval synthesis in the arts – like Aquinas' *Summa* or Dante's *Commedia* – entailed the juxtaposition of diverse and often contrary ingredients, which, although brought into unity, retained their individual identities. This synthesis was the product of an age that believed that God, the Master Architect, had ordered the universe so that no part of it could stand independent of the whole (Figure **13.2**). The arts of the Middle Ages, then, not only pointed the way to salvation; they linked temporal and transcendental realms.

The Carolingian Abbey Church

During the Carolingian Renaissance of the ninth century (see chapter 11), Charlemagne authorized the construction of numerous Benedictine monasteries, or abbeys. Central to each abbey was a church that served as a place of worship and as a shrine that housed sacred relics. Though built on a smaller scale than that of Early Christian churches, most abbey churches of the Carolingian Era were simple basilicas with square towers added at the west entrance and at the crossing of the nave and transept.

In the construction of the abbey church, as in the arrangement of the monastic complex as a whole, Carolingian architects pursued a strict geometry governed by classical principles of symmetry and order. The plan for an ideal monastery, found in a manuscript

from the library of the monastery at Saint Gall, Switzerland, reflects these concerns: Each part of the complex, from **refectory** (dining hall) to cemetery, is fixed on the gridlike plan according to its practical function (Figure **13.1**). Monks gained access to the church, for example, by means of both the adjacent dormitory and the cloister. At the abbey church of Saint Gall, where a

Figure 13.1 A ninth-century plan for an ideal monastery. Monastery Library of Saint Gall, Switzerland.

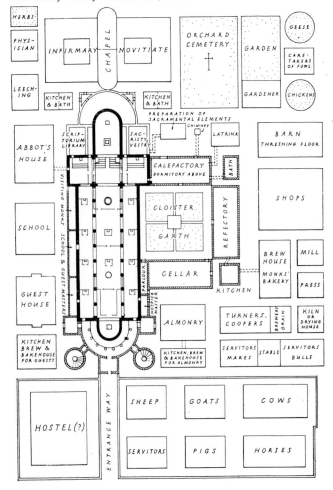

Figure 13.2 God as Architect of the Universe. From the *Bible Moralisée*, thirteenth century. Austrian National Library, Vienna, MS Cod. 2554, f.1.

second transept provided longitudinal symmetry, the monks added chapels along the aisles and transepts to house relics of saints and martyrs, whose bones had been exhumed from the Roman catacombs.

The Romanesque Pilgrimage Church

After the year 1000, devout Christians awaiting the return of Jesus at the end of the millennium reconciled themselves to the advent of a new age. The Benedictine abbey of Cluny in southeast France launched a movement for monastic revitalization that resulted in the construction of more than one thousand monasteries and abbey churches throughout Western Europe within 150 years. The new churches, most of which were modeled on Cluny itself, housed shrines for relics brought back from the Holy Land by the Crusaders. Encased in elaborate **reliquaries** (containers for sacred objects; Figure **13.3**), the remains of saints and martyrs attracted thousands of pilgrims seeking pardon from sins or miraculous cures, or who wished simply to pay homage to a favorite saint. Suppliants afflicted with

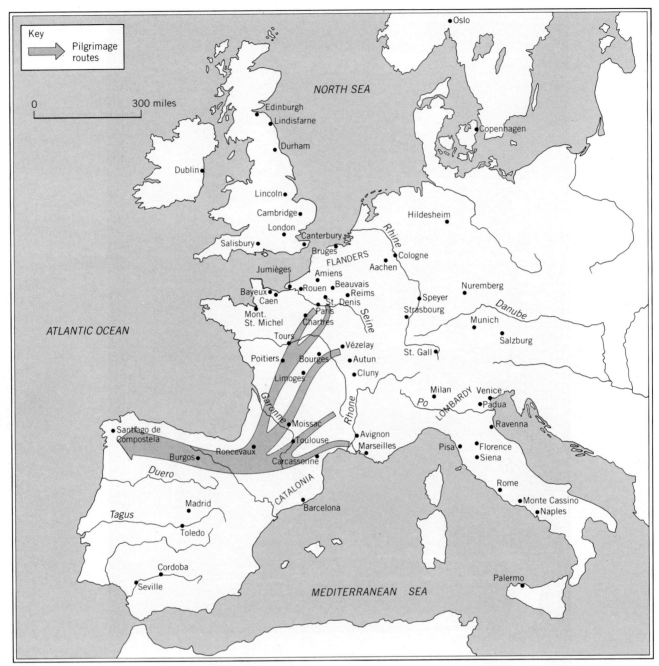

Map 13.1 Romanesque and Gothic sites in Western Europe.

blindness, leprosy, and other ills prayed or slept near the saint's tomb in hope of a healing vision.

There were four major pilgrimage routes that linked the cities of France with the favorite shrine of Christian pilgrims, that of Saint James Major at Santiago de Compostela in northwest Spain (Map **13.1**). Along the roads that carried pilgrims from Paris to the Pyrenees, old churches were rebuilt and new churches erected, prompting one eleventh-century chronicler to observe, "The whole world seems to have shaken off her slumber, cast off her old rags, and clothed herself in a white mantle of new churches."

Like the Crusades themselves, pilgrimages were an expression of increased mobility and economic revitalization (see chapter 11). Since pilgrims, like modern tourists, constituted a major source of revenue for European towns and churches, parishes competed for pilgrims by enlarging church interiors and by increasing the number of reliquary chapels. The practical requirement for additional space in which to house these relics safely and make them accessible to Christian pilgrims determined the character of the pilgrimage church. In the early Christian church, as in the Carolingian abbey, the width of the nave was inhibited by the size and availability of roofing timber, and the wooden superstructure itself was highly susceptible to fire. The use of cut stone as the primary vaulting medium provided a solution to both of these problems. Indeed, the medieval architect's return to stone barrel and groined vaults of the kinds first used by the Romans (see Figure 7.3) inaugurated the *Romanesque style*.

Romanesque architects employed round arches and a uniform system of stone vaults in the upper zones of the nave and side aisles. While the floor plan of the typical Romanesque church adhered to the Latin cross plan of Early Christian and Carolingian churches, the new system of stone vaulting allowed medieval architects to build on a grander scale than ever before. To provide additional space for shrines, architects enlarged the eastern end of the church to include a number of radiating chapels. They also extended the side aisles around the transept and behind the apse to form an ambulatory (walkway) by which the chapels might be

Figure 13.3 Reliquary in shape of head, Rhenish, early twelfth century. Reproduced by courtesy of the Trustees of the British Museum, London.

Figure 13.4 West facade, Abbey of Jumièges, on the lower Seine near Rouen, France, 1037–1067.

reached. In the construction of these new, all-stone structures, the Normans led the way. The technical superiority of Norman stonemasons, apparent in their castles (see Figure 11.10), is reflected in the abbey churches at Caen and Jumièges in northwest France. At the abbey of Jumièges, consecrated in 1067 in the presence of William the Conqueror, little remains other than the **westwork** (west facade) with its 141-foot-high twin towers (Figure 13.4). This noble entrance portal, with its triparte division and three round arches, captures the geometric simplicity and rugged severity that was typical of the Romanesque style in France and England.

The church of Saint Sernin at Toulouse, on the southernmost pilgrimage route to northern Spain, is one of the largest of the French pilgrimage churches (Figure 13.5). Constructed of magnificent pink granite, Saint Sernin's spacious nave is covered by a barrel vault divided by ornamental transverse arches (Figure 13.6). Thick stone walls and heavy piers carry the weight of the barrel vault and provide lateral support (see Figure

Figure 13.5 Collegiate Church of Saint Sernin, Toulouse, France, ca. 1080–1120. Roger Viollet, Paris.

Figure 13.7 Plan of Saint Sernin, Toulouse, France, 1080–1096.

Figure 13.6 Nave and Choir, Saint Sernin, Toulouse, France, twelfth century. Photo: © Snider/The Image Works, Inc.

13.17). Since window openings might have weakened the walls that buttressed the vault, the architects of Saint Sernin eliminated the clerestory. Beneath the vaults over the double side aisles, a gallery that served weary pilgrims as a place of overnight refuge provided additional lateral buttressing.

The formal design of Saint Sernin followed rational and harmonious principles: The square represented by the crossing of the nave and transept was the module for the organization of the building and its parts (Figure 13.7). Each nave **bay** (vaulted compartment) equals one-half the module, while each side aisle bay equals one-fourth of the module. Clarity of design is also visible in the ways in which the exterior reflects the geometry of the interior: At the east end of the building, for instance, five reliquary chapels protrude uniformly from the ambulatory, while at the crossing of the nave and transept, a tower (enlarged in the thirteenth century) rises as both a belfry and a beacon to

approaching pilgrims (see Figure 13.5). Massive and stately in its exterior, dignified and somber in its interior, Saint Sernin conveys the effect of a monumental spiritual fortress.

Romanesque architects experimented with a wide assortment of regional variation in stone vaulting techniques. At the pilgrimage church of Sainte Madeleine (Mary Magdalene) at Vézelay in France, the site from which the second Crusade was launched, the nave was covered with groined vaults separated by pronounced transverse arches. The concentration of weight along the arches, along with lighter masonry, allowed the architect to enlarge the width of the nave to 90 feet and to include a clerestory that admitted light into the dark interior (Figure 13.8). The alternating light and dark stone **voussoirs** (wedges) in the arches of this dramatic interior indicate the influence of Muslim architecture (see Figure 10.7) on the development of the Romanesque church.

Figure 13.8 Nave, Sainte Madeleine, Vézelay, France, ca. 1104–1132. © C.N.M.K.S./S.P.A.D.E.M.

Figure 13.9 (a) Gislebertus, *Last Judgment*, west tympanum, Autun Cathedral, France, ca. 1130—1135. Giraudon. (b) Diagram of a portal.

archivolts

tympanum

lintel

jamb

trumeau

(b)

Romanesque Sculpture

Pilgrimage churches of the eleventh and twelfth centuries heralded the revival of monumental stone sculpture, a medium that, for the most part, had been abandoned since Roman antiquity. Scenes from the Old and New Testaments – carved in high relief and brightly painted – usually appeared on the entrance portals of the church, as well as in the capitals of columns throughout the church and its cloister. Passing beneath the elaborately carved western portal of the church of Saint Lazarus in Autun, medieval Christians were powerfully reminded of the inevitability of death and judgment. The forbidding image of Christ as Judge greeted them from the center of the **tympanum** (the semicircular space within the arch of the portal) just above their heads (Figure 13.9). Framed by an almond-shaped halo, Jesus displays his wounds and points to the realms of the afterlife: Heaven (on his right) and Hell (on his left). Surrounding the awesome Christ, flamelike saints and angels and grimacing devils await the souls of the resurrected. Saint Michael weighs a soul in order to determine its eternal destiny, a motif that looks back to late Egyptian art (see Figure 2.7), while a wraithlike devil tries to tip the scales in his own favor (Figure 13.10). In the **lintel** (the horizontal band below the tympanum), the resurrected are pictured rising from their graves. Just beneath the mouth of Hell, a pair of disembodied claws clutch at the damned, who cower in anticipation of eternal punishment. Like a medieval morality play, the tympanum at Autun served as a *memento mori*, reminding the Christian of the inevitability of divine judgment. Indeed, beneath his signature, the artist Gislebertus added the warning, "Let this terror frighten those bound by earthly sin."

The tympanum at Autun preserves the tradition of abstract stylization that evolved in early medieval manuscripts. With graphic subtlety, Gislebertus carved his figures to fit the shapes of the stone segments that comprise the portal. These lively, elongated figures bend and twist, as if filled with a restless energy appropriate to an age of pilgrimage. Similarly, at the abbey church of Saint Peter in Moissac, the Hebrew prophet Jeremiah stretches and twists like taffy to conform to the shape of the **trumeau** (the post that supports the superstructure) of the west portal (Figure

Figure 13.10 Detail of the *Last Judgment*, Autun Cathedral, France, ca. 1130–1135. Photo: Bulloz, Paris.

Figure 13.11 *Jeremiah the Prophet*, trumeau of south portal, Saint Pierre, Moissac, France, early twelfth century. Giraudon, Paris.

13.11). The Moissac sculptor unites form and content symbolically: The post supports the superstructure just as the Old Testament prophets were said to "support" the New Testament revelation of Final Judgment.

Among the most compelling examples of Romanesque sculpture are those that adorn the capitals of columns in churches and cloisters. These so-called **historiated capitals** feature narrative scenes depicting the life of Christ. One of the largest extant groups of historiated capitals comes from the west porch of the pilgrimage church of Saint Benoit-sur-Loire, which housed the relics of Saint Benedict. In the *Flight to Egypt*, an oval-faced Mary sits awkwardly upon a toy-like donkey led by a bearded Joseph (Figure **13.12**). The cookielike star above Mary's right shoulder and the naively shortened figures — altered to fit into the shape of the capital — give the scene a whimsical quality. Romanesque artisans plumbed their imaginations to generate the legions of fantastic beasts and hybrid demons that embellish church portals and capitals. The popularity of such imagery moved medieval churchmen to debate whether the visual arts inspired or distracted the faithful from contemplation and prayer. Nevertheless, the fusion of dogma and fantasy that characterizes so much Romanesque sculpture must have made a tremendous impact on the great percentage of people, who could neither read nor write.

Figure 13.12 *The Flight to Egypt*, capital, Saint Benoit-sur-Loire, France, late eleventh century. Photo: James Austin.

The Gothic Cathedral

Where Romanesque architecture reflected Greco-Roman principles and building techniques, Gothic architecture represented a clear break with the classical past. Whereas classical temples seemed to hug the earth, Gothic cathedrals soared heavenward; whereas classical structures enforced a static relationship between building parts, Gothic structures engaged a dynamic system of thrusts and counterthrusts; and whereas classic architects rationalized form, Gothic architects infused form with symbolism. Seventeenth-century neoclassicists coined the term "Gothic" to condemn a style they judged to be a "rude and barbarous" alternative to the classical style. But modern critics have recognized the *Gothic style* as the sophisticated and majestic expression of an age of faith.

The Gothic style was born in northern France and spread quickly throughout medieval Europe. In France alone, eighty Gothic cathedrals and nearly five hundred cathedral-class churches were constructed between 1170 and 1270. Like all Christian churches, the Gothic cathedral was the religious center in which priests conducted Masses for all occasions. But, reflecting a shift of intellectual life from the monastery to the town, the Gothic cathedral was also the administrative seat or throne (*cathedra*) of a bishop, the site of ecclesiastic authority, and an educational center – a fount of theological doctrine and divine precept. The Gothic cathedral was a monumental shrine that honored one or more saints, including and especially the Virgin Mary – the principal intercessor between God and the Christian believer. Indeed, most of the prominent churches of the Middle Ages were dedicated to Notre Dame ("Our Lady"). On a symbolic level, the church was the Heavenly Jerusalem, the City of God, and a model of the Virgin as Womb of Christ and Queen of Heaven. In the cathedral, the various types of religious expression converged: Sculpture appeared in its portals, capitals, and choir screens; stained glass diffused divine light through its windows; painted altarpieces embellished its chapels; religious drama was enacted both within its walls and outside its portals; liturgical music filled its choirs.

Figure 13.13 Chartres Cathedral, France, begun 1194.

Figure 13.14 Thirteenth-century masons. Miniature from an Old Testament building scene, French, ca. 1240. Stones, shaped by the two men, bottom right, are lifted by a hoisting engine, powered by the tread-wheel on the left. Another man is carrying mortar up the ladder on his back. The J. Pierpont Morgan Library, New York, 1991. MS. 638 f.3.

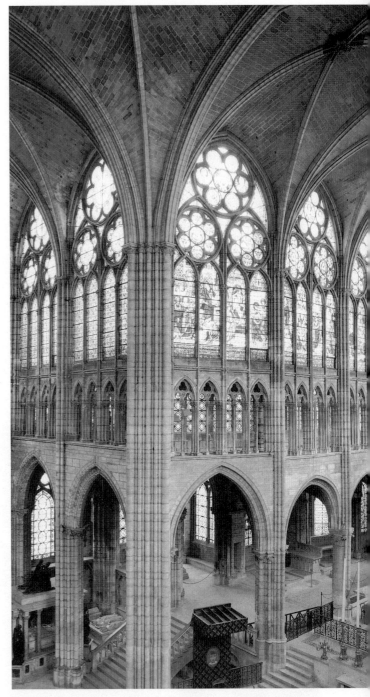

Figure 13.15 Choir and ambulatory, Abbey Church of Saint Denis, France, 1140–1144. © Hirmer Fotoarchiv.

Finally, the Gothic cathedral, often large enough to hold the entire population of a town, was a municipal center. While the Romanesque church was essentially a rural retreat for monastics and pilgrims, the Gothic cathedral served as the focal point for an urban community. Physically dominating the town, its spires soaring above the houses and shops below (Figure **13.13**), the cathedral attracted civic events, public festivals, and even local business. The construction of a Gothic cathedral was a town effort, supported by the funds and labors of local citizens and guild members, including stonemasons, carpenters, metalworkers, and glaziers (Figure **13.14**).

The definitive features of the Gothic style were first assembled in a monastic church just outside Paris: the abbey church of Saint Denis — for centuries, the burial place of French royalty. Between 1122 and 1144, Abbot Suger (1085–1151), the personal friend and adviser of the French Kings Louis VI and VII, enlarged and remodeled the original church of Saint Denis. At the east end of the church, Suger ingeniously combined three architectural innovations that heretofore had been employed only occasionally or experimentally: the pointed arch, the rib vault, and stained glass windows (Figure **13.15**). The result was an ambulatory free of heavy stone supports and flooded with light. These features, along with flying buttresses (first used at the Cathedral of Notre Dame in Paris around 1170), became the essential elements of the Gothic style.

The floor plan of the Gothic cathedral remained basically a Latin cross plan — the only major modification involved moving the transept further west to create a larger choir area (Figure **13.16**). The combination of rib vault and pointed arch had a major impact on

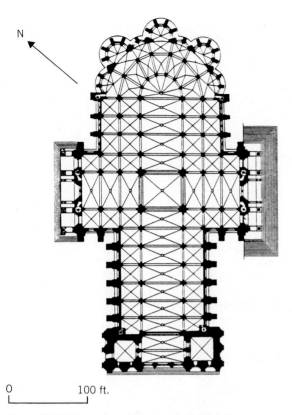

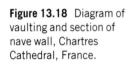

Figure 13.16 Floor plan of Chartres Cathedral, France.

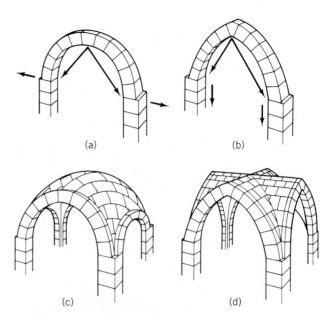

Figure 13.17 Round and pointed arches and vaults.
The round arch (a) spreads the load laterally, while the pointed arch (b) thrusts its load more directly toward the ground.
The pointed arch can rise to any height while the height of the semicircular arch is governed by the space it spans. Round arches create a dome-shaped vault (c). The Gothic rib-vault (d) permits a lighter and more flexible building system with larger wall-openings that may accommodate windows.

size and elevation. Stone ribs replaced the heave stone masonry of Romanesque vaults, and pointed arches raised these vaults to new heights. While the rounded vaults of the Romanesque church demanded extensive lateral buttressing, the steeply pointed arches of the Gothic, which directed weight downward, required only the combination of slender vertical piers and thin lateral ("flying") buttresses (Figures **13.17**, **13.18**). In

place of masonry, broad areas of glass filled the interspaces of this "cage" of stone. The nave wall consisted of an arcade of pier bundles that swept from floor to ceiling, an ornamental **triforium** gallery (the arcaded passage between the nave arcade and the clerestory), and a large clerestory consisting of **rose** (from "*roue*" or "wheel") and **lancet** (vertically pointed) windows (Figure **13.18**). Above the clerestory hung elegant

Figure 13.18 Diagram of vaulting and section of nave wall, Chartres Cathedral, France.

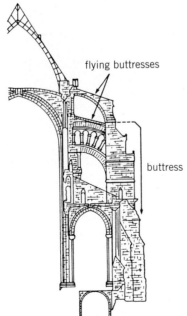

flying buttresses

buttress

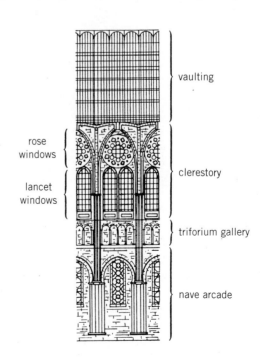

vaulting

rose windows

lancet windows

clerestory

triforium gallery

nave arcade

Figure 13.19 Nave facing east, Chartres Cathedral, France, begun 1194.

canopies of **quadripartite** (four-part) (Figure **13.19**) or **sexpartite** (six-part) rib vaults. Lighter and more diaphanous than Romanesque churches, Gothic cathedrals seemed to soar heavenward, their interiors expanding and unfolding in space.

Medieval towns competed with one another in the grandeur of their cathedrals: At Chartres, a town located fifty miles southwest of Paris (see Map 13.1), the nave of the cathedral rose to a height of 122 feet (Figures **13.13**, **13.20**); architects at Amiens took the space from the floor to the apex of the vault to a breathtaking 144 feet. At Beauvais, the 157-foot nave collapsed twelve years after its completion and had to be reconstructed over a period of forty years. These major

Figure 13.20 West facade, Chartres Cathedral, France, lower parts 1134–1150, mainly after 1194.

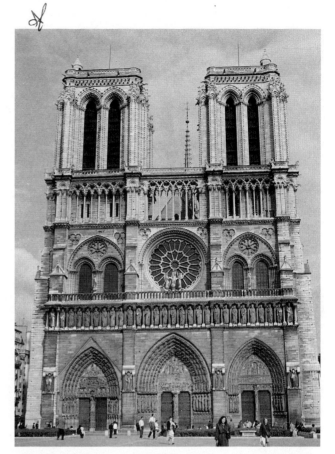

Figure 13.21 West facade, Notre Dame, Paris, ca. 1200–1250. Photo: © Museum of Notre Dame de Paris.

Figure 13.22 Grotesques and a gargoyle waterspout on a tower terrace of the cathedral of Notre Dame, Paris. Alinari/Art Resource, New York.

enterprises in engineering design and craftsmanship often took decades to build, and many were never finished. In contrast to the Romanesque church, with its well-defined cubic volumes and its simple geometric harmonies, the Gothic cathedral was an intricate web of stone, a dynamic network of open and closed spaces that evoked a sense of unbounded extension. Despite its visual complexity, the Gothic interior revealed its principal divisions in the articulation of the facade. At the Cathedral of Notre Dame in Paris, for instance, the height of the nave arcade corresponds to that of the west portals; the triforium arcade is echoed in the rows of saints standing above those portals; and the clerestory is marked by a majestic rose window (Figure **13.21**).

Gothic architects embellished the structural extremities of the cathedral with stone **crockets** (stylized leaves) and **finials** (crowning ornamental details). At the upper portions of the building, **gargoyles**, waterspouts in the form of grotesque human beings or hybrid beasts, warded off evil (Figure **13.22**). During the

Figure 13.23 West facade, Notre Dame of Amiens, France, ca. 1220–1288. Scala/Art Resource, New York.

thirteenth century and thereafter, cathedrals increased in structural and ornamental complexity (Figure **13.23**). Flying buttresses became ornate stone wings terminating in minichapels that housed individual statues of saints and martyrs. Crockets and finials sprouted in greater numbers from gables and spires (compare the facades of Chartres and Amiens – Figures 13.20 and 13.23), and sculptural details became more numerous. But, like an Aquinan proposition, the final design represents the reconciliation of all individual parts into a majestic and harmonious synthesis.

Stained Glass

Stained glass was to the Gothic cathedral what mosaics were to the Early Christian church: a source of religious edification, a medium of divine light, and a delight to the eye. Produced on the site of the cathedral by a process of mixing metal oxides into molten glass, colored sheets of glass were cut into fragments to fit preconceived designs. They were then fixed within lead bands, bound by a grid of iron bars, and set into stone **mullions** (vertical frames). Imprisoned in this lacelike armature, the glass vibrated with color, sparkling in response to the changing natural light and casting rainbows of color that seemed to dissolve the stone walls. The faithful of the High Middle Ages regarded the cathedral windows as precious objects – glass tapestries

that clothed the House of God with radiant light. They especially treasured the windows that were filled with rich blues, which, in contrast to other colors, required a cobalt oxide that came from regions outside France. Legend had it that Abbot Suger, the first churchman to exploit the aesthetic potential of stained glass, produced blue glass by grinding up sapphires – a story that, although untrue, reflects the popular equation of precious gems with sacred glass.

Suger described stained glass as the medium through which divine light poured in upon the faithful. The light of the Heavenly Kingdom was identical with Christ ("I am the light of the world," [John 8:12]) and with the gift of salvation. Light symbolism was as distinctive to medieval sermons and treatises as it was to the everyday liturgy of the church; recall the words of Ambrose's sixth-century song of praise, the "Ancient Morning Hymn" (see chapter 9),

> O Splendor of God's Glory bright
> O thou who bringest light from light,
> O light of light, light's living spring,
> O Day, all days illumining!

Drawing on this mystical bond between Jesus and light, Suger identified the *lux nova* ("new light") of the Gothic church as the symbolic equivalent of God and the windows as mediators of God's love. On the wall of the ambulatory at Saint Denis, Suger inscribed these words: "That which is united in splendor, radiates in splendor/ And the magnificent work inundated with a new light shines."

The Windows at Chartres

The name "the golden age of stained glass" may be given to the late twelfth and early thirteenth centuries. At Chartres, the 175 surviving glass panels with representations of more than four thousand figures comprise a cosmic narrative of humankind's religious and secular history. Chartres' windows, which were removed for safekeeping during World War II and thereafter returned to their original positions, followed a carefully organized theological program designed, as Abbot Suger explained, "to show simple folk . . . what they ought to believe." Like most Gothic cathedrals, Chartres was dedicated to the Virgin Mary. Chartres housed the tunic Mary was said to have worn when she gave birth to Jesus; and since that tunic had survived the late twelfth-century fire that destroyed most of the old church – a miracle that was taken to indicate the Virgin's desire to see the cathedral rebuilt – her image dominated the iconographic program. In one of Chartres' oldest windows, whose vibrant combination of red and blue glass inspired the title *Notre Dame de la Belle Verrière* ("Our Lady of the Beautiful Glass"), the Virgin

Figure 13.24 *Notre Dame de la Belle Verrière* ("Our Lady of the Beautiful Glass"), stained glass window, Chartres Cathedral, France, twelfth century. Photo: Sonia Halliday, Weston Turville.

Figure 13.25 South rose and lancets, Chartres Cathedral, France, thirteenth century. Photo: Sonia Halliday, Weston Turville.

Figure 13.26 Sainte Chapelle, Paris, view from southwest, 1245–1248. Photo: A. F. Kersting, London.

Figure 13.27 Interior, upper chapel, Sainte Chapelle, Paris, 1245–1248. © Ciccione/Photo Researchers, Inc.

appears in her dual role as Mother of God and Queen of Heaven (Figure **13.24**). Holding the Christ Child on her lap and immediately adjacent to her womb, she also symbolizes the Seat of Wisdom. In the lancet windows below the rose of the south transept wall (Figure **13.25**), Mary and the Christ Child are flanked by four Old Testament prophets who carry on their shoulders the four evangelists, a symbolic rendering of the Christian belief that the Old Dispensation upheld the New (compare Figure 13.10). Often, the colors chosen for parts of the design carried symbolic value. For instance, in scenes of the Passion from the west-central lancet window, the cross carried by Jesus is green – the color of vegetation – to symbolize rebirth and regeneration.

Many of Chartres' windows were donated by members of the nobility – their coats-of-arms are prominently depicted below the images of the saints (Figure **13.25**) – and by guilds of craftspeople and merchants. Scenes depicting the activities of bakers, butchers, stonemasons, and other workers often appear among the windows commemorating the patron saints of each guild (see Figure 11.14).

Sainte Chapelle: Medieval "Jewelbox"

The art of stained glass reached its apogee in Sainte Chapelle, the small palace chapel commissioned for the Ile de France by King Louis IX ("Saint Louis") (Figure **13.26**). Executed between 1245 and 1248, the chapel was designed to hold the Crown of Thorns, a relic that Christian Crusaders recovered along with other symbols of Christ's Passion. The lower level of the chapel is richly painted with frescoes that imitate the canopy of heaven, while the upper level consists almost entirely of 49-foot-high lancet windows dominated by ruby red and purplish blue glass (Figure **13.27**). More than a thousand individual stories are depicted within the stained glass windows that make up two-thirds of the upper chapel walls. In its vast iconographic program and its dazzling, ethereal effect, this medieval "jewelbox" is the crowning example of French Gothic art.

Figure 13.28 Central doorway, Royal Portal, west facade, Chartres Cathedral, France, ca. 1140–1150.

Figure 13.29 Scenes from the life of the Virgin Mary, tympanum of the right door of the Royal Portal, west facade, Chartres Cathedral, France, between 1145 and 1170. Photo: © James Austin.

Figure 13.30 *Coronation of the Virgin*, tympanum of Central portal, north porch, Chartres Cathedral, France, ca. 1225. © Hirmer Fotoarchiv.

Gothic Sculpture

The sculpture of the Gothic cathedral was an exhaustive compendium of Old and New Testament history, classical and Christian precepts, and secular legend and lore. Like the stained glass of the Gothic cathedral, the sculptural program of the cathedral – that is, the totality of its carved representations – conveyed Christian doctrine and liturgy in terms that were meaningful to both scholars and laity. Learned churchmen might glean from these images a profound symbolic message, while less educated Christians might see in them a history of their faith and a mirror of daily experience. The Gothic facade was both a "bible in stone" and an encyclopedia of the religious and secular life of an age of faith.

In the sculpture of the cathedral, as in the stained glass window scenes, the Virgin Mary held a prominent place. At Chartres, the west facade, or Royal Portal – so called for its statue-columns of kings and queens from the Old Testament (Figure 13.28) – honored Mary as Queen of the Liberal Arts. Like the Virgin of *La Belle Verrière* (see Figure 13.24), the Mother of God appears in the south tympanum of the Royal Portal as the Seat of Wisdom (Figure 13.29). The archivolts (the relief bands that frame the tympanum) pursue the theme of education with allegorical representations of grammar, rhetoric, arithmetic, and so on. Each discipline is accompanied by the appropriate historical authority. In the inner archivolt on the lower right, for instance, Music, shown holding a **psaltery** (a stringed instrument) and striking a set of bells, appears just above the image of Pythagoras, shown hunched over his lap desk.

On cathedral facades, the Virgin Mary appears frequently as Mother of God and Queen of Heaven (Figure 13.30). The central trumeau of the west portal

Figure 13.31 Virgin and Child (above), Temptation of Adam and Eve (below). Trumeau, central portal, west porch, Notre Dame, Paris, thirteenth century. Photo: Bulloz, Paris.

at Notre Dame in Paris shows Mary proudly holding the Christ Child in her arms (Figure **13.31**). Below this triumphant image is the fallen Eve, depicted alongside Adam in the Garden of Eden. The conjunction of Mary and Eve alluded to the popular medieval idea that Mary was the "new Eve," who brought salvation as a remedy to the sentence of death resulting from the disobedience of the "old Eve."

The thousands of individually carved figures on the facades of the cathedrals at Chartres, Paris, Amiens, and elsewhere required the labor of many sculptors working over long periods of time. Often, the variety of styles on a single facade combined the efforts of different workshops and different eras. The present cathedral at Chartres, the fifth (at least) on that site, was the product of numerous building campaigns: Its west portal survived the devastating fire of 1194, while its north and south portals were added in the early thirteenth century. The Royal Portal retains the linear severity of the Romanesque style (see Figure 13.28). In the central tympanum sits a rigidly posed Christ in Majesty flanked by symbols of the four evangelists and framed by the twenty-four elders. In the lintel below, the apostles are ordered into formal groups of threes. Yet, if one compares this late-twelfth-century image with that at Autun, carved only a few decades earlier (see Figure 13.9), it is apparent that medieval sculpture was moving in the direction of greater repose and heightened realism.

During the thirteenth century, figural representation became gradually more detailed and lifelike. The figures of Chartres' north porch (1200–1220), a veritable throng of angels, prophets, kings, and patriarchs, assume natural poses, their robes shifting with the positions of their bodies and their gestures varied and subtle. Rather than conform stiffly to the architectural framework, the figures seem to detach themselves from the stone, a fact quickly grasped when one observes the pigeons darting in and out of the spaces behind and between the stone figures of the Virgin Mary and Jesus seated on the central tympanum (see Figure 13.30). The trend toward greater realism in Gothic sculpture accompanied the proliferation of figures and architectural details—indeed, at Amiens, the entire west facade seems to dissolve into a lacy skein of stone (see Figure 13.23).

Medieval Painting

Medieval painting shared the graphic character of Romanesque sculpture. Responsive to the combined influence of Germanic, Islamic, and Byzantine art, medieval artists developed a taste for decorative abstraction through line. In fresco, manuscript illumination, and panel painting, line worked to flatten form,

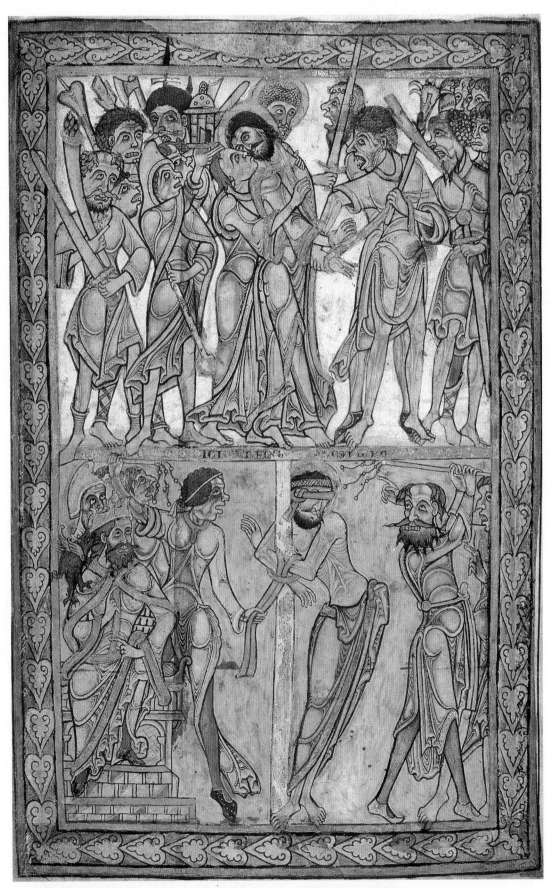

Figure 13.32 Capture of Christ and the Flagellation. From the *Psalter of Saint Swithin*, ca. 1250. Reproduced by permission of the British Library, London.

eliminate space, and enhance the symbolic nature of the image. Line also helped to emphasize gesture, an important symbolic device. In an age dominated by sermons, liturgical chant, and other oral genres, a single, symbolic gesture was truly "worth a thousand words."

Graceful draftsmanship characterizes the illustrations in the thirteenth-century *Psalter of Saint Swithin* (Figure **13.32**). Like the figures at Moissac and Autun, those depicted in the Capture and Flagellation of Christ are tall, thin, and lively, their gestures and facial expressions exaggerated to emphasize the contrasting states of arrogance and humility. The artist who painted the Crucifixion and Deposition of Christ for the *Psalter of Blanche of Castile* (the mother of Saint Louis) imitates

the geometric compositions and strong, simple colors of stained glass windows (Figure **13.33**). To the right and left of Jesus are depicted the Church (representing the New Dispensation) and the Synagogue (representing the Old Dispensation). Book illuminators often used pattern books filled with stock representations of standard historical and religious subjects, a practice that encouraged stylistic conservatism. Nevertheless, in the preparation of thousands of miniatures and marginal illustrations for secular and religious manuscripts, the imagination of medieval artists usually prevailed.

Some of the finest examples of medieval painting appear in thirteenth-century altarpieces. The typical Gothic altarpiece consisted of a wooden panel or panels covered with **gesso** (a chalky white plaster), on which

Figure 13.33 Crucifixion and Deposition of Christ with the Church and the Synogogue. From the *Psalter of Blanche of Castile*, ca. 1235. Bibliothèque de l'Arsenal, Paris, MS 1186, f. 24.

Figure 13.34 Cimabue, *Madonna Enthroned*, ca. 1280–1290. Panel 12 ft. 7 in. × 7 ft. 4 in. Uffizi Gallery, Florence. Scala/Art Resource, New York.

images were painted in **tempera** (a powdered pigment that produces dry, flat surface colors), and embellished with gold leaf. Installed on or behind the church altar, the altarpiece usually displayed scenes from the life of Jesus, the Virgin Mary, or a favorite saint or martyr. The late-thirteenth-century altarpiece by the Florentine painter Cimabue (1240–1302) shows the Virgin and Child elevated on a monumental seat that is both a throne and a tower (Figure **13.34**). Angels throng around the throne, while beneath the Virgin's feet, four Hebrew prophets display scrolls predicting the coming of Jesus. To symbolize their lesser importance, angels and prophets are pictured considerably smaller than the enthroned Mary. Such hierarchic grading, which was typical of medieval art, also characterized Egyptian and Mesopotamian art (see Figures 2.8 and 2.12).

Cimabue's lavishly gilded devotional image has a schematic elegance: Line elicits the sharp, metallic folds of the Virgin's dark blue mantle, the crisp wings of the angels, the chiseled features of the Christ Child, and the decorative surface of the throne. The figure of the Virgin combines the hypnotic grandeur of Byzantine icons (by which many Italian artists were influenced) and the bodiless symmetry and static resolution of Gislebertus' Christ in Majesty on the tympanum at Autun (see Figure 13.9). Although Cimabue's Virgin is more humanized than the Autun image, she is every bit as regal an object of veneration.

Medieval artists often imitated the ornamental vocabulary of Gothic architecture and the bright colors of stained glass windows. The Sienese painter Simone Martini (1284–1344) made brilliant use of Gothic architectural motifs in his Annunciation altarpiece of 1333 (Figure **13.35**). The frame of the altarpiece consists of elegant Gothic spires and heavily gilded **ogee** arches (pointed arches with **S**-shaped curves near the apex) sprouting finials and crockets. Set on a gold leaf ground, the petulant Virgin, the Angel Annunciate, and the vase of lilies (symbolizing Mary's purity) seem suspended in time and space. Martini's composition depends on a refined play of lines: The graceful curves of the angel Gabriel's wings are echoed in his fluttering vestments, in the contours of the Virgin's body as she shrinks from the angel's greeting, and in the folds of her mantle, the pigment for which was ground from semiprecious lapis lazuli.

Medieval Music

Early Medieval Music and Liturgical Drama

The major musical developments of the Early Middle Ages, like those in architecture, came out of the monasteries. In Charlemagne's time, monastic reforms in church liturgy and in sacred music accompanied the Renaissance in the visual arts. One early medieval monk wrote in the margin of his songbook, "The tedious plainsong grates my tender ears." Perhaps to remedy such complaints, the monks at Saint Gall enlarged the range of expression of the classical Gregorian chant by adding **antiphons**, or verses sung as responses to the text. Carolingian monks also embellished plainsong with the **trope**, an addition of music or words to the established liturgical chant. Thus, "Lord, have mercy upon us" became "Lord, *omnipotent Father, God, Creator of all*, have mercy upon us." A special kind of trope, called a **sequence**, added words to the long, melismatic passages — such as the alleluias and amens — that occurred at the end of each part of the Mass.

By the tenth century, singers began to divide among themselves the parts of the liturgy for Christmas and Easter, now embellished by tropes and sequences. As more and more dramatic incidents were added to

Figure 13.35 Simone Martini, *Annunciation*, 1333. Tempera on wood, 8 ft. 8 in. × 10 ft. (Saints in side panels by Lippo Memmi.) Uffizi Gallery, Florence. Scala/Art Resource, New York.

the texts for these masses, full-fledged music-drama emerged. Eventually, liturgical plays broke away from the liturgy and were performed in the intervals between the parts of the Mass. Such was the case with the eleventh-century *Play of Herod*, whose dramatic "action" brought to life the legend of the three Magi[◊] and the massacre of the innocents by King Herod of Judaea – incidents surrounding the Gospel story of the birth of Christ appropriate to the Christmas season. By the twelfth century, as spoken dialogue and possibly musical instruments were introduced, church drama moved outside the walls of the church itself.

Medieval Musical Notation

Musical notation was invented in the monasteries. As with Romanesque architecture, so with medieval musical theory and practice, Benedictine monks at Cluny and elsewhere were especially influential. During the eleventh century, they devised the first efficient Western system of musical notation, thus facilitating the performance and transmission of liturgical music. They arranged the tones of the commonly used scale in progression from A through G and developed a formal system of notating pitch. The Italian Benedictine Guido of Arezzo (ca. 990–ca. 1050) introduced a staff of colored lines (yellow for C, red for F, etc.) on which he registered neumes, marks traditionally written above the words to indicate tonal ascent or descent (see chapter 9). Guido's system established a precise means of indicating shifts in pitch. Instead of relying on memory alone, singers could consult songbooks inscribed with both words and music. Such advances encouraged the kinds of compositional complexity represented by medieval polyphony.

[◊]See Music Listening Selections at end of chapter.

Medieval Polyphony

Although our knowledge of early medieval music is sparse, there is reason to believe that even before the year 1000, choristers were experimenting with multiple lines of music as an alternative to the monophonic style of the Gregorian chant. **Polyphony** (music consisting of two or more lines of melody) was a Western invention; it did not make its appearance in Asia and the Far East until modern times. The earliest polyphonic compositions consisted of Gregorian melodies sung in two parts simultaneously, with both voices moving note for note in parallel motion (parallel **organum**)[◊] or with a second voice moving in contrary motion (free organum), perhaps also adding many notes to the individual syllables of the text (melismatic organum).[◊] Consistent with rules of harmony derived from antiquity, the second musical voice usually was pitched at a fourth or a fifth above or below the first.

Throughout the High Middle Ages, northern France — and the city of Paris in particular — was the center of the art of polyphonic composition. From the same area that produced the Gothic cathedral came a new musical sound that featured several lines of melody arranged in simultaneous but counterpoised rhythms. The foremost Parisian composer of the twelfth century was Perotin. A member of the Notre Dame School, Perotin enhanced the splendor of the Christian Mass by writing three- and four-part polyphonic compositions based on Gregorian chant. Perotin's music usually consisted of a principal voice or "tenor" (from the Latin *tenere*, meaning "to hold") that sang the "fixed song" (the *cantus firmus*) and one or more independent voices that moved in shorter-phrased and usually faster tempos.[◊] The combination of two or three related but independent voices, a musical technique called **counterpoint**, enlivened thirteenth-century music. Indeed, the process of vertical superimposition of voice on voice — a careful conciliation of simultaneous voice lines — augmented sonority and enriched the melodic complexity of medieval music, much in the way the counterpoised parts of the Gothic cathedral enriched its visual texture.

As medieval polyphony encouraged the addition of voices and voice parts, the choir areas of Gothic cathedrals were enlarged to accommodate more singers. Performed within the acoustically resonant body of such cathedrals as Notre Dame in Paris, the polyphonic Mass produced an aural effect as resplendent as that of the multicolored glass that shimmered throughout the interior. Like the cathedral itself, the polyphonic Mass was a masterful synthesis of carefully arranged parts — a synthesis achieved in *time* rather than in space.

The "Dies Irae"

One of the best examples of the medieval synthesis, particularly as it served the Christian immortality ideology, is the *Dies irae* ("Day of Wrath"). The fifty-seven-line hymn, which originated among the Franciscans during the thirteenth century, was added to the Roman Catholic **Requiem** (the Mass for the Dead) and quickly became a standard part of the Christian funeral service. Invoking a powerful vision of the end of time, the *Dies irae* is the musical counterpart of the church sermons (see Reading 16) and Last Judgment portals (see Figure 13.9) that issued forth solemn warnings of final doom. The hymn opens with the words,

> Day of Wrath! O day of mourning!
> See fulfilled the prophets' warning,
> Heaven and earth in ashes burning!

But as with most examples of apocalyptic art, including Dante's *Commedia*, the hymn held out hope for absolution and deliverance:

> With Thy favored sheep, oh, place me!
> Nor among the goats abase me,
> But to Thy right hand upraise me.
>
> While the Wicked are confounded,
> Doomed to flames of woe unbounded,
> Call me, with Thy saints surrounded.

Like so many other forms of medieval expression, the *Dies irae* brought into vivid contrast the destinies of sinners and saints. In later centuries, it inspired the powerful Requiem settings of Mozart, Berlioz, and Verdi, and its music became a familiar symbol of apocalyptic death and damnation.

The Motet

The thirteenth century also witnessed the invention of a new religious musical genre, the **motet**, a short, polyphonic choral composition based on a sacred text. Performed both inside and outside the church, the motet was the most popular kind of medieval religious song. Like the trope, the motet — from the French word *mot*, meaning "word" — began from the practice of adding words to the melismatic parts of the melody. Medieval motets usually juxtaposed two or more uncomplicated melodies, each with its own lyrics and metrical pattern, in a manner that was lilting and lively.[◊] Motets designed to be sung outside the church often borrowed secular tunes with vernacular lyrics. A three-part motet might combine a love song in the vernacular, a well-known hymn of praise to the Virgin, and a Latin liturgical text in the *cantus firmus*.

[◊]See Music Listening Selections at end of chapter.

[◊]See Music Listening Selections at end of chapter.

Figure 13.36 Music and Her Attendants. From Boethius, *De Arithmetica*, fourteenth century. Scala/Art Resource, New York. Holding a portable pipe organ, the elegant lady who symbolizes the civilized art of courtly music is surrounded by an ensemble of female court musicians. In the circle at the top, King David plays a psaltery, the instrument named after the Psalms (Psaltery) of David. Clockwise from right: lute, clappers, trumpets, nakers (kettledrums), bagpipe, shawm, tambourine, rebec (viol).

Thirteenth-century motets were thus polytextual, as well as polyphonic and polyrhythmic. A stock of melodies (like the stock of images in medieval pattern books) were available to musicians for use in secular and sacred songs, and the same melody might serve both types of song. Subtle forms of symbolism occurred in many medieval motets, as for instance where a popular song celebrating spring might be used to refer to the Resurrection of Jesus, the awakening of romantic love, or both.

Instrumental Music of the Middle Ages

Medieval music exalted the human voice. Musical instruments first appeared in religious music not for the purpose of accompanying songs, as with troubadour poems and folk epics, but to substitute for the human voice in polyphonic compositions. Medieval music depended on **timbre** (tone color) rather than volume for its effect, and medieval instruments produced sounds that were gentle and thin by comparison with their modern (not to mention electronically amplified)

counterparts. Medieval string instruments included the harp, the psaltery, and the lute (all three are plucked), and bowed fiddles such as the vielle and the rebec (Figure **13.36**). Wind instruments included portable pipe organs, recorders, and bagpipes. Percussion was produced by chimes, cymbals, bells, tambourines, and drums. Instrumental music performed without voices accompanied medieval dancing. Percussion instruments established the basic rhythms for a wide variety of high-spirited dances, including the *estampie*⁶, a popular round dance consisting of short, repeated phrases.

SUMMARY

Medieval churches and cathedrals were the monumental expressions of an age of faith. In Carolingian times, the church was the focal point of monastic life as well as the repository of sacred relics that drew pilgrims from neighboring areas. After the year 1000, Romanesque pilgrimage churches were constructed in great numbers throughout Western Europe. They featured all-stone masonry with round arches and thick barrel and groined vaults. The sculptures on their stone portals and capitals illustrated the Christian themes of redemption and salvation.

While the Romanesque church was essentially a rural phenomenon, the Gothic cathedral was the focus and glory of the medieval town. First developed in the region of Paris, the cathedral was an ingenious synthesis of three structural elements: rib vaults, pointed arches, and flying buttresses, the combination of which permeated the extensive use of stained glass. Raised to breathtaking heights, the Gothic cathedral was – in the words recited at the Mass for consecration of the Catholic church – "the Court of God and the Gate of Heaven." The sculptural facade, a "bible in stone," presented a panorama of Christian history, medieval lore, and everyday life. Medieval sculpture and painting were generally abstract, symbolic, and characterized by expressive linearity, the use of bright colors, and a decorative treatment of form. Gradually, however, medieval art moved in the direction of greater realism and descriptive detail.

As in the visual arts, the music of the Middle Ages was closely related to religious ritual. In Carolingian times, tropes and sequences came to embellish the melismatic passages of Christian chant, a process that led to the birth of liturgical drama. In the eleventh century, Benedictine monks devised a system of musical notation that facilitated performance and made possible the accurate transmission of music from generation to generation. At about the same time, polyphony,

---

⁶See Music Listening Selections at end of chapter.

a uniquely Western form of musical expression, emerged. In polyphonic compositions, a second, third, or fourth melodic line provided counterpoint to the fixed melody. Polyphonic religious compositions known as motets often borrowed vernacular texts and secular melodies.

Like the Gothic cathedral, the polyphonic motet may be said to illustrate the medieval habit of juxtaposing and reconciling opposing elements. Collectively, all of the arts worked to form a coherent whole – a synthesis that projected the medieval view of nature as the expression of a preordained, divine order.

GLOSSARY

antiphon   a verse sung in response to the text; see also *antiphonal* in glossary to chapter 9

bay   a regularly repeated spatial unit of a building; in medieval architecture, a vaulted compartment

crocket   a stylized leaf used as a terminal ornament

counterpoint   a musical technique that involves two or more independent melodies; the term is often used interchangeably with "polyphony"

finial   an ornament, usually pointed and foliated, that tops a spire or pinnacle

gargoyle   a waterspout usually carved in the form of a grotesque figure

gesso   a chalky white plaster used to prepare the surface of a panel for painting

historiated capital   the uppermost member of a column, ornamented with figural scenes

lancet   a narrow window that is topped with a pointed arch

lintel   a horizontal beam or stone that spans an opening; (see Figures 1.9 and 13.9b)

motet   a short, polyphonic religious composition based on a sacred text

mullion   the slender, vertical pier dividing the parts of a window, door, or screen

ogee   a pointed arch having on each side an s-shaped curve

organum   the general name for the oldest form of polyphony: in *parallel organum*, the two voices move exactly parallel to one another; in *free organum* the second voice moves in contrary motion; *melismatic organum* involves the use of multiple notes for the individual syllables of the text

polyphony   (Greek, "many voices") a musical texture

consisting of two or more lines of melody that are of equal importance

psaltery   a stringed instrument consisting of a flat soundboard and strings that were plucked

quadripartite   consisting of or divided into four parts

refectory   the dining hall of a monastery

reliquary   the container for a sacred object or objects

Requiem   a mass for the dead; a solemn chant to honor the dead

rose   a large circular window with stained glass and stone tracery

sequence   a special kind of trope consisting of words added to the melismatic passages of the Gregorian chant

sexpartite   consisting of or divided into six parts

tempera   a powdered pigment that produces dry, flat colors

timbre   tone color; the distinctive tone or quality of sound made by a voice or a musical instrument

triforium   in a medieval church, the shallow arcaded passageway above the nave and below the clerestory; (see Figure 13.18)

trope   an addition of words, music, or both to the Gregorian chant

trumeau   the pillar that supports the superstructure of a portal; (see Figure 13.9b)

tympanum   the semicircular space enclosed by the lintel over a doorway and the arch above it; (see Figure 13.9b)

voussoir   (French, "wedge") a wedge-shaped block or unit in an arch or vault

westwork   (or *westwerk*) the elaborated west end of a Carolingian or Romanesque church

SUGGESTIONS FOR READING

Boney, Jean. *French Gothic Architecture of the Twelfth and Thirteenth Centuries*. Berkeley, Calif.: University of California Press, 1983.

Calkins, Robert. *Monuments of Medieval Art*. Ithaca, N.Y.: Cornell University Press, 1989.

Gimpel, Jean. *The Cathedral Builders*, trans. D. King. Ithaca, N.Y.: Cornell University Press, 1980.

Macauley, David. *Cathedral: The Story of its Construction*. Boston: Houghton Mifflin, 1973.

Mâle, Emile. *The Gothic Image: Religious Art in France of the Thirteenth Century*. New York: Harper, 1958.

Seay, Albert. *Music in the Medieval World*. 2d ed. Englewood Cliffs, N.J.: Prentice-Hall, 1975.

Simson, Otto von. *The Gothic Cathedral*. New York: Harper 1964.

Snyder, James. *Medieval Art*. New York: Abrams, 1989.

MUSIC LISTENING SELECTIONS

Cassette I Selection 6   Medieval Liturgical Drama: *The Play of Herod*, Scene 2: "The Three Magi."

Cassette I Selection 7   Three Examples of Early Medieval Polyphony (ca. 900–1150). Parallel Organum: "*Rex caeli, Domine*." Free Organum: Trope, "*Agnus Dei*." Melismatic Organum: "*Benedicamus Domino*."

Cassette I Selection 8   Three-part Organum, twelfth century, Perotin, "*Alleluya*" (*Nativitas*).

Cassette I Selection 9   Motet, thirteenth century, Anonymous, "*En non Diu! Quant voi; Eius in Oriente*," excerpt.

Cassette I Selection 10   *Estampie*, thirteenth century.

PART
III
THE WORLD BEYOND THE WEST

Western students often overlook the fact that Europe – home of the culture that is most familiar to them – occupies only a tiny area at the far western end of the vast continental landmass of Asia. At the eastern end of that landmass lie two geographic and cultural giants: India and China (see Maps 14.1 and 14.2). During the European Middle Ages, East and West had little contact with each other, apart from periodic exchanges of goods and technology facilitated by Arab intermediaries. Although neither India nor China had a direct impact on the West, their indirect influence was considerable. Moreover, India and China produced unique forms of expression, forms that provide a broader perspective on the humanistic tradition. The arts of East Asia offer a holistic view of nature that has continued to dominate the cultures of modern-day India and China.

Between 500 and 1300 C.E., India was the homeland of some of the finest Sanskrit literature ever written. Hindu temple architecture and sculpture reached its apogee, and Indian music flourished. In China, during roughly the same period, the T'ang and Sung dynasties fostered a Golden Age in poetry and painting. The Chinese surpassed the rest of the world in technological invention and led the way in the production of fine pottery and textiles. A brief examination of these achievements puts our study of the humanistic tradition in a global perspective and provides the basis for a sympathetic appreciation of the two greatest of Asian cultures.

(opposite) Siva Nataraja, early Chola Dynasty, ca. 1000 C.E. Bronze. The Metropolitan Museum of Art, New York. Harris Brisbane Dick Fund, 1964.

14

The Civilizations
of India and China

The Medieval Period in India

During the late fifth century, central Asian Huns destroyed the remains of two of Asia's greatest cultures – an event that paralleled the decline of Rome in the West and the collapse of the Han Empire in China. Although the term *medieval* does not apply to the history of India in the Western sense of an interlude between classical and modern times, some scholars have used that term to designate the era between the end of the Gupta dynasty (ca. 500) and the Mongol conquest of India in the fourteenth century, a thousand-year period that roughly approximates the Western Middle Ages.

Following the fall of the Gupta Empire, India experienced widespread political turmoil and anarchy. It became a conglomeration of fragmented, rival local kingdoms dominated by a warrior caste not unlike the feudal aristocracy of medieval Europe. The ruling hereditary chiefs or *rajputs* (literally, "sons of kings") followed a code of chivalry that set them apart from the lower classes. The caste system (see chapter 3), which had been practiced in India for many centuries, worked to enforce the distance between rulers and the ruled. And as groups were subdivided according to occupation and social status, caste distinctions became more rigid and more fragmented. Extended families of the same caste were ruled by the eldest male, who might take a number of wives. Children were betrothed early in life and women's duties – to tend the household and raise children (preferably sons) – were carefully prescribed. In a society where males were masters, a favorite Hindu proverb ran, "A woman is never fit for independence." The devotion of the upper caste Hindu woman to her husband was dramatically expressed in *sati*, a custom by which the wife threw herself on her mate's funeral pyre.

Early in the eighth century, the Arabs entered India and zealously labored to convert the native population to Islam. Muslim authority was established in northern India, and Muslims rose to power as members of the ruling caste. During the tenth century, the invasions of Turkish Muslims brought further chaos to India, resulting in the capture of Delhi (Map 14.1) in 1192 and the destruction of the Buddhist University of Nalanda in the following year. Despite widespread persecution of the Hindu population and continuous contention between the monotheistic Muslims and the polytheistic Hindus, the native traditions of India and

Map 14.1 India in the eleventh century.

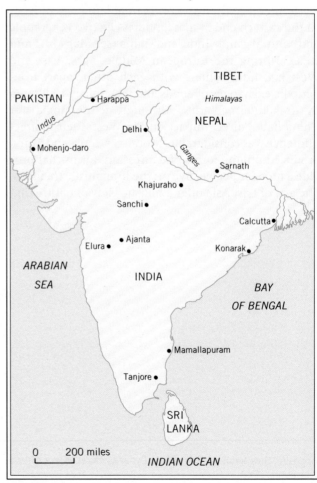

the Hindu religion itself prevailed. Buddhism, on the other hand, virtually disappeared from India by the twelfth century. And Islam – while implanted firmly in some parts of India – became the faith of only a minority of India's population. Most of India – especially the extreme south, which held out against the Muslims until the fourteenth century – retained the Hindu faith, which today is followed by approximately eighty-five percent of India's population.

Hinduism in Medieval India

In the medieval period, the philosophic aspects of Hinduism, as expressed in the Upanishads, the *Bhagavad-Gita*, and elsewhere, were overshadowed by growing devotion to the gods and goddesses of Hindu mythology (see chapter 2). These personal deities, associated with the life-giving aspects of nature, were rooted in India's ancient past and honored in the Vedas. Hindu pantheism, which emphasized the oneness of nature, taught that all aspects of the universe – human beings, animals, plants, insects – belonged to the same divine substance: the impersonal Absolute Spirit known as Brahman. Hence, Hindus viewed the gods of Indian mythology as **avatars** ("incarnations") of Brahman, much in the way that Christians regarded Jesus as the incarnate form of God. Indeed, since Hindus believed that the avatars of Brahman might assume different names and forms (even those of animals), they freely honored the Buddha and Jesus as human guises of the Divine Reality. Having no priesthood comparable to that of medieval Christianity, nor any uniform set of devotional practices, Hinduism encouraged its devotees to seek union with Brahman in their own fashion, whether through meditation or by paying homage to the many gods of Hindu myth and legend. Hinduism, however, cannot be called polytheistic, since Hindus identify all gods and spirits as manifestations of the all-pervading Absolute Spirit.

The three principal gods of medieval India were Brahma, Vishnu, and Shiva. Hindus saw in this trinity the divine expression of Brahman in its three major functions: creation, preservation, and destruction. They honored Brahma as the creator of the world. The preserver god Vishnu, associated with the sun in ancient Vedic hymns, was prized for his special concern for humanity. Hindu mythology recounts his appearance on earth in nine different incarnations, including that of Krishna, the hero-god of the *Mahabharata* (see chapter 2). Icons of Vishnu often resemble those of the Buddha, who was himself accepted by most Hindus as an avatar of Vishnu (Figure 14.1). Such images, cast in bronze and produced in large numbers in Tamil Nadu in southern India, were carried in ceremonial processions. (Note the rings at the four corners of the base of

Figure 14.1 *Standing Vishnu*, South Indian School, Chola Dynasty, tenth century. Bronze, with greenish-blue patination, height 33¾ in. The Metropolitan Museum of Art, New York, Purchase 1962, Mr. and Mrs. John D. Rockefeller Gift.

the *Standing Vishnu*, which once held poles for transporting the statue.)

The third god of the trinity, Shiva, was the Hindu god of fertility and regeneration. A god of destruction and creation, of disease and death, and of sexuality and rebirth, Shiva symbolized the dynamic rhythms of the universe. While often represented in a dual male and female aspect, Shiva was most commonly portrayed as Lord of the Dance, an image that evokes the Hindu notion of time. Unlike the Western view of time, which is linear and progressive, the Hindu perception of time is cyclical, like an ever-turning cosmic wheel. Hindus believe that devotion to Shiva or Vishnu, their avatars, and their female consorts ultimately leads to release from the cycle of death and rebirth. Reverence for these and the innumerable other deities of Hindu mythology

Figure 14.2 Shiva Nataraja, Lord of the Dance, South Indian School, Chola Period, eleventh century. Copper, height 43⅞ in. The Cleveland Museum of Art, Purchase from the J. H. Wade Fund, 30.331.

is mirrored in the literature of medieval India, as well as in its magnificent temple architecture and sculpture.

The four-armed figure of Shiva as Lord of the Dance is the most famous of Hindu icons (Figure **14.2**), so popular that Tamil sculptors cast multiple versions of the image. Framed in a celestial circle of fire, Shiva turns in a gyric movement symbolizing cosmic energy. His serpentine body bends at the neck, waist, and knees in accordance with specific and prescribed dance movements (Figure **14.3**). In Figure **14.2** every gesture and object has symbolic meaning: In one right hand he carries a small drum, the symbol of creation; a second right hand (the arm wreathed by a snake) makes the *mudra* meaning protection; one left hand holds a flame, the symbol of destruction; the second left hand points downward to the "released" left foot and to the right foot that crushes a dwarf, symbolizing ignorance. Shiva thus exhibits the five activities of the godhead: creation, protection, destruction, release from destiny, and enlightenment.

Indian Religious Literature

Medieval Indian literature drew heavily on the mythology and legends of early Hinduism as found in the Vedic hymns and in India's two great epics, the *Mahabharata* and the *Ramayana* (see chapter 2). This body of classic Indian literature was recorded in Sanskrit, the language of India's educated classes. Occupying much the same position in Indian literature that Latin occupied in the medieval West, Sanskrit served for centuries as a cohesive force amidst a wide variety of vernacular dialects.

Among the most popular forms of Hindu literature in the medieval period were the *Puranas*, eighteen religious books that preserved the myths and legends of the Hindu gods. Many of the tales in the *Puranas* illustrate the special powers of the gods Vishnu and Shiva. In the *Vishnu Purana*, for instance, Krishna is pictured as a lover who courts his devotees with sensual abandon. In contrast to medieval Christianity's somber

Figure 14.3 Temple sculptures. Classical dance postures, inspired by the *Karanas*, from the Devi temple, Chidambaram, India, thirteenth century. © Government of India, Department of Archaeology.

condemnation of the sensual life, Hinduism celebrated the erotic union of male and female as symbolic of the eternal mingling of flesh and spirit and as a sublime metaphor for the fusion of the Self (Atman) and the Absolute Spirit (Brahman). In the Upanishads (see chapter 2), we read:

> In the embrace of his beloved a man forgets the whole world – everything both within and without. In the same manner, he who embraces the Self knows neither within nor without.

The Hindu view that sexuality lay at the heart of existence recalls the spirit of pre-Christian fertility cults, which proclaimed the life-affirming aspects of erotic love. In the following passage from the *Vishnu Purana*, Krishna's cajoling and sensuous courtship, culminating in the circle of the dance, symbolizes God's love for the human soul and the soul's unswerving attraction to the One.

READING 49

From the *Vishnu Purana*

. . . . [Krishna], observing the clear sky, bright with the   1
autumnal moon, and the air perfumed with the fragrance of the wild water-lily, in whose buds the clustering bees were murmuring their songs, felt inclined to join with the milkmaids [Gopis] in sport . . . .

Then Madhava [Krishna], coming amongst them, conciliated some with soft speeches, some with gentle looks; and some he took by the hand: and the illustrious deity sported with them in the stations of the dance. As each of the milkmaids, however, attempted to keep in one   10
place, close to the side of Krishna, the circle of the dance could not be constructed; and he, therefore, took each by the hand, and when their eyelids were shut by the effects of such touch, the circle was formed. Then proceeded the dance, to the music of their clashing bracelets, and songs that celebrated, in suitable strain, the charms of the autumnal season. Krishna sang of the moon of autumn – a mine of gentle radiance; but the nymphs repeated the

praises of Krishna alone. At times, one of them, wearied by the revolving dance, threw her arms, ornamented with tinkling bracelets, round the neck of the destroyer of Madhu [Krishna]; another, skilled in the art of singing his praises, embraced him. The drops of perspiration from the arms of Hari [Krishna] were like fertilizing rain, which produced a crop of down upon the temples of the milkmaids. Krishna sang the strain that was appropriate to the dance. The milkmaids repeatedly exclaimed "Bravo, Krishna!" to his song. When leading, they followed him; when returning they encountered him; and whether he went forwards or backwards, they ever attended on his steps. Whilst frolicking thus, they considered every instant without him a myriad of years; and prohibited (in vain) by husbands, fathers, brothers, they went forth at night to sport with Krishna, the object of their affection.

    Thus, the illimitable being, the benevolent remover of all imperfections, assumed the character of a youth among the females of the herdsmen of [the district of] Vraja; pervading their natures and that of their lords by his own essence, all-diffusive like the wind. For even as the elements of ether, fire, earth, water, and air are comprehended in all creatures, so also is he everywhere present, and in all . . . .

20

30

40

———————◆———————

Indian Poetry

If the religious literature of India is sensuous in nature, so is the secular literature, much of which gives attention to physical pleasures. Sanskrit lyric poetry is the most erotic of all world literatures. Unlike the poetry of most ancient cultures, Sanskrit poetry is independent of music: Most Sanskrit poems are meant to be spoken, not sung. On the other hand, Sanskrit poetry shares with most ancient Greek and Latin verse a lack of rhyme. It also exploits such literary devices as **alliteration** (the repetition of initial sounds in successive words, as in *panting* and *pale*) and **assonance** (similarity between vowel sounds, as in *lake* and *fate*).

    In Sanskrit poetry, implication and innuendo are more important than direct statement or assertion. The multiplicity of synonyms in Sanskrit permits a wide range of meanings, puns, and verbal play. And although this wealth of synonyms and near-synonyms contributes to the richness of Indian poetry, it makes English translation quite difficult. For example, there are some fifty expressions for the Sanskrit word for lotus, whereas in English there is but one. Sanskrit poets employ a large number of stock similes: The lady's face is like the moon, her eyes resemble lotuses, and so on. Sanskrit poems are rarely intimate or personal; rather, they describe general and universal conditions. But classical rules of style dictate that every poem must exhibit a single characteristic sentiment, such as anger, courage, wonder, or passion. Grief, however, the emotion humans seek to avoid, may not dominate any poem or play.

A great flowering of Indian literature occurred between the fourth and tenth centuries, but it was not until the eleventh century and thereafter that the renowned anthologies of Sanskrit poetry appeared. One of the most honored of these collections, an anthology of 1,739 verses dating from between 700 and 1050, was produced by the twelfth-century Buddhist monk Vidyakara. It is entitled *The Treasury of Well-Turned Verse*. As with most Indian anthologies, poems on the subject of love outnumber those in any other category, and many of the love lyrics feature details of physical passion. As suggested by the three selections that follow, Indian poetry is more frank and erotic than ancient or medieval European love poetry and less romantic than Islamic verse.

READING 50

From *The Treasury of Well-Turned Verse*

When we have loved, my love,   1
Panting and pale from love,
Then from your cheeks my love,
Scent of the sweat I love:
And when our bodies love   5
Now to relax in love
After the stress of love,
Ever still more I love
Our mingled breath of love.

———————◆———————

When he desired to see her breast   1
She clasped him tight in an embrace;
And when wished to kiss her lip
She used cosmetics on her face.
She held his hand quite firmly pressed   5
Between her thighs in desperate grip;
   Nor yielded to his caress,
   Yet kept alive his wantonness.

———————◆———————

If my absent bride were but a pond,   1
her eyes the water lilies and her face the lotus,
her brows the rippling waves, her arms the lotus stems;
then might I dive into the water of her loveliness
and cool of limb escape the mortal pain   5
exacted by the flaming fire of love.

———————◆———————

Indian Architecture

The medieval period generated some of the finest works of Hindu art and architecture in India's history. Buddhist imagery influenced the style of Hindu art, and Buddhist rock-cut temples and caves provided models for Hindu architects. Between the sixth and fourteenth centuries, Hindus built thousands of temple-shrines to honor Vishnu and Shiva. These structures varied in shape from region to region, but generally they took the form of square or rectangular mounds topped with lofty towers or spires. They were constructed of stone or brick with iron dowels often taking the place of mortar. Like the early Buddhist *stupas* (see Figure 9.18), medieval Hindu temples symbolized the sacred mountain. Some were even painted white to resemble the snowy peaks of the Himalayas. But whereas the *stupa* was a solid mound, designed to be circumscribed by the Buddhist, the Hindu temple (more akin to the *chaitya* cave; see Figure 9.19) featured a series of interior spaces leading into a shrine – the dwelling place for the god on earth. One entered the temple by way of an ornate porch or series of porches, each with its own roof and spire. One then arrived at a large hall designed for sacred dancing, and, finally, at the dim, womblike sanctuary that held the cult figure of the god. While Hindu temples did not serve as places for congregational worship, they acted as cosmic diagrams; sacred

Figure 14.5 Celestial deities, Kandariya Mahadeo Temple, Khajuraho, India, ca. 1000. Stone. Photo: © Richard Lucas/The Image Works, Inc.

Figure 14.4 Kandariya Mahadeo temple, Khajuraho, India, ca. 1000. Archaeological Survey of India. Reproduced by courtesy of the British Library, London.

numerology dictated the design of the building and its embellishment. Thus, like the Gothic cathedral, the Hindu temple reflected the profound human impulse to forge a link between heaven and earth and between matter and spirit.

The Kandariya Mahadeo temple in Khajuraho is but one of twenty remaining Hindu temple-shrines that rise like stone mountains out of the dusty plains of north-central India (see Map 14.1). Dedicated in the early eleventh century to the god Shiva, the temple, some 102 feet high, rests on a high masonry terrace and is entered through an elevated porch (Figure 14.4). Like most Indian temples, Kandariya Mahadeo consists of a series of extensively ornamented horizontal cornices that ascend in narrowing diameter to their lotus-shaped peaks. At each tier of the beehive-like tower is a row of figures: Human beings and animals drawn from India's great epics appear at the lower levels, while divine nymphs and celestial deities adorn the upper levels (Figure 14.5).

Like the Gothic cathedral, the Hindu temple hosted a multitude of relief sculptures that covered almost the entire surface of the building. Yet, concep-

Figure 14.6 Mithuna Couple, Orissa, India, twelfth to thirteenth century. Stone, height 6 ft. The Metropolitan Museum of Art, New York. Florance Waterbury Fund, 1970.

tually, no two artistic enterprises could have been further apart. For whereas the medieval Church regarded the nude human form as symbolic of sexual pleasure and sinfulness and thus discouraged its representation, Hinduism saw in the human body and in sexual union expressions of the universal life force. The sinuous nudes that animate the surface of the temple at Kandariya Mahadeo assume languid, erotic poses. Deeply carved, and endowed with supple limbs, and swelling breasts and buttocks, their volumetric bodies convey the divine attributes of life breath and sexual "fullness." The popular *mithuna*, a man and woman shown in passionate embrace (Figure **14.6**), like the imagery of the dance in the *Vishnu Purana*, is symbolic of the ultimate oneness of human and divine energy.

Indian Music and Dance

As noted in chapter 9, the music of India is inseparable from its religious history. Indeed, a single musical tradition, one that goes back some three thousand years and is still in use today, nourished both secular and religious music. In ancient times, India developed a system of music characterized by modes (*ragas*) and rhythms (*talas*). Over the centuries, hundreds of *ragas* have evolved, of which sixty remain in standard use and nine are considered primary. Each *raga* comprises a series of seven basic notes arranged in a specific order. As with the Greek modes (see chapter 6), each of the basic Indian *ragas* is associated with a different emotion, mood, or time of day. A famous Indian anecdote tells how a sixteenth-century court musician once sang at noontime so beautiful a night *raga* that darkness instantly fell where he stood. Governing the rhythm of an Indian musical composition is the *tala* or rhythmic pattern, which, in union with the *raga*, shapes the mood of the piece. Indian music divides the octave into twenty-two principal tones and many more microtones, all of which are treated equally. There is, therefore, no tonal center and no harmony in traditional Indian music. Rather, the character of a musical composition depends on the exposition of the *raga* and the *tala*. A typical *raga* opens with a slow portion that establishes a particular mood, moves into a second portion that explores rhythmic variations, and closes with rapid, complex, and often syncopated improvisations that culminate in a breathtaking finale.[§]

India developed a broad range of stringed instruments that were either bowed or plucked. The most popular of these was the *sitar*, a long-necked, stringed instrument with a gourd resonator, which came into use during the thirteenth century (Figure **14.7**). Re-

---

[§]See Music Listening Selections at end of chapter.

Figure 14.7 Ravi Shankar playing the sitar (right); others with tabla (hand drums) and tamboura (plucked string instrument). Photo: © Silverstone/Magnum Photos, Inc.

lated to the *cithara*, an instrument used in ancient Greece (see Figure 6.27), the *sitar* provided a distinctive rhythmic "drone," while its strings were plucked for melody. Accompanied by flutes, drums, bells, and horns, sitar players were fond of improvising patterns of notes in quick succession against a resonating base sound.

Since the Sanskrit word for music (*sangeeta*) means both "sound" and "rhythm" we may assume that the music of India, like that of ancient Greece, was inseparable from the art of dance. Usually designed to set a mood or tell a story – like the *raga* it accompanied – Indian dance involved rigidly observed steps and hand gestures (*mudra*). The professional dancer was trained in achieving difficult leg and foot positions (see Figure 14.3), some of which may be seen on the facades of Indian temples (see Figure 14.5). Each of some thirty traditional dances requires a novel combination of complex body positions, of which there are more than one hundred. The close relationship among the arts of medieval India provides something of a parallel with the medieval synthesis in the West. On the other hand, the sensual character of the arts of India distinguishes them rather sharply from the arts of Christian Europe.

Chinese Civilization

Nowhere else in the world has a single cultural tradition dominated so consistently and for so long a time as in China. When European merchants visited China in the thirteenth century, the Chinese had already enjoyed 1,700 years of civilization, the essentials of which would survive with few changes until 1911. China's agrarian landmass, rich in vast mineral, vegetable, and animal resources, readily supported a large and self-sufficient population. Despite internal shifts of power

and repeated barbarian attacks, China experienced a single form of government, that of imperial monarchy, and a large degree of political order until the invasion of the Mongols in the thirteenth century. But even after the establishment of Mongol rule under Kublai Khan (1215–1294), the governmental bureaucracy on which China had long depended remained intact, and Chinese culture continued to flourish.

China During the T'ang Era

T'ang China (618–907 C.E.) was a unified, centralized state that had no equal in India or the West. In contrast with India, class distinctions in China were flexible and allowed a fair degree of social mobility: Even commoners could rise to become members of the ruling elite. Nevertheless, like all Asian and European civilizations of premodern times, the great masses of Chinese people had no voice in political matters.

Despite the success of Buddhism in China (see chapters 8 and 9), Confucianism remained China's foremost moral philosophy. Confucian teachings encouraged social harmony and respect for the ruling patriarch, whom the Chinese called the "Son of Heaven." The Confucian equation of virtue and authority, which linked the destiny of the community with its leader's adherence to moral law (see chapter 3), and the Chinese respect for universal order (expressed in the creative interaction of *yin* and *yang*) were humanizing forces in Chinese culture. Confucianism was generally tolerant of all religious creeds, though it disapproved of the Buddhist commitment to celibacy, which contravened the Confucian esteem for family. The growth of Buddhist sects and the popularity of a religion that attracted large numbers of talented men to the cloister encouraged eighth-century emperors to

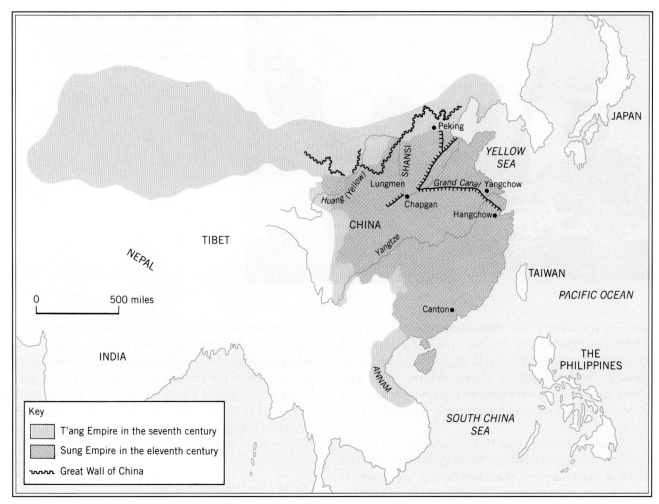

Map 14.2 The T'ang and Sung Empires in China.

restrict the number of Buddhist monasteries and to limit the ordination of new monks and nuns. In contrast to medieval Europe, however, where transcendental Christianity guided the soul's journey to the hereafter, China held firmly to a secular ethic that emphasized proper conduct (*li*) and the sanctity of human life on earth. These Confucian tenets – renewed in the Neo-Confucian movement of the eleventh century – challenged neither the popular worship of a large number of Chinese nature deities nor the ancient belief that the souls of the dead, wandering in the spirit world, must be honored and appeased. Likewise, Confucian ideals of order, harmony, and filial duty were easily reconciled with the holistic outlook of the Taoists (see chapter 2). Tolerant of all religious beliefs, the Chinese never engaged in religious wars or massive crusades of the kind that disrupted both Christian and Islamic civilizations.

Under the rule of the T'ang emperors, China experienced a flowering of culture that was unmatched anywhere in the world. Often called the greatest dynasty in Chinese history, the T'ang brought unity and wealth to a vast Chinese empire (Map **14.2**). T'ang emperors perpetuated the economic reforms of their immediate predecessors. They completed the Grand Canal connecting the lower valley of the Hwang (Yellow) River to the eastern banks of the Yangtze, a project that facilitated shipping and promoted internal cohesion and wealth. They initiated a full census of the population (some four centuries before a similar survey was undertaken in Norman England), which was repeated every three years. They also humanized the penal code and tried to guarantee farmlands to the peasants. They stimulated agricultural production, encouraged the flourishing silk trade, launched a tax reform that based assessments on units of land rather than agricultural output, and commuted payments from goods to coins.

The T'ang Empire dwarfed the Carolingian Empire in the West not only by its geographic size and population but also by its intellectual and educational accomplishments. T'ang bureaucrats, steeped in Confucian traditions and rigorously trained in the literary classics, were members of an intellectual elite that rose to service on the basis of merit. Beginning in the seventh century (but rooted in a long tradition of leadership based on merit; see chapter 3), every government official was subject to a rigorous civil service examination. A young man gained a political position by passing three levels of examinations (district, provincial, and national) that tested his familiarity with the Chinese classics as well as his grasp of contemporary political issues. For lower ranking positions, candidates took exams in law, mathematics, and calligraphy. Because Chinese characters changed very little over the centuries, students could read 1,500-year-old texts as easily as they could read contemporary texts. Chinese classics were thus accessible to Chinese scholars in a way that the Greco-Roman classics were not accessible to Western scholars. Though training for the arduous civil service exams required a great degree of memorization and a thorough knowledge of the Chinese literary tradition, originality was also important: Candidates had to prove accomplishment in the writing of prose and poetry, as well as in the analysis of administrative policy. Strict standards applied to grading, and candidates who failed the exams (only one to ten percent passed the first level) could take them over and over, even into their middle and old age.

During the seventh century, the imperial college in the capital city of Changan prepared some 3,000 men for the civil service exams. (As in the West, women were excluded from education in colleges and universities.) Such scholar officials (sometimes called **mandarins**) constituted China's highest social class. And while the vast population of Chinese peasants lived in relative ignorance and poverty, the mandarins generally enjoyed lives of wealth and position. Nowhere else in the world at this time in history was such prestige attached to education and intellectual achievement. Despite instances in which family connections influenced political position, the imperial examination system remained the main route to official status in China well into the twentieth century.

China in the Sung Era

After a brief period of turmoil resulting from barbarian attacks, the Sung dynasty (960–1279) restored political unity to China. The three centuries of Sung rule corresponded roughly to the period of Norman domination in Europe (see chapter 11). While the feudal West glorified the values of heroism and military prowess, the Chinese despised military life. During the Sung Era, mercenaries were often hired to replace peasant-soldiers. A Chinese proverb claimed that "superior" men should no more serve as soldiers than high-grade iron should be used to forge common nails. And Chinese poets frequently lamented the disruption of family life as soldiers left home to defend remote regions of the empire. In combat, the Chinese generally preferred starving out their enemies to confronting them in battle. The peaceful nature of the Chinese impressed its first Western visitors: Arriving in China a half century after the end of the Sung Era, the Venetian merchant Marco Polo (1254–1324) observed with some astonishment that no one carried arms.

The Sung Era was a period of population growth, agricultural productivity, and commercial trade centering on the exportation of tea, silk, and porcelain.

Figure 14.8 *Lady Wen-chi's Return to China*, Chinese, Northern Sung dynasty, ca. 1100. Ink, gold, and colors on silk. The Museum of Fine Arts, Boston. Denman Waldo Ross collection. © 1990. All rights reserved.

Figure 14.9 Attributed to Emperor Hui Tsung, *Ladies Preparing Newly Woven Silk*, Chinese, Sung Dynasty, early twelfth century (signed 1101–1126). Ink and color on silk handscroll, 14½ × 56½ in. Courtesy, Museum of Fine Arts, Boston. Chinese and Japanese Special Fund.

China's new economic prosperity caused a population shift from the countryside to the city. Port cities like Hangchow and Changan (see Map 14.2), with populations of over two million people, boasted luxurious shops, restaurants, teahouses, temples, and gardens (Figure 14.8). Chinese cities were larger and more populous than those in the West. But while medieval European town life offered new opportunities to both men and women, urbanization in China led to a decline in the social standing of women. Traditionally, Chinese women participated in agricultural activities as well as in the manufacture of silk (Figure 14.9), and many were trained in musical performance (Figure 14.10). During the Sung Era, however, as women became less essential to economic productivity, they assumed a more ornamental place in Chinese society. To indicate that their female offspring were exempt from common labor, prosperous urban families bound the feet of their infant daughters, a practice that broke the arch and dwarfed the foot to half its normal growth. This cruel means of signifying social status continued until the twentieth century.

Figure 14.10 Girls' ensemble performing yen-yüeh (court banquet music) during the reign of Emperor Hsuan-tsung, with (upper group, left to right) lute, angular harp, long zither, stone-chime, mouth organ, hourglass drum, transverse flute, and clapper. Detail from a silk handscroll, Sung dynasty (960–1279). Attributed to Zhou Wenju, United by Music, Ming dynasty, sixteenth century, ink and colors on silk handscroll, 16⅜ in. × 71⅞ in. Kate S. Buckingham Purchase Fund, 1950. 1370 right side. Photograph © 1994 The Art Institute of Chicago. All rights reserved.

Technology in the T'ang and Sung Eras

Chinese civilization is exceptional in the extraordinary number of its technological inventions, many of which came into use elsewhere in the world only long after their utilization in China. A case in point is printing, which originated in ninth-century China but was not perfected in the West until the fifteenth century. The earliest printed document, the *Diamond Sutra*, dated 868, is a Buddhist text produced from large woodcut blocks (Figure 14.11). In the mid-eleventh century, the Chinese invented movable type, and by the end of the century, the entire body of Buddhist and Confucian classics, including the commentaries, were available in printed editions. One such classic (a required text for civil service candidates) was *The Confucian Book of Odes*, a venerable collection of over three hundred poems dating from the first millennium B.C.E. By the twelfth century, the Chinese were also printing paper money—a practice that inevitably gave rise to the profession of counterfeiting. Although in China movable type did not inspire a revolution in the communication of ideas (as it would in Renaissance Europe), it encouraged literacy, fostered scholarship, and facilitated the preservation of the Chinese classics.

Chinese technology often involved the intelligent application of natural principles to produce labor-saving devices. Examples include the water mill (devised to grind tea leaves and to provide motive power for textile machinery), the wheelbarrow (used in China from at least the third century but not found in Europe until more than ten centuries later), and the stern-post rudder and magnetic compass (Sung inventions that facilitated maritime trade). The latter two devices had revolutionary consequences for Western Europeans, who used them to inaugurate an age of exploration and discovery (see chapter 18). Other devices, such as the abacus and the hydromechanical clock, and such processes as iron casting (used for armaments, for suspension bridges, and for the construction of some T'ang and Sung pagodas) were unknown in the West for centuries or were invented independently of Chinese prototypes. Not until the eighteenth century, for instance, did Western Europeans master the technique of steel casting, which had been in use in China since the sixth century C.E.; and the seismograph (invented in China around 100 B.C.E.) remained unknown to Europe until modern times.

Figure 14.11 The world's earliest printed book, the *Diamond Sutra*, dated 868 C.E., 6 ft. × 2½ ft. Reproduced by courtesy of the British Library, London, Department of Oriental Manuscripts and Books.

Some of China's most important technological contributions, such as the foot stirrup (in use well before the fifth century) and gunpowder (invented during the ninth century), improved China's ability to withstand the attacks of Huns, Turks, and other tribal people that repeatedly attacked China's northern frontiers. While T'ang emperors used gunpowder for fireworks, Sung armies employed it during the tenth century to launch projectiles to a range of some three hundred yards. In the West, the foot stirrup and gunpowder had revolutionary effects, the former ushering in the military aspect of medieval feudalism, the latter ultimately undermining siege warfare and inaugurating modern combat.

In addition to their ingenuity in engineering and metallurgy, the Chinese were in the forefront in the practice of medicine. From the eleventh century on, they used vaccination to prevent diseases, thus establishing the science of immunology. Their understanding of human anatomy and their assumption that illness derives from an imbalance of *ch'i* (life energy) gave rise to acupuncture, the practice of applying needles to specific parts of the body to regulate and restore proper energy flow. Chinese medical encyclopedias dating from the twelfth century were far in advance of any produced in the medieval West.

Chinese Literature

Chinese literature owes little to other cultures. It reflects at every turn a high regard for native traditions and for the concepts of universal harmony expressed in Confucian and Taoist thought. Philosophic in nature, it is, however, markedly free of religious sentiment. Even between the fifth and ninth centuries, when Buddhism was at its height in China, Chinese literature was largely secular, hence, very different from most of the literature of medieval Europe and the rest of Asia.

The literature of the T'ang and Sung Eras embraced a wide variety of genres including treatises on history, geography, religion, economics, and architecture; monographs on botany and zoology; essays on administrative and governmental affairs; drama, fiction, and lyric poetry. Masters in the art of compiling information, the Chinese produced a vast assortment of encyclopedias, manuals of divination and ritual, ethical discourses, and anthologies based on the teachings of Confucius and others. Like the medieval scholastics in the West, Chinese scholars esteemed their classical past, but unlike European schoolmen, they encountered no conflict between (and therefore no need to reconcile) faith and reason.

During the twelfth and thirteenth centuries, in the urban centers of the Sung Era, storytelling flourished, and popular theater arose in the form of dramatic performance. Popular genres included comedy, historical plays, and tales of everyday life — many of which featured love stories. As dramatists began to adapt literary plots to music, **opera** (musical drama) became the fashionable entertainment among ordinary townspeople and at the imperial court.[§] The first Chinese **novels** – products of a long tradition of oral narrative – also appeared during the twelfth century, their themes focusing on the adventures of contemporary heroes.

The novel, however, was not original to China. Rather, it was a product of the aristocratic and feudal culture of medieval Japan. During the tenth and eleventh centuries, Japan produced some of its greatest literature, including the world's first novel, *The Tale of Genji* (ca. 1004). Its author, Murasaki Shikibu (978–1016), was one of a group of outstanding female writers and members of Japanese court society. Unique in East Asian literary history, were upper-class Japanese women, like Murasaki, who won so much acclaim as prose masters (especially in diary-writing) that one tenth-century male diarist pretended his work was penned by a woman. The achievement of medieval Japanese women is all the more remarkable in that (like their Chinese counterparts) they were excluded from the world of scholarship. Nevertheless, using a system of phonetic symbols derived from Chinese characters, these women produced the classic works of Japanese prose, works in which the refined, ceremonial life of the Japanese court is captured.

In China, early fiction writing reaches its apogee with the monumental historical novel entitled *Three Kingdoms* (attributed to the fourteenth-century playwright Luo Guanzhong). This one-thousand-page novel, filled with hundreds of characters and lengthy, epic descriptions of martial prowess, brings alive the turbulent era that followed the breakup of the Han dynasty (168–265 C.E.).

Chinese Music and Poetry

A 1978 archeological excavation in central China uncovered a set of sixty-four large bells that proved to be the oldest fixed-pitch instruments in the world. More than two thousand years old, these bells were tuned to the twelve-note scale that formed the basis of China's musical system. The Chinese drew from these twelve basic notes a series of five-tone scales. Each of the five notes was held to correspond to one of the five elements (earth, metal, wood, fire, and water), as well as to Chinese geographic, astronomical, and social divisions. For the Chinese, the function of music was to imitate and sustain the harmony of nature. Both

---

§See Music Listening Selections at end of chapter.

Taoists and Confucians regarded music as an expression of cosmic order, and Taoists even made distinctions between *yin* and *yang* notes. Like most of the music of the ancient world, Chinese music was monophonic, but it assumed a unique timbre produced by nasal tones that were often high in pitch and subtle in inflection. The sliding nasal tones of Chinese music resemble those of the zither. Frequently used for Buddhist chant (see chapter 9), the zither was the favorite of Chinese instruments and notation for it was devised as early as the second century B.C.E. The Chinese employed the zither, along with the short-necked lute and various flutes, bells, and chimes in instrumental ensembles (see Figure 14.10). But the most popular Chinese musical genre was the solo song, performed with or without instrumental accompaniment.

A close kinship between Chinese music and speech was enforced by the unique nature of the Chinese language. Consisting of some eight hundred characters, the Chinese language demands of its speaker subtle intonation: The pitch or tonal level at which any word is pronounced gives it its meaning. A single word, depending on how it is uttered, may have more than a hundred meanings. In this sense, all communication in the Chinese language is musical, a phenomenon that has particular importance for Chinese poetry. Chinese poetry is a kind of vocal music: A line of spoken poetry, is – like music – essentially a series of tones that rise and fall in various rhythms. Moreover, since Chinese is a monosyllabic language with few word endings, rhyme is common to speech. All Chinese verse is rhymed, often in long runs that are almost impossible to imitate in English. And finally, Chinese verse is characterized by extraordinary kinds of condensation and innuendo that most English translations cannot capture.

During the T'ang Era, China produced some of the most beautiful poetry in world literature. The poems of the eighth and ninth centuries, an era referred to as the Golden Age of Chinese poetry, resemble diary entries that record the intimate experience of everyday life. Unlike the poetry of India, Chinese lyrics are rarely sensuous or erotic and only infrequently attentive to either physical affection or romantic love. Restrained and sophisticated, the poetry of the T'ang period was written by scholar-poets who considered verse making a mark of educational and intellectual refinement. From earliest times, nature and natural imagery played a large part in Chinese verse. T'ang poets continued this long tradition: Their poems are filled with the meditative spirit of Taoism and a sense of oneness with nature.

Two of the greatest poets of the T'ang period, Li Po (ca. 700–762: Figure **14.12**) and Tu Fu (712–770) belonged to the group of cultivated individuals who made up China's cultural elite. Although Li Po was not a scholar official, as was his friend, Tu Fu, he was

Figure 14.12 Lian K'ai, *The Poet Li Po*, thirteenth century. Ink on paper, 42⅞ × 13 ins. Tokyo National Museum.

familiar with the Chinese classics. Both Li Po and Tu Fu were members of the Eight Immortals of the Wine Cup, an informal association of poets who celebrated the kinship of ink and drink and the value of inebriation to poetic inspiration. Tu Fu, often regarded as China's greatest poet, wrote some 1,400 poems, many of which are autobiographical reflections that impart genuine emotion and humor. In contrast with these T'ang poets, the ninth-century poet, Po Chu-i, who headed the Bureau of War, brought to his poetry a cynicism and worldliness that is particularly typical of the Sung Era. Like most of the poets of his time, he was a statesman, a calligrapher, an aesthetician, and a moralist. He thus epitomized the ideal of the well-rounded individual long before that concept became important among Renaissance Europeans.

READING 51
Selections from the Poetry of the T'ang and Sung Eras

Watching the Mt. Lushan Waterfall

Incense-Burner Peak shimmers in the sun,   1
Purple mist slowly rising.
A flying stream, seen from below,
Hangs like clouds down the crag.
The waterfall pours itself   5
Three thousand feet straight down,
Roaring like the Milky Way
Tumbling from high heaven.

Li Po (translator B. Raffel)

Chuang Chou and the Butterfly

Chuang Chou[1] in dream became a butterfly,   1
And the butterfly became Chuang Chou at waking.
Which was the real — the butterfly or the man?
Who can tell the end of the endless changes of things?
The water that flows into the depth of the distant sea   5
Returns anon to the shallows of a transparent stream.
The man, raising melons outside the green gate of the city,
Was once the Prince of the East Hill,[2]
So must rank and riches vanish.
You know it, still you toil and toil, — What for?   10

Li Po (translator S. Obata)

Spring Rain

Oh lovely spring rain!   1
You come at the right time, in the right season.
Riding the night winds you creep in,
Quietly wetting the world.
Roads are dark, clouds are darker.   5
Only a light on a boat, gleaming.
And in the morning the city is drunk with red flowers,
Cluster after cluster, moist, glistening.

Tu Fu (translator B. Raffel)

[1]A fourth-century follower of Lao Tzu (see chapter 2), whose writings describe how, in a dream, he became a butterfly.
[2]The Marquis of Tung-ling, a third-century B.C.E. official, lost his exalted position at court after the fall of the Ch'in dynasty, and retired to grow melons outside of the city of Changan.

Farewell Once More
(To my friend Yen at Feng Chi Station)

Here we part.   1
You go off in the distance,
And once more the forested mountains
Are empty, unfriendly.
What holiday will see us   5
Drunk together again?
Last night we walked
Arm in arm in the moonlight,
Singing sentimental ballads
Along the banks of the river.   10
Your honor outlasts three emperors.
I go back to my lonely house by the river,
Mute, friendless, feeding the crumbling years.

Tu Fu (translator K. Rexroth)

On His Baldness

At dawn I sighed to see my hairs fall;   1
At dusk I sighed to see my hairs fall.
For I dreaded the time when the last lock should go . . .
They are all gone and I do not mind at all!
I have done with that cumbrous washing and getting dry;   5
My tiresome comb forever is laid aside.
Best of all, when the weather is hot and wet,
To have no topknot weighing down on one's head!
I put aside my dusty conical cap;
And loose my collar fringe,   10
In a silver jar I have stored a cold stream;
On my bald pate I trickle a ladle-full.
Like one baptized with the Water of Buddha's Law,
I sit and receive this cool, cleansing joy.
Now I know why the priest who seeks repose   15
Frees his heart by first shaving his head.

Po Chu-i (translator Arthur Waley)

Madly Singing in the Mountains

There is no one among men that has not a special failing: 1
And my failing consists in writing verses.
I have broken away from the thousand ties of life:
But this infirmity still remains behind.
Each time that I look at a fine landscape: 5
Each time that I meet a loved friend,
I raise my voice and recite a stanza of poetry
And am glad as though a god had crossed my path.
Ever since the day I was banished to Hsün-yang
Half my time I have lived among the hills.   10
And often, when I have finished a new poem,
Alone I climb the road to the Eastern Rock.
I lean my body on the banks of white stone:
I pull down with my hands a green cassia branch.
My mad singing startles the valleys and hills: 15
The apes and birds all come to peep.
Fearing to become a laughing-stock to the world,
I choose a place that is unfrequented by men.

Po Chu-i (translator Arthur Waley)

Figure 14.13 Mi Yu-jen, *Cloudy Mountains*, 1130. Handscroll, ink, white lead, and slight touches of color on silk, 16¹⁵⁄₁₆ × 75¾ in. The Cleveland Musuem of Art, Purchase from the J.H. Wade Fund.

Chinese Landscape Painting

During the T'ang Era, figural subjects presented in a pictorial and representational style dominated Chinese art (see Figure 14.9), but by the tenth century, landscape painting became the favorite genre. The Chinese often refer to landscape paintings as wordless poems, and, in fact, Chinese painting and poetry are intimately related. Both seek to evoke mood rather than describe or narrate events, and both embrace a cosmic view of nature. T'ang and Sung landscapes convey the harmony of heaven, earth, and humankind, an idea fundamental to both Taoism and Buddhism. The contemplative landscapes of Chinese artists reflect a self-conscious effort to integrate complementary elements: dark and light shapes, bold and muted strokes, dense and sparse textures, large and small forms, and positive and negative spaces, each pair interacting in imitation of the *yin/yang* principle that symbolizes cosmic wholeness.

Chinese paintings generally assume one of three basic formats: the handscroll, the hanging scroll, and the album leaf (often used as a fan). Between one and forty feet long, the handscroll is viewed continuously from right to left (Figure 14.13). Like a poem, the visual "action" unfolds in time – an object of meditation and delight. Vertical in format, the hanging scroll is meant to be read from the bottom up, from earth to heaven, so to speak (Figures 14.14, 14.15). The album leaf usually belongs to a book that combines poems and paintings in a sequence (Figure 14.15). Chinese scrolls and books may be made of silk, cotton, paper, or bamboo, and ornamented with either ink or thin washes of paint applied in monochrome or in muted colors. An unusual feature of the Chinese painting is the addition of the seals or signatures of collectors who have owned the work of art. These appear along with occasional marginal comments or poems inspired by the painting. Thus, the Chinese painting is a repository of the personal experiences of both the artist and the art lover.

In contrast to the art produced in the West before the nineteenth century, much of which is religious in

Figure 14.14 Attributed to Li Ch'eng, A *Solitary Temple Amid Clearing Peaks*, Northern Sung dynasty (960–1127). Hanging scroll, ink and slight color on silk, 44 × 22 in. The Nelson-Atkins Museum of Art, Kansas City, Missouri (Purchase: Nelson Trust) 47–71.

content, Chinese art is almost exclusively secular. And whereas Western artists exalt the heroic deeds and historical achievements of human beings, Chinese artists rarely glorify human actions. Indeed, in Chinese paintings, the landscape tends to dwarf the figures so that their occupations seem mundane and incidental to the larger view of nature (see Figures 14.13, 14.14, 14.15). Chinese artists were disinterested in the world of physical appearance; rather, they tried to capture the spirit of things. Instead of copying nature, they combined pictographic marks that caught the essence of natural objects. Specific brushstrokes – each bearing an individual name – were prescribed for different natural phenomena: pine needles, rocks, mountains, and so forth. Resembling Chinese calligraphy, the artist's brushstrokes are the "bones" of the Chinese landscape. Economy, gestural expressiveness, and spontaneity are hallmarks of the finest Chinese paintings, as they are of the best Chinese poems. In Chinese art, tradition rather than originality governed creativity: Artists spent many years copying the works of the masters and frequently honored their forebears by "quoting" from their poems or paintings.

Chinese landscape paintings are generally meditative in mood and subtle in composition. There is no single viewpoint from which to observe the mountains, trees, waters, and human habitations pictured in Figure 14.14. Rather, we perceive the whole from what one eleventh-century Chinese art critic called the "angle of totality." We look down upon some elements, such as the rooftops, and up to others, such as the mountains. As our eye moves over the scroll, we tend to read the misty areas between mountains as an indication of depth. Our voyage through discontinuous pictorial space engages our recognition of the subtle relationships between all parts of the painting and puts us in touch with the physical and spiritual energies of nature. The lofty mountains and gentle waterfall seem protec-

Figure 14.15 Chao Meng-fu, *River Village – Fisherman's Joy*, Yuan dynasty (1254–1322). Album leaf, ink and color on silk, 11¼ × 11¹³⁄₁₆ in. The Cleveland Museum of Art, Leonard C. Hanna, Jr., Bequest.

Figure 14.16 Mu Ch'i, *Swallow and Lotus*, Sung dynasty. Hanging scroll, ink on silk, 36⅛ × 18½ in. The Cleveland Museum of Art, Purchase from the J.H. Wade Fund.

tive of the infinitely smaller images of houses and people. As with Chinese poetry, in which a few well-chosen words may convey a distinct mood, the virtue of the Chinese painting lies in its remarkable economy of line and color – that is, in the artist's ability to evoke a powerful image by means of a limited number of brushstrokes and tones.

More meticulous in detail, yet equally simple in composition and in its extraordinary balance of positive and negative space, *Swallow and Lotus* by Mu Ch'i (Figure 14.16) reflects the Sung taste for a decorative style that featured brightly colored flowers and birds. Refined nature studies like this one, executed on silk or on paper, became popular during the Sung period, even as artists sought a greater simplicity of brushwork in landscape painting.

Chinese Crafts

From earliest times, the Chinese excelled in the production of ceramic wares. For centuries, they manufactured fine terra-cotta objects both for everyday use and for burial in the tombs of the dead (see Figure 7.27). During the T'ang Era, Chinese craftspeople produced thousands of realistic clay images of horses, servants and entertainers. These figures were cast from moulds, assembled in sections, and glazed with green, yellow, and brown (Figure 14.17).

In addition to earthenware, stoneware of the T'ang and Sung periods was noted for its extraordinary quality (Figure 14.18). The crowning achievement was **porcelain** – a hard, translucent clay fired at high heat. Describing the magnificent porcelains of the T'ang Era, a ninth-century merchant observed that one could see the sparkle of water through Chinese bowls that were "as fine as glass." Exported along with silk, lacquerware, and carved ivory, porcelain became one of the most sought-after of Chinese luxury goods – indeed, so popular that Westerners still call their dishes and plates "china." Noted for their refined contours, some classic Chinese ceramics look back to early bronze vessels, while the gray-green glazes of others recall the color

Figure 14.17 Tomb figurine, horse, T'ang dynasty (618–907 C.E.). Glazed pottery, 30¼ × 31⅝ in. The Cleveland Museum of Art, Anonymous gift, 55.295.

Figure 14.18 Flower vase, Northern Sung dynasty (1127–1279). Tz'u-chou ware, glazed stoneware with sgraffito decoration, 22⅜ × 10 in. The Nelson-Atkins Museum of Art, Kansas City, Missouri (Purchase: Nelson Trust) 35–116.

and texture of Chinese jades. In subtlety and poetic restraint, these ceramics compare favorably with the most sublime Chinese landscape paintings.

The somber restraint of Chinese ceramics stand in sharp contrast to the profuse richness of Chinese metalwork, inlaid wood, and textiles. So famous was Chinese silk that the eight-thousand-mile overland trade route connecting West and East (from Cadiz on the Atlantic to Shanghai on the Pacific) was dubbed "the Silk Road." Between 500 B.C.E. and roughly 1450 C.E., this route (and the nomadic peoples that traversed it) facilitated the exchange of goods and ideas between China and the great cities of the Near East (see Map 7.2).

Chinese Architecture

Chinese architects embraced a system of design that reflected the ancient Chinese quest for harmony with nature. Structures were emphatically horizontal – built to hug the earth – and both whole towns and individual buildings were laid out according to a cosmic axis that ran from north to south. House doors faced the "good" southerly direction of the summer sun and rear walls were closed to the cold north, homeland of barbarian hordes that had threatened China throughout its history. Symbolic perhaps of the aloof and self-absorbed nature of Chinese society, Chinese homes were self-enclosed "boxes" that looked inward to courtyards or gardens.

During the T'ang and Sung Eras, the multi-roofed pagoda, a shrine sheltering the relics of the Buddha or the *bodhisattvas*, remained the principal center of Buddhist worship (see chapter 9). From earliest times, pagodas were constructed of wood, a medium that was plentiful in China and one that was highly valued for its natural beauty. Chinese architectural ingenuity lay in the invention of a unique timber frame that – in place of walls – bore the entire weight of the roof while making the structure earthquake resistant (Figure **14.19**). Perfected during the T'ang Era, the Chinese

Figure 14.19 Seven-tiered bracket for a Chinese palace hall. Woodcut. Illustration from the Sung dynasty architectural manual, Ying-tsao fa-shin (1925 edition).

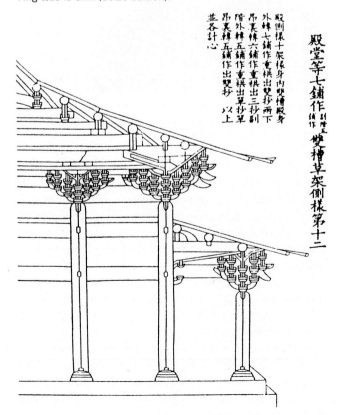

Figure 14.20 East pagoda of Yakushiji, Nara, Japan, ca. 720 C.E. Photo: Ancient Art and Architecture, Middlesex.

system of vaulting consisted of an intricate series of wooden cantilevers (horizontal brackets extending beyond the vertical supports) that provided support for centrally pitched, shingled or glazed tile roofs. This timber style spread to Japan, where it inspired some of the most refined and graceful pagodas ever built (Figure **14.20**). By the tenth century, the aesthetics of wood construction were firmly established in China and Japan, and during the following century, scholars enshrined these principles in the first great manual on architecture.

Since wooden buildings were highly vulnerable to fire, Chinese architects also built in brick and in cast iron. Regardless of medium, however, Chinese pagodas, pavilions, and domestic structures, with their projecting upturned eaves, were masterful achievements in elegant design. And, as indicated by the many magnificent pagodas found throughout Japan and southeast Asia, the Chinese were influential in disseminating an architectural style that, in its dependence on the wooden cantilever and its harmonious relationship with the natural site, remains stylistically distinct from that of the West.

SUMMARY

Between roughly 500 and 1300, India and China produced a wealth of arts and ideas that, although markedly different from those of the European West, contributed to the character of the humanistic tradition. Both India and China generated forms of expression that revealed a profound respect for the interdependence of natural and divine forces, of body and mind, and of matter and spirit. The sacred literature of Hinduism, as well as the rich fund of Sanskrit secular poetry manifest a distinctly sensual approach to nature. In literature, architecture, and sculpture, the Hindu gods are identified with the creative, cyclical, and regenerative forces of the Absolute Spirit. The Hindu notion that nature and humankind belong to one and the same unifying, organic order differed sharply from the medieval Christian view that humankind was distinct and separate from both lower (animal) and higher (divine) forms of reality. In Indian visual art, as in Indian music and dance, the holistic view is expressed as a celebration of cyclical and natural universal rhythms.

The arts of China blossomed under the centralized leadership of the T'ang and Sung dynasties. Chinese religious philosophy, a synthesis of Buddhist, Confucian, and Taoist precepts, emphasized natural harmony and the unity of all living things. These concepts found sublime expression in Chinese poetry and landscape painting – two of China's greatest contributions to world culture. During the T'ang and Sung Eras, the Chinese imperial examination system produced an elite class of scholar officials. China manufactured high-quality luxury goods and exported these to the rest of the world. Until at least the fourteenth century, China's technological and commercial achievements (such as the invention of printing, the magnetic compass, and gunpowder and the manufacture of magnificent porcelains and silks) far outstripped those of the West.

The civilizations of India and China perceived time as cyclical rather than as linear or progressive, that is, moving toward a specific end or goal. Repetition, harmony, and continuity are motifs that characterize the arts of these cultures. The circle, a universal symbol, and one that also frequently appears in medieval European art, is particularly characteristic of Asian expression, where it becomes a metaphor for the powerful forces of creation, destruction, and regeneration. In Krishna's dance and in Shiva's cosmic fire, as in the *yin/yang* unities of Chinese landscapes and poems, the circle symbolizes the concepts of continuity and completion. Deeply committed to these concepts of natural harmony, the civilizations of India and China produced arts and ideas that were quintessentially humanistic. As modern forms of communication have worked to bring all parts of the world closer together, the Asian contributions to the humanistic tradition have gained greater recognition, better understanding, and deeper appreciation in the West.

GLOSSARY

alliteration a literary device involving the repetition of initial sounds in successive or closely associated words or syllables

assonance a literary device involving a similarity in sound between vowels followed by different consonants

avatar the incarnation of a Hindu deity

mandarin a Chinese scholar-official

mithuna the Hindu representation of a male and a female locked in passionate embrace

novel an extended fictional prose narrative

porcelain fine ceramic ware made from a hard, translucent clay fired at high heat

opera a drama set to music and making use of vocal pieces with orchestral accompaniment

raga a mode or melody type in Hindu music; a particular combination of notes associated with a particular mood or atmosphere

tala a set rhythmic formula in Hindu music

sitar a long-necked, stringed instrument popular in Indian music

SUGGESTIONS FOR READING

Bhavnani, Enakshi. *The Dance in India*, 2nd ed. Bombay: Taraporevala, 1970.

Bussagli, Mario. *Oriental Architecture*, trans. by J. Shepley. New York: Abrams, 1973.

Coomaraswamy, Ananda. *The Dance of Shiva*. New York: Sunwise Turn, 1913.

Dawson, Robert, ed. *The Legacy of China*. New York: Oxford University Press, 1964.

Hookham, Hilda. *A Short History of China*. New York: New American Library, 1972.

Massey, Reginald. *The Music of India*. New York: Crescendo, 1977.

Murck, Alfreda and Wen Fong. *Words and Images: Chinese Poetry, Calligraphy, and Painting*. Princeton, N.J.: Princeton University Press, 1991.

Wu, N. I. *Chinese and Indian Architecture*. New York: Braziller, 1963.

MUSIC LISTENING SELECTIONS

Cassette I Selection 11 The Music of India: *Thumri*, played on the sitar by Ravi Shankar.

Cassette I Selection 12 The Music of China: Cantonese Music Drama: "Ngoh Wai Heng Kong" ("I'm Mad About You"). Male solo, zither, and other instruments.

Selected
General Bibliography

Baker, Herschel. *The Image of Man: A Study in the Idea of Human Dignity in Classical Antiquity, the Middle Ages, and the Renaissance.* New York: Harper, 1961.

Bugner, Ladislas, ed. *The Image of the Black in Western Art.* Vol. 2, *From the Early Christian Era to the Age of Discovery.* Cambridge, Mass.: Harvard University Press, 1976.

Bentley, Jerry H. *Old World Encounters: Cross-Cultural Contacts and Exchanges in Pre-Modern Times.* New York: Oxford University Press, 1993.

Clark, Kenneth. *Civilisation: A Personal View.* New York: Harper, 1970.

———. *The Nude: A Study in Ideal Form.* Princeton, N.J.: Princeton University Press, 1956.

Craven, Roy C. *Indian Art.* London: Thames and Hudson, 1985.

De la Croix, Horst, Richard G. Tansey, and Diane Kirkpatrick. *Gardner's Art Through the Ages*, 9th ed. San Diego: Harcourt, 1991.

Esposito, John L. *Islam: The Straight Path.* New York: Oxford University Press, 1988.

Ferguson, George. *Signs and Symbols in Christian Art.* New York: Oxford University Press, 1966.

Hopfe, L. M. *Religions of the World*, 4th ed. New York: Macmillan, 1987.

Kostoff, Spiro. *A History of Architecture: Settings and Rituals.* New York: Oxford University Press, 1985.

Lee, Sherman E. *A History of Far Eastern Art*, 4th ed. New York: Abrams, 1982.

Lund, Erik, Mogens Pihl, and Johannes Sløk. *A History of European Ideas*, trans. W. G. Jones. Reading, Mass.: Addison-Wesley, 1962.

May, Elizabeth, ed. *Music of Many Cultures.* Berkeley, Calif.: University of California Press, 1980.

Morton, W. Scott. *China: Its History and Culture.* New York: Cromwell, 1980.

———. *Japan: Its History and Culture.* New York: Cromwell, 1970.

Nuttgens, Patrick. *The Story of Architecture.* Englewood Cliffs, N.J.: Prentice-Hall, 1983.

O'Faolain, Julia, and Lauro Martines, eds. *Not in God's Image: Women in History from the Greeks to the Victorians.* New York: Harper, 1973.

Quadir, C.A. *Philosophy and Science in the Islamic World: From Origins to the Present Day.* London: Routledge, Chapman, and Hall, 1988.

Schirokauer, Conrad. *A Brief History of Chinese and Japanese Civilizations.* San Diego, Calif.: Harcourt Brace, 1978.

Sorrell, Walter. *The Dance Through the Ages.* New York: Grosset and Dunlap, 1967.

Spencer, Harold. *The Image Maker: Man and His Art.* New York: Scribners, 1975.

Sternfeld, F. W., gen. ed. *Praeger History of Western Music.* 5 vols. New York: Praeger, 1973.

Sullivan, Michael. *The Arts of China*, 3d ed. Berkeley, Calif.: University of California Press, 1984.

Tidworth, Simon. *Theatres: An Architectural and Cultural History.* New York: Praeger, 1973.

Tregear, Mary. *Chinese Art.* London: Thames and Hudson, 1980.

Books in Series

Daily Life in the Five Great Ages of History: The Horizon Books of Daily Life. New York: American Heritage Pub. Co., 1975.

Great Ages of Man: A History of the World's Cultures. New York: Time-Life Books, 1965–1969.

Time-Frame. 25 vols. (projected). New York: Time-Life Books, 1990–.

Credits

Calmann & King, the author, and the literature researcher wish to thank the publishers and individuals who have kindly allowed their copyright material to be reproduced in this book, as listed below. Every effort has been made to contact copyright holders, but should there be any errors or omissions, Calmann & King would be pleased to insert the appropriate acknowledgment in any subsequent edition of this publication.

CHAPTER 8

Reading 29 (p. 4): Reprinted by permission of the publishers and the Loeb Classical Library from Apuleius, *Initiation Into the Cult of Isis*, in *Metamorphoses*, Vol. II, translated by J. Arthur Hanson. Cambridge, Mass.: Harvard University Press, 1989.

Reading 30 (p. 6): From *The New Jerusalem Bible* (Reader's edition). Biblical text © 1985, Reader's edition © 1990 by Darton, Longman & Todd, Ltd., and Doubleday, a division of Bantam Doubleday Dell Publishing Group, Inc. Used by permission of Doubleday, a division of Bantam Doubleday Dell Publishing Group, Inc.

Reading 31 (p. 8): From *The New Jerusalem Bible* (Reader's edition). Biblical text © 1985, Reader's edition © 1990 by Darton, Longman & Todd, Ltd., and Doubleday, a division of Bantam Doubleday Dell Publishing Group, Inc. Used by permission of Doubleday, a division of Bantam Doubleday Dell Publishing Group, Inc.

Reading 32 (p. 11): From *Wisdom of China and India* by Lin Yutang. Copyright © 1942 and renewed 1970 by Random House, Inc. Reprinted by permission of Random House, Inc.

CHAPTER 9

Reading 33 (p. 16): From *The Nicene Creed*, in *Documents of the Christian Church*, edited Henry Bettenson (2nd. ed., 1963). Reprinted by permission of Oxford University Press.

Reading 35 (p. 18): From Saint Augustine's *Confessions*, in *The Confession of St. Augustine*, translated by Rex Warner (NAL, 1963).

Reading 36 (p. 19): Reprinted by permission of the publishers and the Loeb Classical Library from St. Augustine, *City of God Against the Pagans*, translated by Philip Levine. Cambridge, Mass.: Harvard University Press, 1966.

CHAPTER 10

Reading 37 (p. 40) Source: *Tacitus: Historical Works*, volume II, translated by Arthur Murphy, 315–325. London: J. M. Dent Co., 1907.

Reading 38 (p. 45): From *The Koran*, from Ahmed Ali, *Al-Qur'an*. Copyright © 1990 by Princeton University Press.

Reading 39 (p. 52) Source: *Poetry of the Orient; An Anthology of the Classic Secular Poetry of the Major Eastern Nations*, edited by Eunice Tietjens, 1928. New York: Alfred A. Knopf.

Reading 40 (p. 53) Source: *Poetry of the Orient: An Anthology of the Classic Secular Poetry of the Major Eastern Nations*, edited by Eunice Tietjens, 1928. New York: Alfred A. Knopf.

CHAPTER 11

Reading 41 (p. 64): Reprinted with the permission of Macmillan College Publishing Company from *The Song of Roland*, translated by Patricia Terry. Copyright 1965 by Macmillan College Publishing Company, Inc.

Reading 42 (p. 72): From Chrétien de Troyes, *Lancelot*, translated by W. W. Comfort (David Campbell Publishers Ltd., Everyman's Library 1970). Reprinted with permission.

Reading 43 (p. 76): Bernart de Ventadour "When I Behold the Lark" in Jack Lindsay, *The Troubadours and Their World*. London: Frederick Muller Ltd., 1976. Peire Cardenal, "Lonely the Rich Need Never Be" in Jack Lindsay, *The Troubadours and Their World*. London: Frederick Muller Ltd., 1976.

Reading 44 (p. 78): From "The Vices of Women" in *Three Medieval Views of Women*, translated by Gloria Fiero et al. Copyright © Yale University Press, New Haven, Conn. Reprinted with permission.

CHAPTER 12

Reading 45 (p. 81): Reprinted with the permission of Macmillan College Publishing Company from *On the Misery of the Human Condition* by Pope Innocent III, edited by Donald R. Howard. Copyright © 1969 by Macmillan College Publishing Co., Inc.

Reading 47 (p. 92): *The Inferno* by Dante Alighieri, translated by John Ciardi, 1954. Copyright John Ciardi 1954. Reprinted with permission.
(p. 95): *The Paradiso* by Dante Alighieri, translated by John Ciardi, 1954. Copyright John Ciardi 1954. Reprinted with permission.

Reading 48 (p. 99): From *Basic Writing of Saint Thomas Aquinas*, Vol. I, edited by Anton C. Pegis. Copyright 1945 Random House Inc. Reprinted by permission of the Estate of A. C. Pegis.

CHAPTER 14

Reading 49 (p. 135) Source: *The Vishnu Purana*, volume III, translated by H. H. Wilson, pp. 217–221. London: Trubner and Co., 1868.

Reading 50 (p. 136): Reprinted by permission of the publishers from *Anthology of Sanskrit Court Poetry*, translated by Daniel H. Ingalls. Cambridge, Mass.: Harvard University Press, © 1965 by the President and Fellows of Harvard College.

Reading 51 (p. 146): From Kenneth Rexroth, *One Hundred Poems from the Chinese*. Copyright © 1971 by Kenneth Rexroth. Reprinted by permission of New Directions Publishing Corporation.

Index